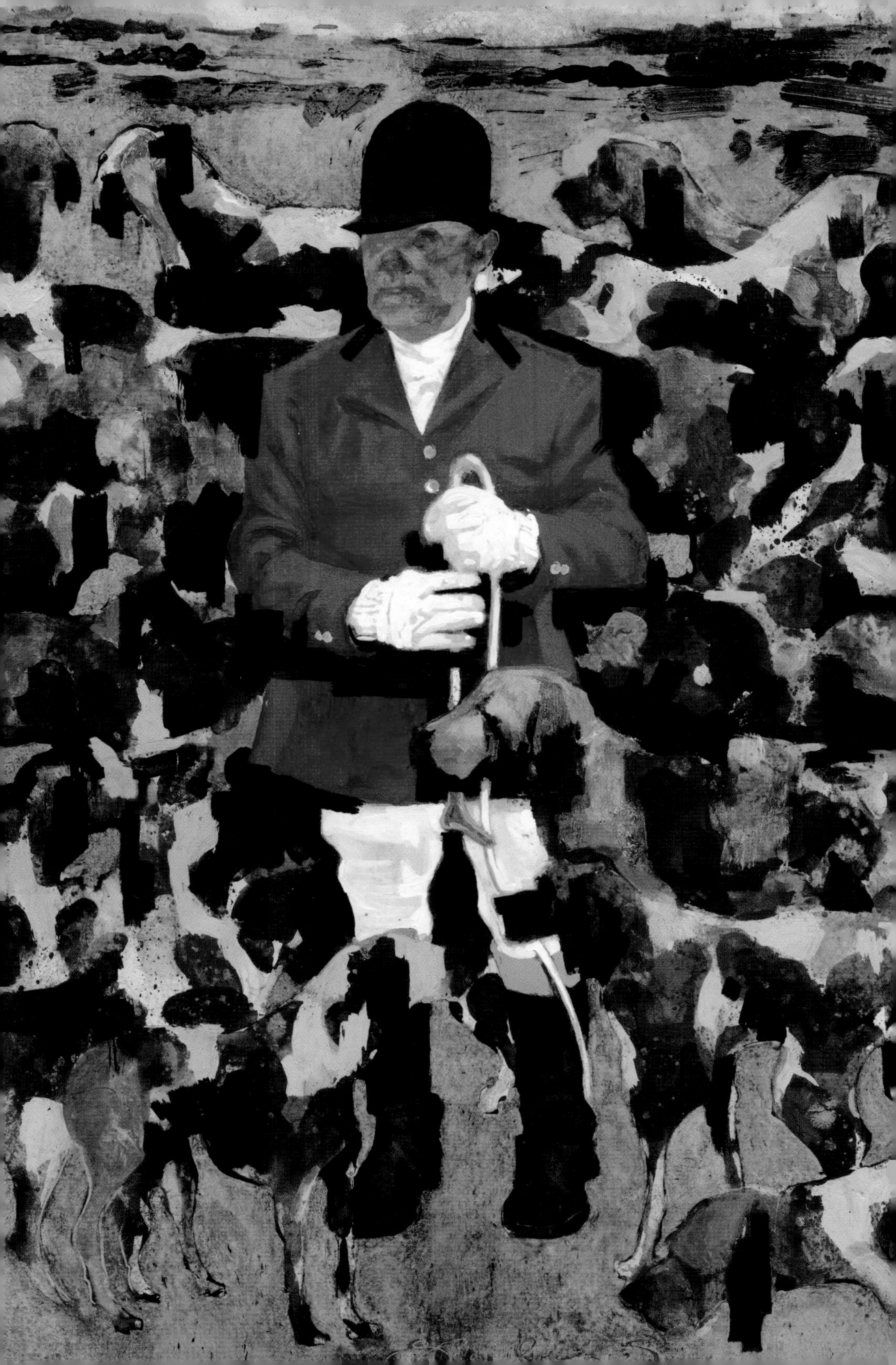

STERLING HUNDLEY

AdHouse Books
Richmond, VA

Foreword

Illustration is Blue Collar – both pervasive and accessible. It is art that must survive in spite of commerce and function. There is a desperation to the thing; illustration that doesn't work doesn't eat. Given limitations in time to communicate and the space in which to do it, illustration must *answer a question.*

Fine Art is White Collar – reclusive with airs of mystery and sophistication. It is pursued. Given the abundance of space in which it is viewed and the time which it is afforded, fine art has the luxury of *asking a question.*

As innovators that communicate, we are between two opposing fronts, searching for that anomaly that is both recognizable and never-before-seen. Ideas are born of the union of such unrelated things.

In a time when access has reached the Faustian ideal, *information* is often confused with *knowledge.* I refuse to accept that appropriation and homogenization are the movements that will define our generation. The search for original thought is a journey of faith – a belief that art is necessary because it isn't necessary. The compulsion to create is emblematic of life that has moved beyond the base functions of survival. *Art is evolution.*

If life moved at a steady speed and constant direction, then art would not survive. We need only lead the beast with the proper trajectory to take it down. But life *lives,* and we must choose to take it or to tame it. Art is us run-through-the-world and the world-run-through-us.

"Art is the transfer of emotion from one person to another." – Leo Tolstoy

Blue Collar / White Collar
Published by AdHouse Books.

Content is © copyright 2011 Sterling Hundley.
www.sterlinghundley.com
AdHouse logo is © copyright 2011 AdHouse Books.

ISBN 1-9352331-5-7
ISBN 978-1-935233-15-2
10 9 8 7 6 5 4 3 2 1

Design: Pitzer + Hundley
Assist: Jeffrey Alan Love

AdHouse Books
1224 Greycourt Ave.
Richmond, VA 23227-4042
www.adhousebooks.com

First Printing, August 2011

Printed in Singapore

To my wife, Shelly.

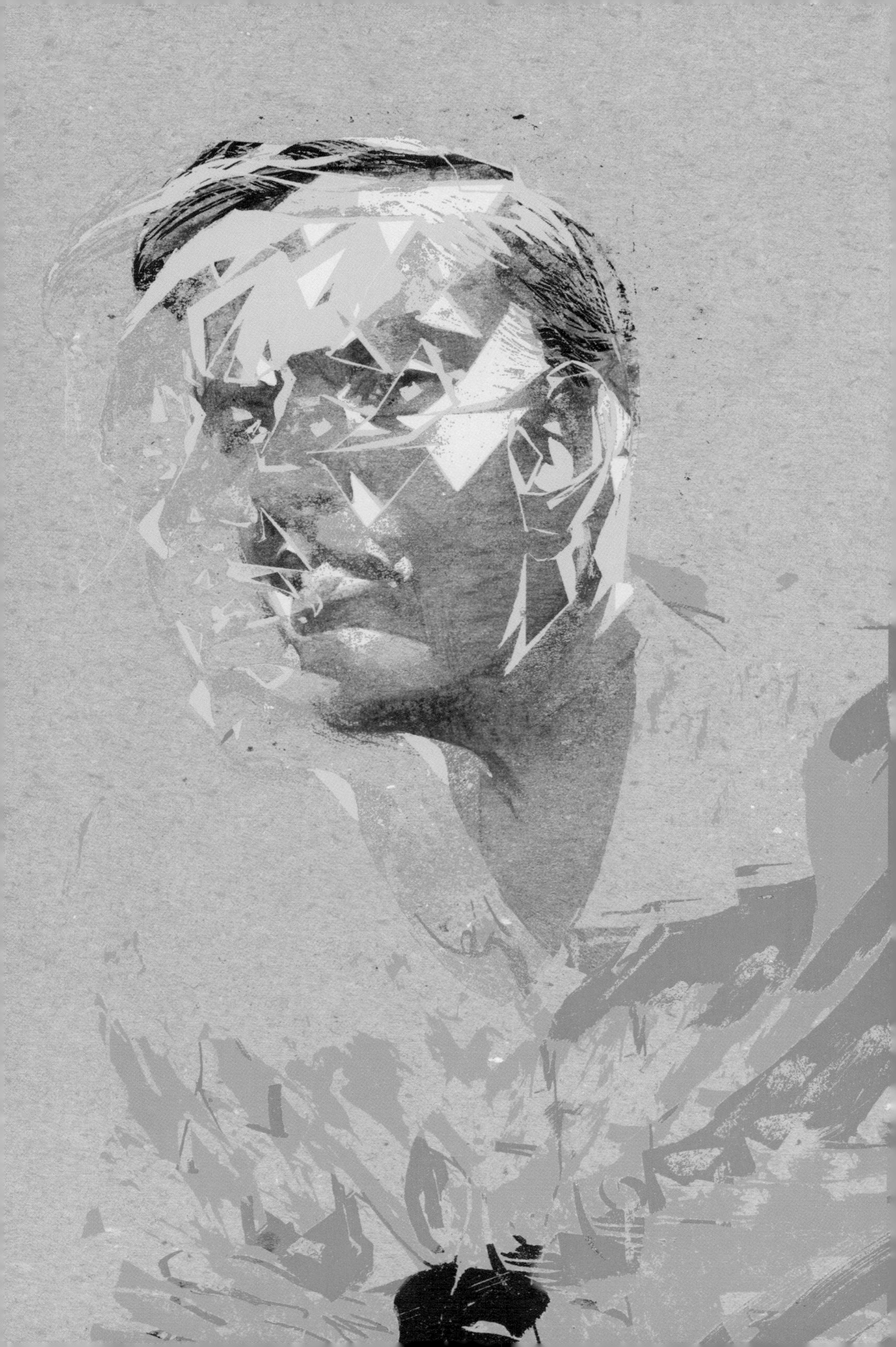

Introduction by David Apatoff

One's self must never give way — that is the final substance — that out of all is sure.
Out of politics, triumphs, battles, life, what at last finally remains?
When shows break up what but One's Self is sure?

— *Walt Whitman*

In this book, Sterling Hundley writes about combining a blue collar work ethic with a white collar aesthetic. But as his career demonstrates, sometimes it's the backbone within that collar that matters the most.

The field of illustration has been on a volatile path for many years. The digital revolution radically transformed the role of the illustrator, as well as the market for illustration. Clients have changed their expectations; editors interject themselves into decisions once made by artists, "tweaking" artwork with Photoshop to satisfy the whims of corporate sponsors or bookstore chains. Even before computers, television siphoned off the advertising revenue that had previously fueled an entire century of beautiful picture magazines. Publications such as *Colliers, The Saturday Evening Post* and *Life,* which employed illustrators such as Norman Rockwell, N.C. Wyeth and Maxfield Parrish, are all gone today. Much of the print journalism and book market are headed in the same direction. Photography has taken many of the remaining assignments previously performed by illustrators.

So how does a genuine artist adapt to this evolving world?

Many illustrators have wobbled in their search for a new identity. Some became caught in the gravitational pull of photography, and are now doomed to orbit the photographic process with photorealistic pictures or computer manipulated photographs (what *Time* magazine euphemistically refers to as "photo illustration"). Other illustrators intentionally moved in the opposite direction, disavowing photorealism but in the process throwing out skill, technique, or anything else that might hint they were competing with a camera. Some illustrators sought refuge in childish or willfully ugly images, or inflated the prominence of personal opinion and editorial concepts (many of which were barely worthwhile in the first place).

I admire the fact that Hundley has a center of gravity which enables him to face this changing world with artistic integrity. He was not one of those quickly spooked into believing that the value of good drawing was extinguished by some invention. He understood that good taste and fundamental skills are not obsolete.

Hundley thoughtfully selects what he finds relevant and appropriate from both the old and new worlds. Some older illustrators might tend to create lovely, polished images with no thought for the philosophical content of the subject. Some newer illustrators might prefer to focus on content or depict gritty, "relevant" ideas complete with warts and scars. (This is sometimes known as the "I'm so smart I don't have to draw well" school.)

Hundley's work embodies his belief that you can have both – you don't need to throw out classical concerns with design, balance, color, harmony, anatomy, or the other qualities important to image making in order to make thoughtful and relevant philosophical statements. Hundley's pictures don't move, blink, or explode. They don't require a digital soundtrack or 3D glasses. Instead, they come from the tradition where the picture holds still and your brain moves. Such art sometimes seems to be in short supply these days.

In the following book, you will see how Hundley incorporates words directly into the design of an image (as with *My Lady of Richmond* on pages 36 & 37 or *Hair* on page 42), or by working with symbols and double entrendres (as with *God Eyes* on page 9). But mostly, he uses imagery to achieve content, as with his award winning *Death of a Salesman* on page 26. Here he depicts Arthur Miller's tragic hero as nothing more than an empty suit, someone whose only value to society was his handshake and his clean tie for selling merchandise. Willy Loman's secret personal self is hidden away behind that "Do Not Disturb" sign; his mind, his face, his individual personality were of no concern to society, and once he was used up he was simply hung up on a rack out of the way. Norman Rockwell and Maxfield Parrish never had to incorporate their opinions into their work in this fashion. Their world of illustration was something very different.

But Hundley doesn't limit himself to servicing the field of illustration as it is currently configured. He questions and explores, working on "personal" art which he displays in gallery exhibitions; he works on digital variations of the popular "graphic novel" medium; he is an educator and a critic and a writer. He creatively explores these venues simultaneously, so that his work is not confined to the current version of the illustration market. That market will continue to evolve, and tomorrow may look nothing like it does today. As an artist of substance, Hundley does not let himself be defined by that market. He takes the initiative and develops his art around his own broader taste and judgment.

Returning to the vertebrae inside that white collar / blue collar, Hundley is an artist who sticks his neck out to be protective of his own talent so that he can do his best. He sticks his neck out to help and defend young art students. He lifts his neck up to survey the larger landscape of art, rather than simply following the tail of the pack mule ahead of him on the trail. And he is stiff necked and determined about growing his talent.

Whether his collar is blue or white at the time he paints any particular work, this is artwork to be enjoyed.

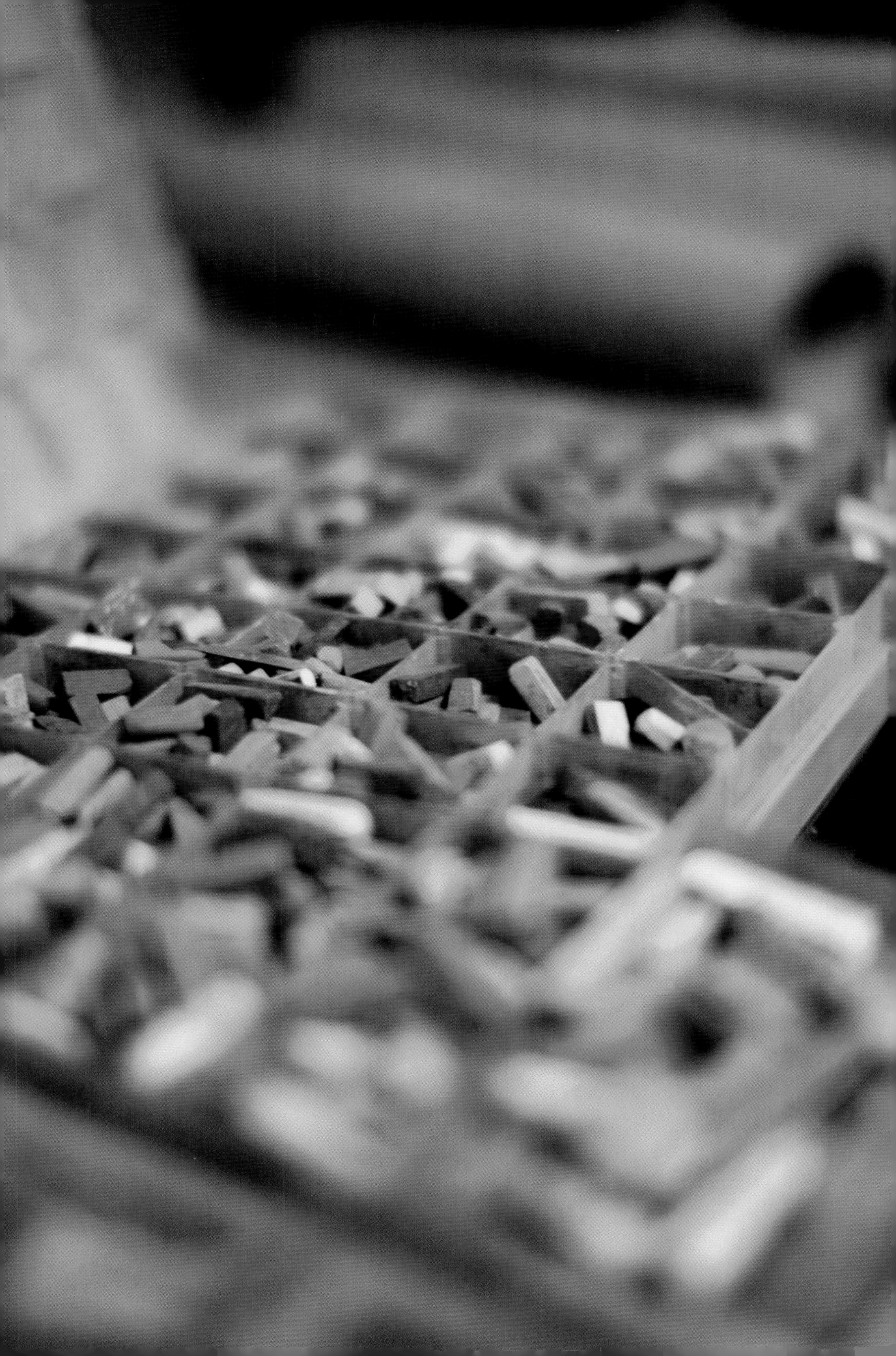

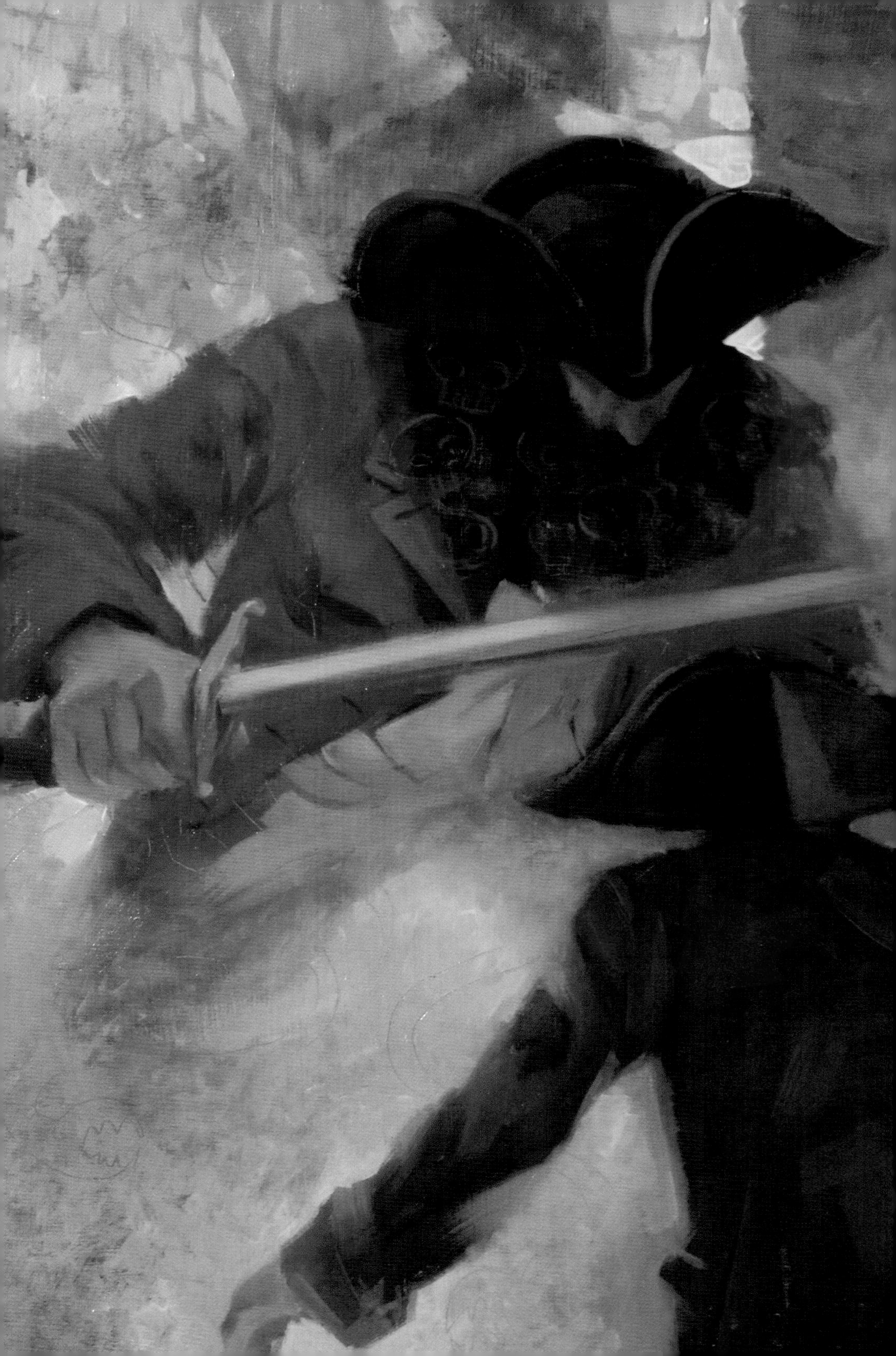

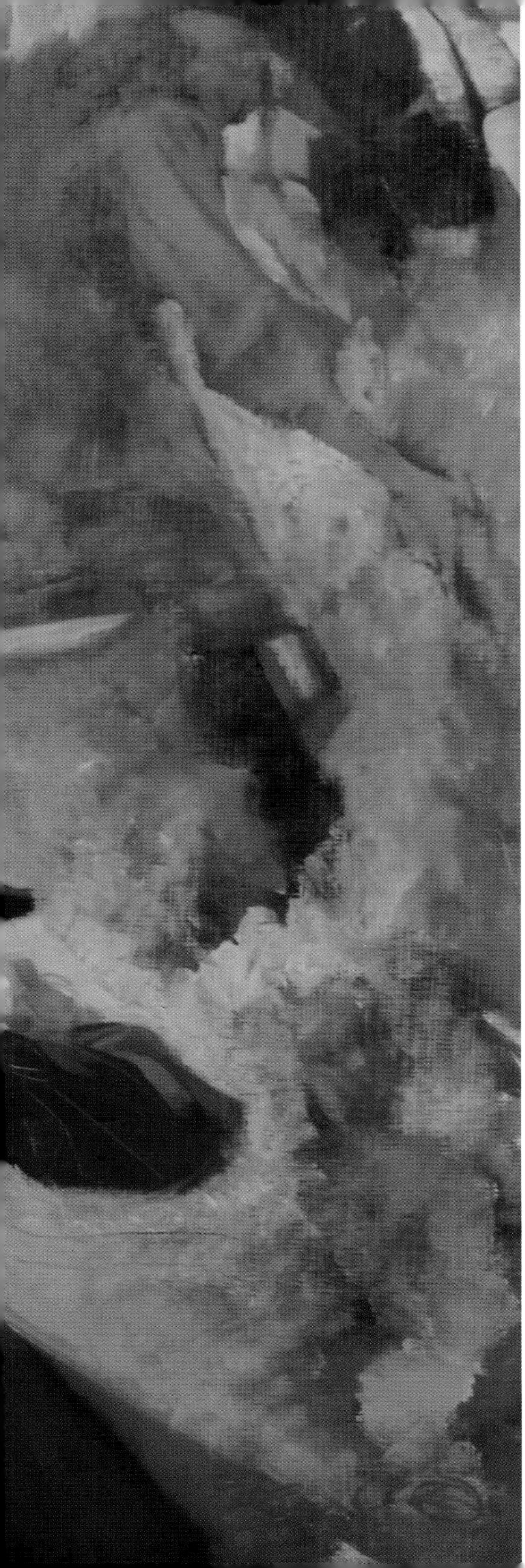

LEGEND

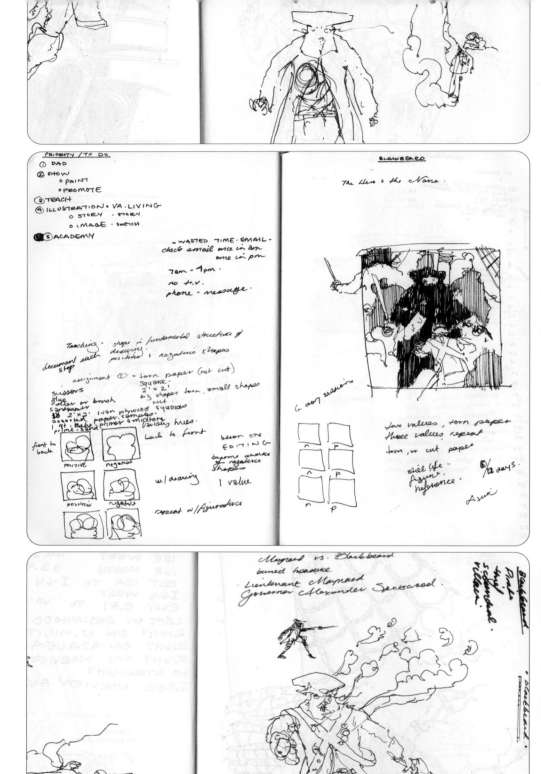

PRIORITY / TO DO

① DAD
② SHOW
  ○ PAINT
  ○ PROMOTE
③ TEACH
④ ILLUSTRATION • VA. LIVING
  ○ STORY · STORY
  ○ IMAGE · SKETCH
⑤ ACADEMY

- WASTED TIME · EMAIL -
check email once in am
once in pm

7am - 4pm.
no t.v.
phone - message.

Teaching - shape in fundamental structure of drawing.
positive + negative shapes
document each step

assignment ① - torn paper (not cut)
square.
2' × 2'
big shapes torn, small shapes cut.

scissors
glue
roller or brush
sandpaper
18 2'×2' luan plywood squares
assorted paper. samples.
1 qt. Behr primer & midtone
prime - sand.

various hues.

back to front

front to back
POSITIVE
negative
positive
negative

become one
EDITING
become aware of negative shapes

w/ drawing

1 value

repeat w/ figurative

BLACKBEARD

The Hero's the Name.

6 day sessions

n
p
n
p
n
p

two values, torn paper
three values, repeat
torn, or cut paper

still life.
figure.
reference.

5/12 days.

Asuni

Maynard vs. Blackbeard
buried treasure
Lieutenant Maynard
Governor Alexander Spotswood.

Blackbeard
Pirate
thief
scoundrel.
villain.

• blackbeard.

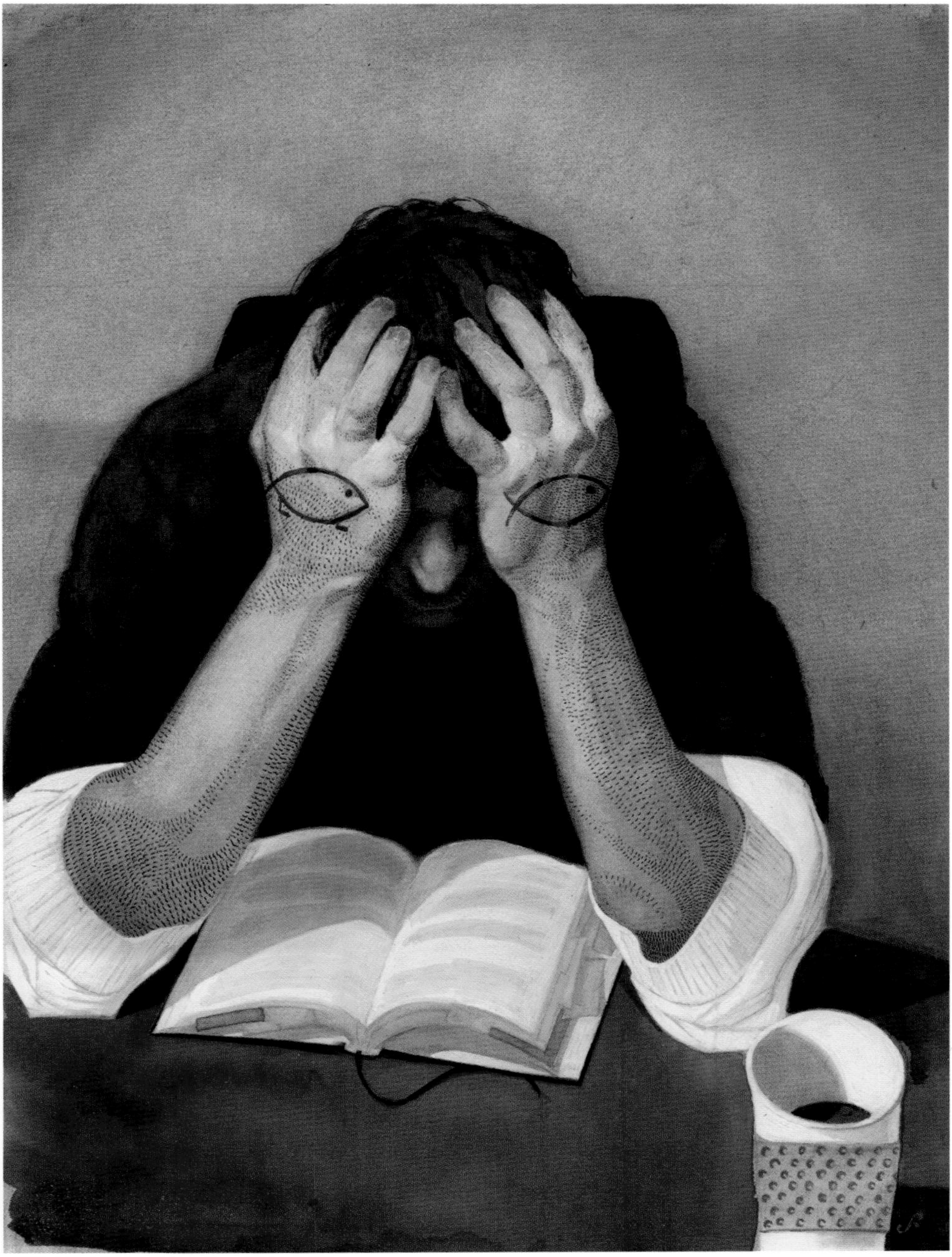

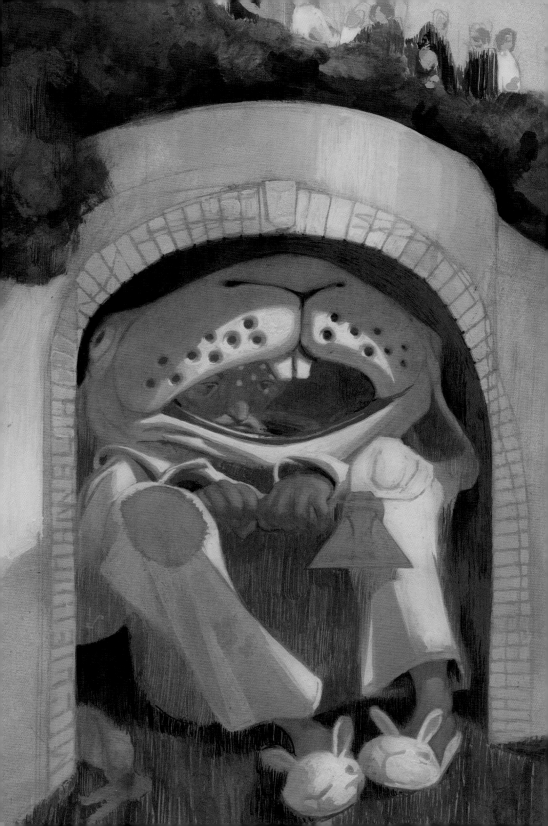

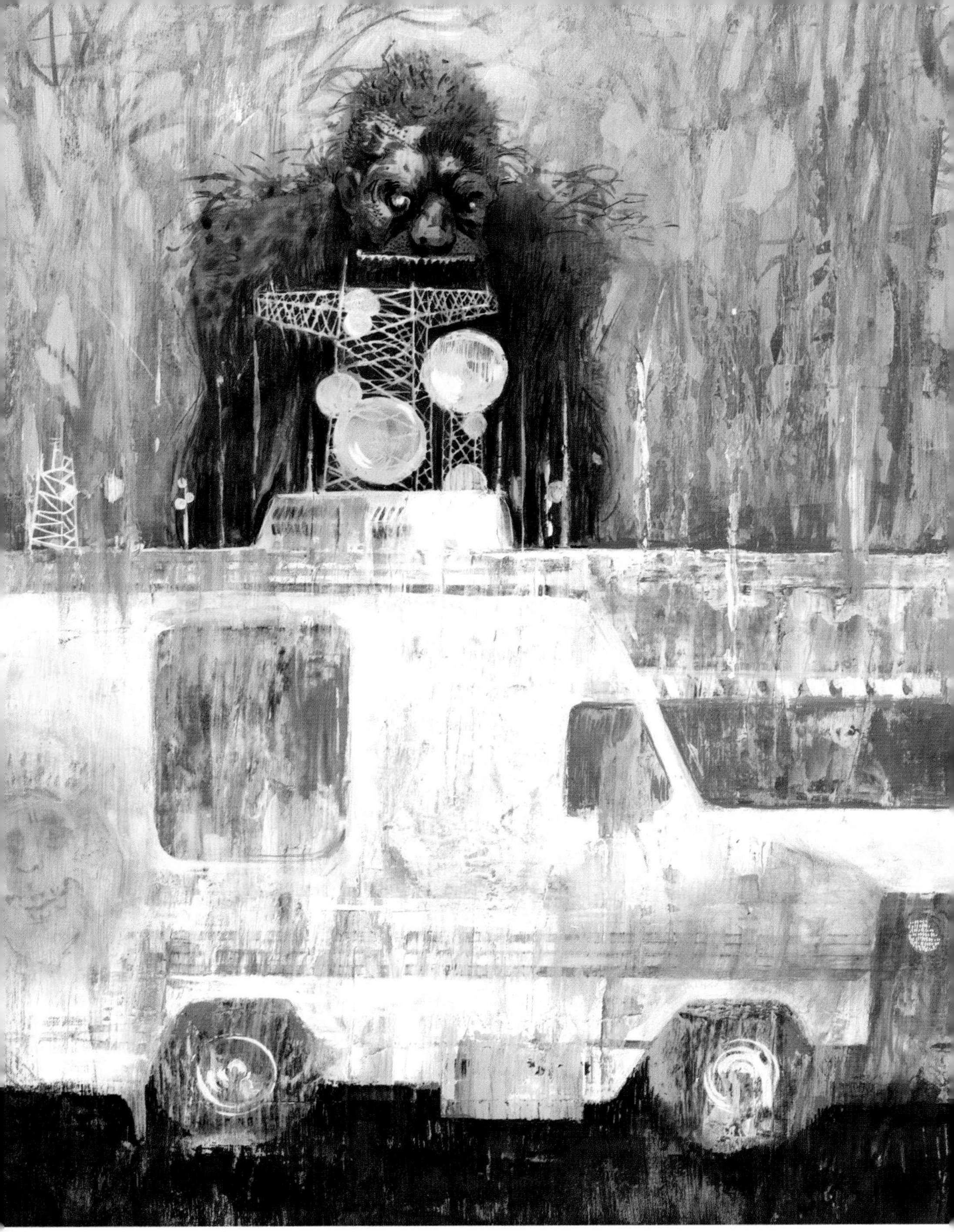

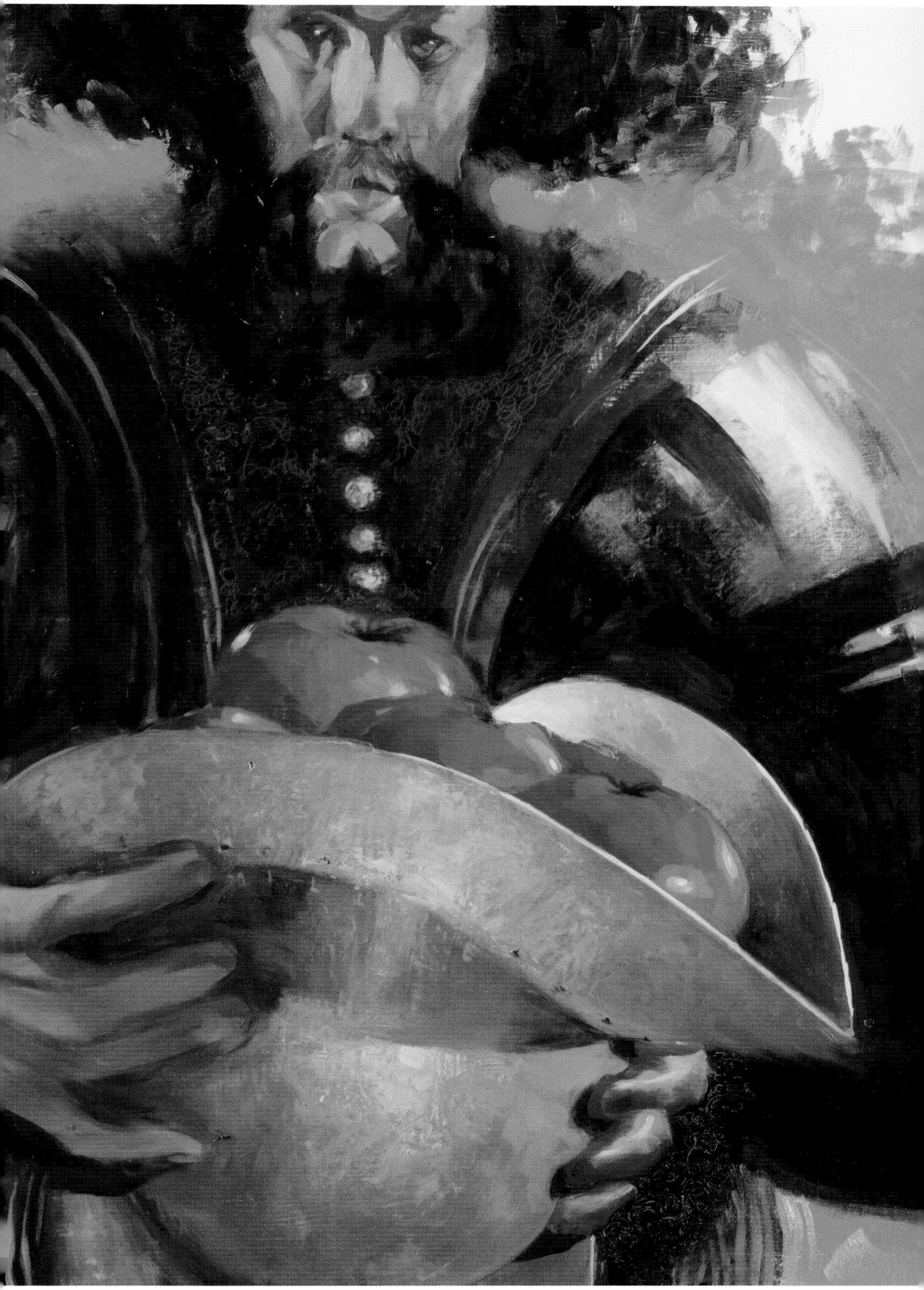

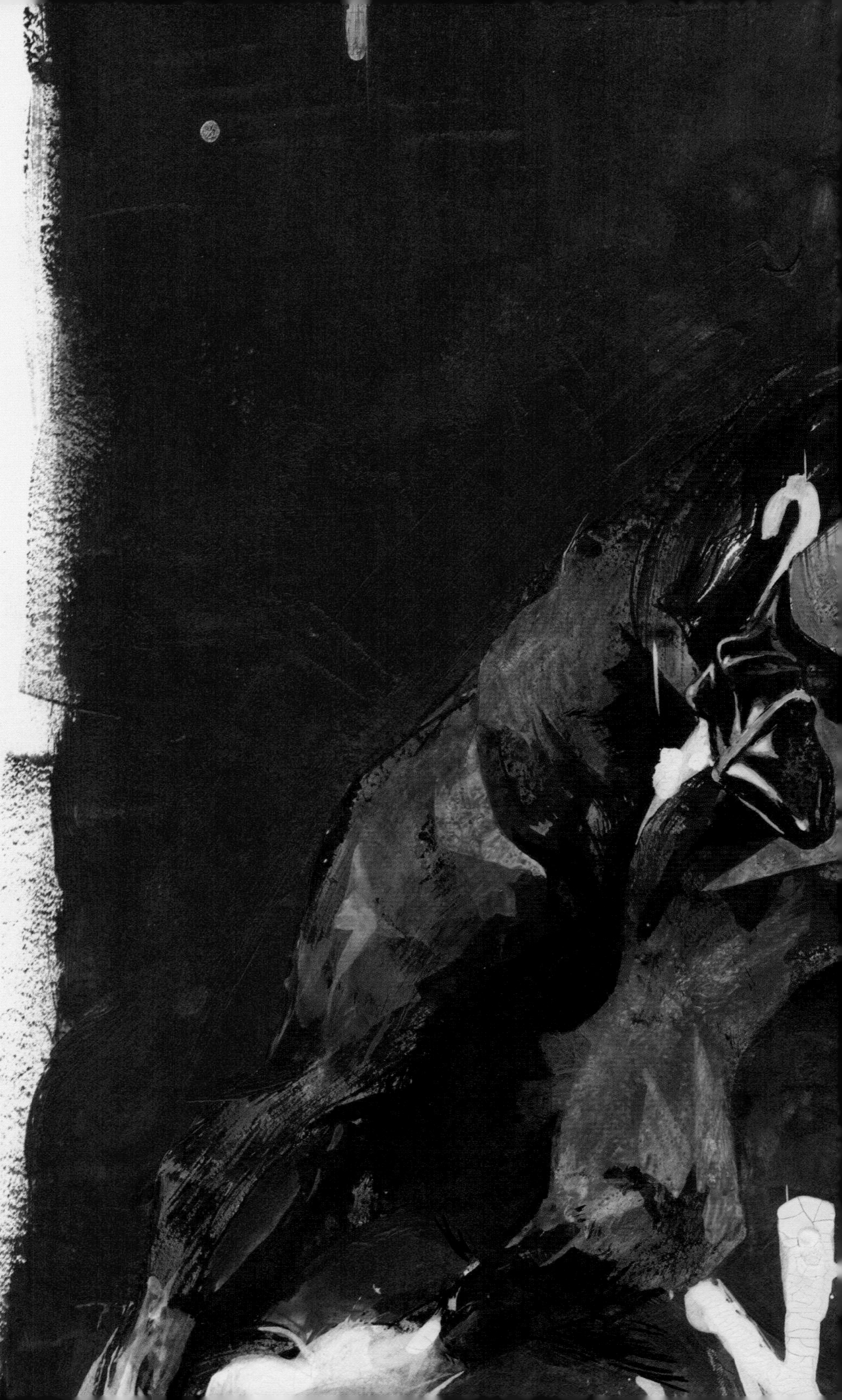

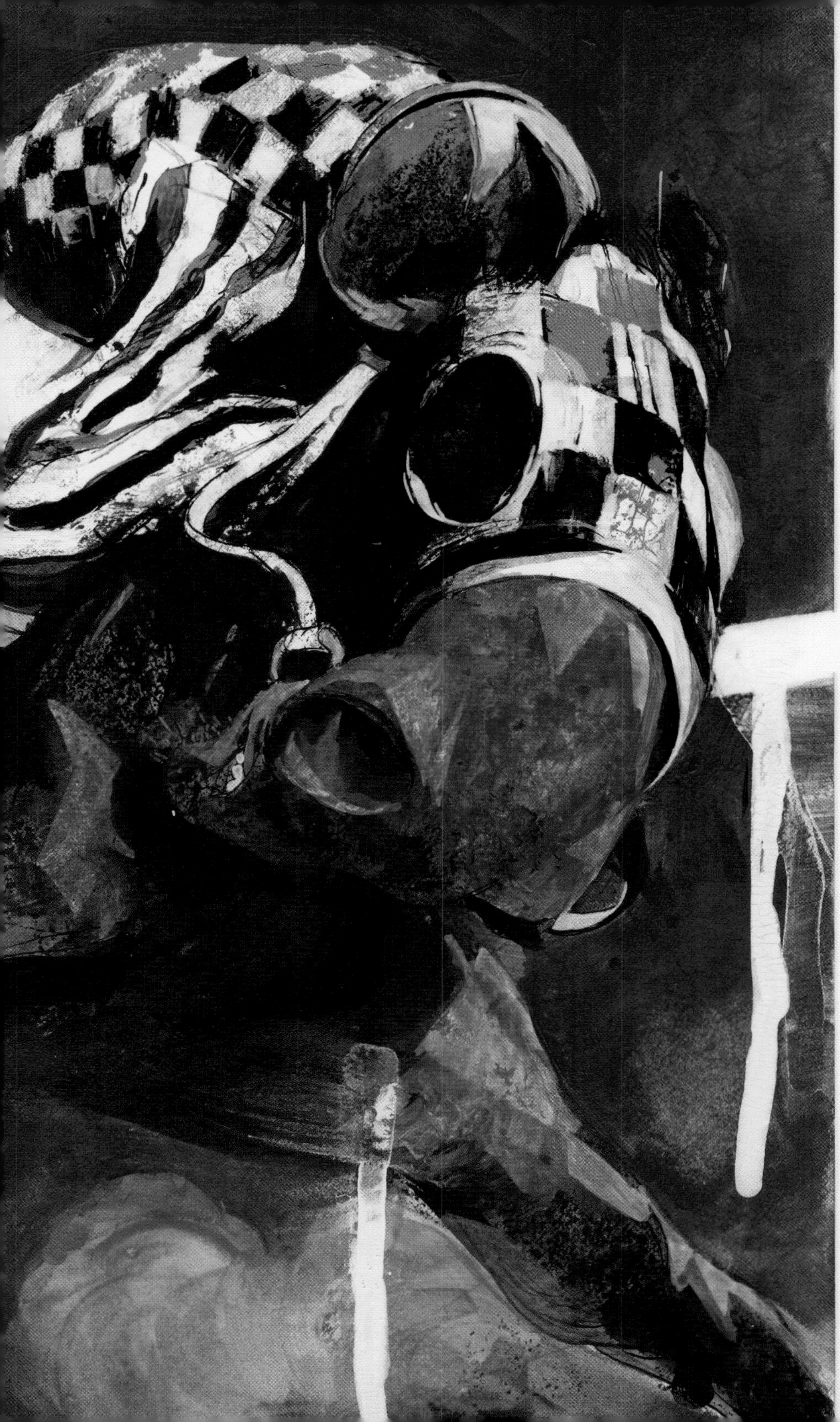

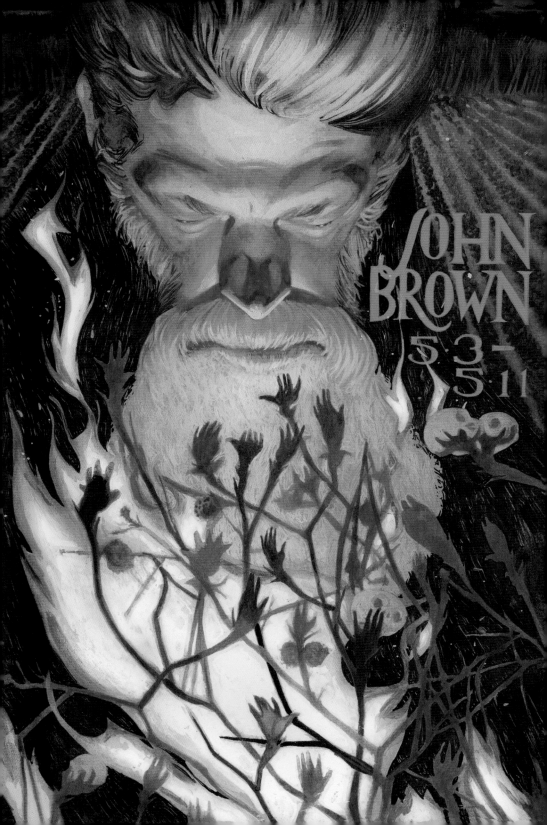

JOHN
BROWN
5·3–
5·11

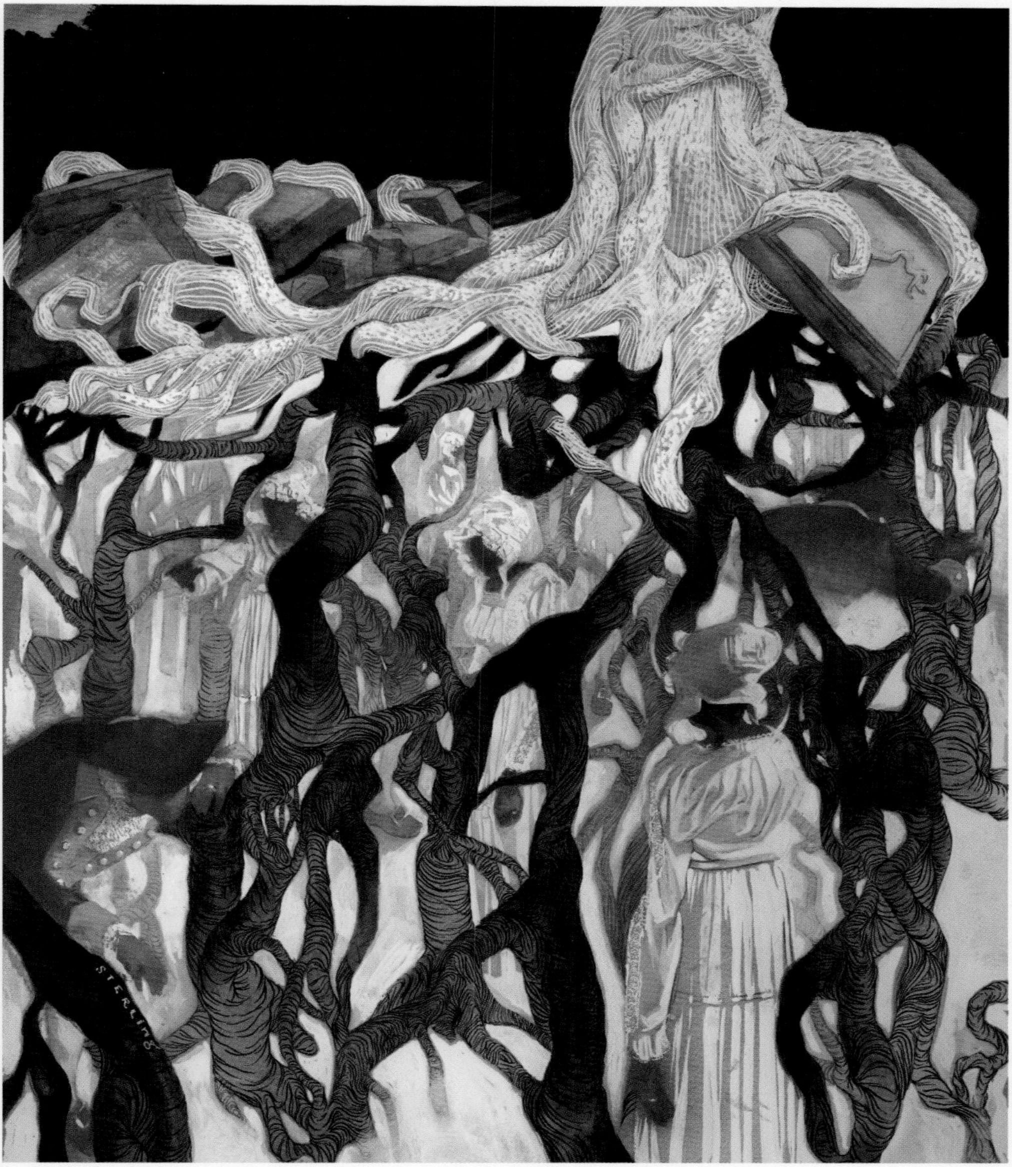
STERLING

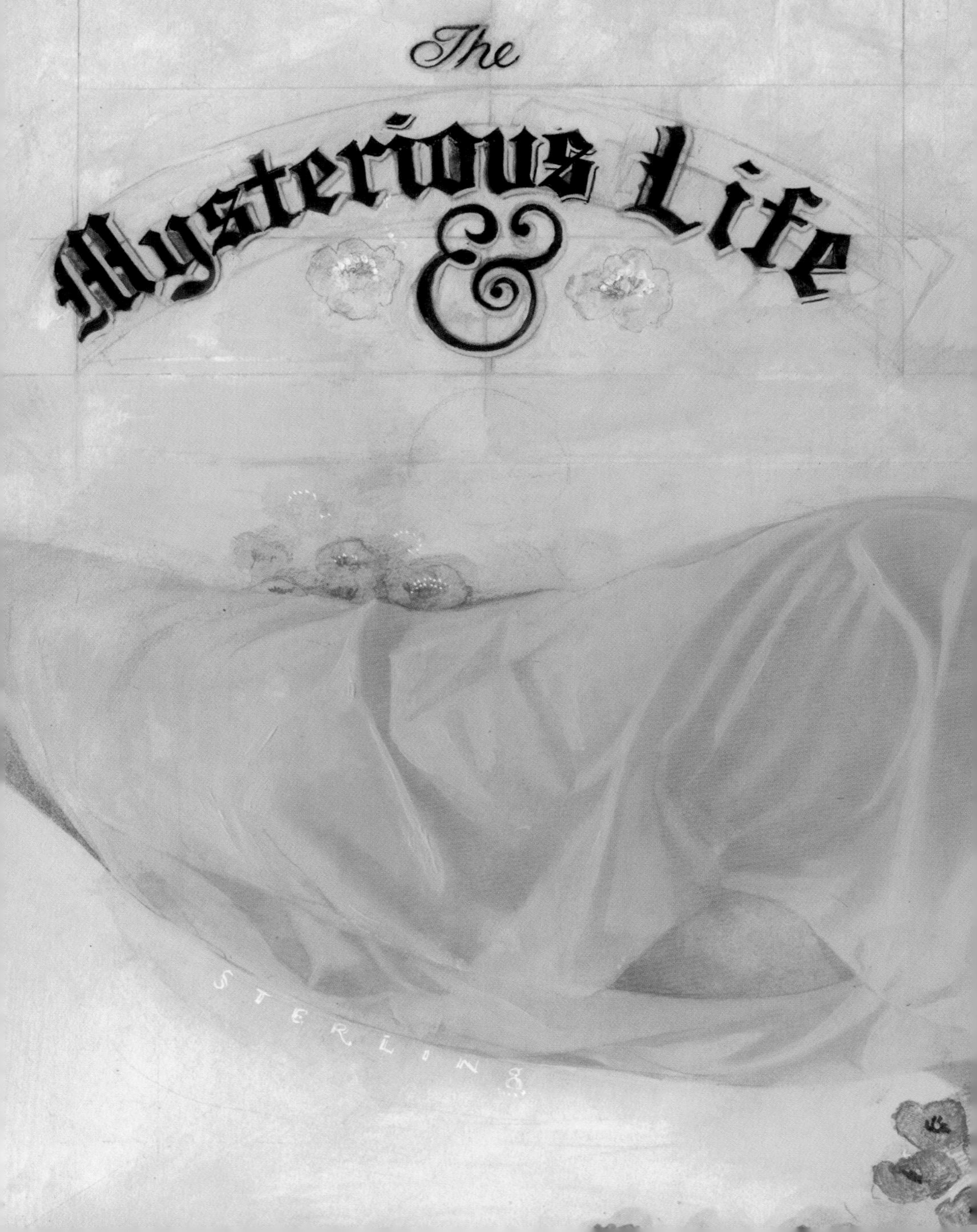
The
Mysterious Life
&
STERLING

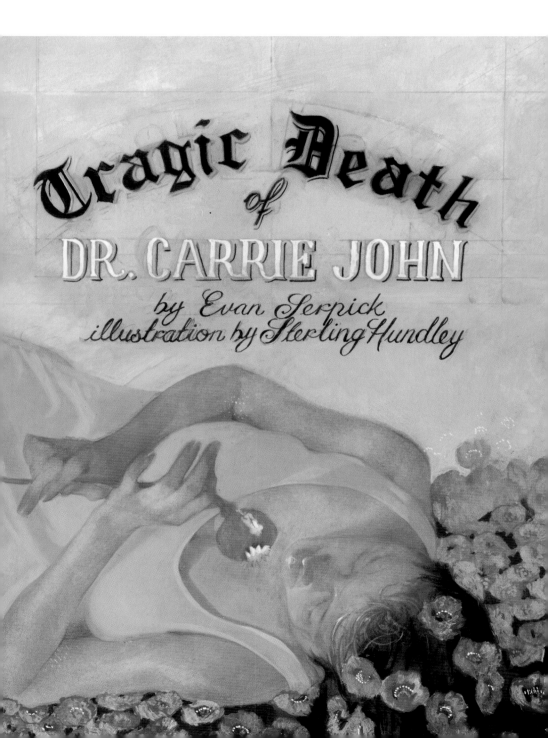

Tragic Death of DR. CARRIE JOHN

by Evan Serpick

illustration by Sterling Hundley

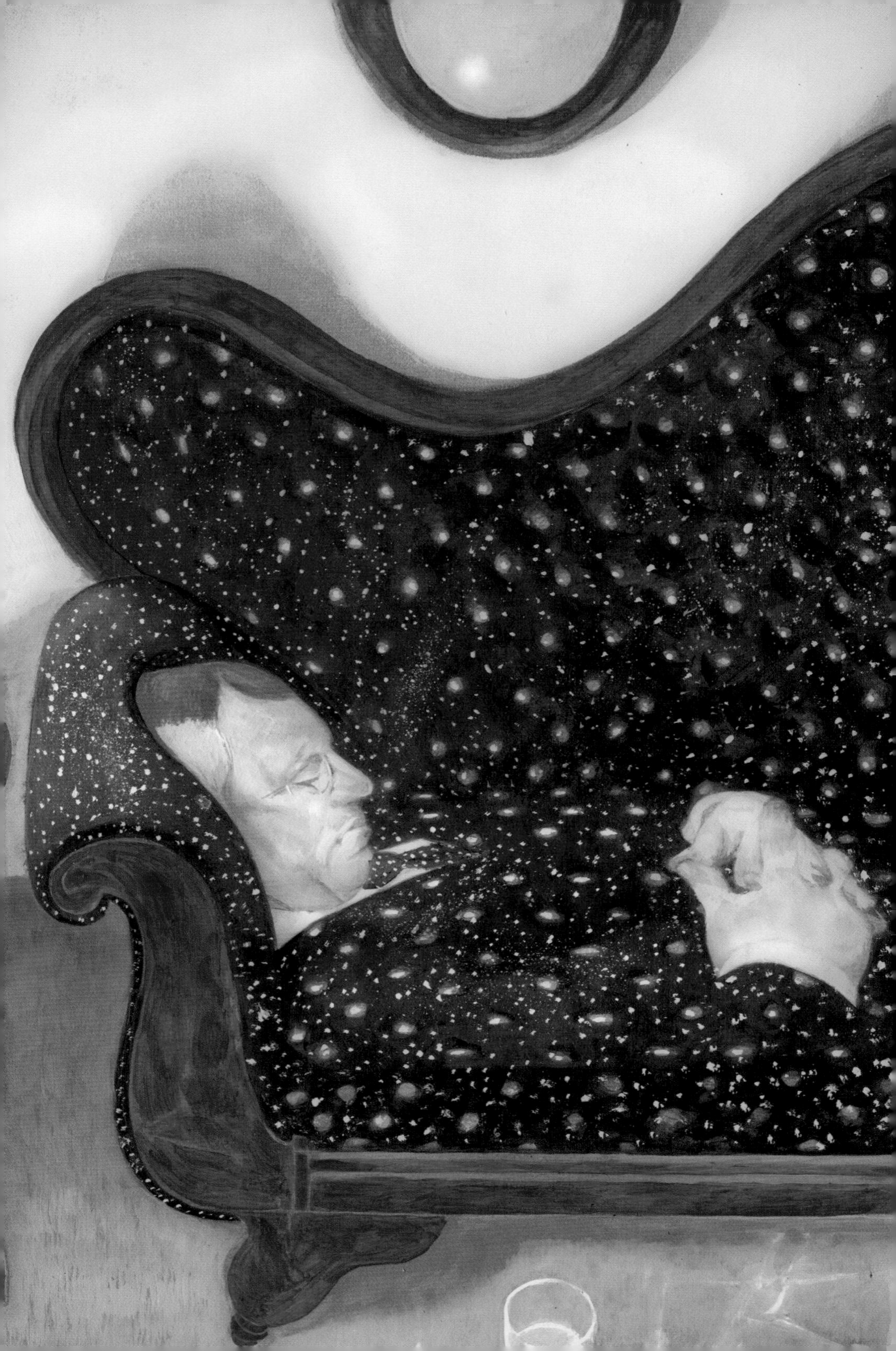

STERLING

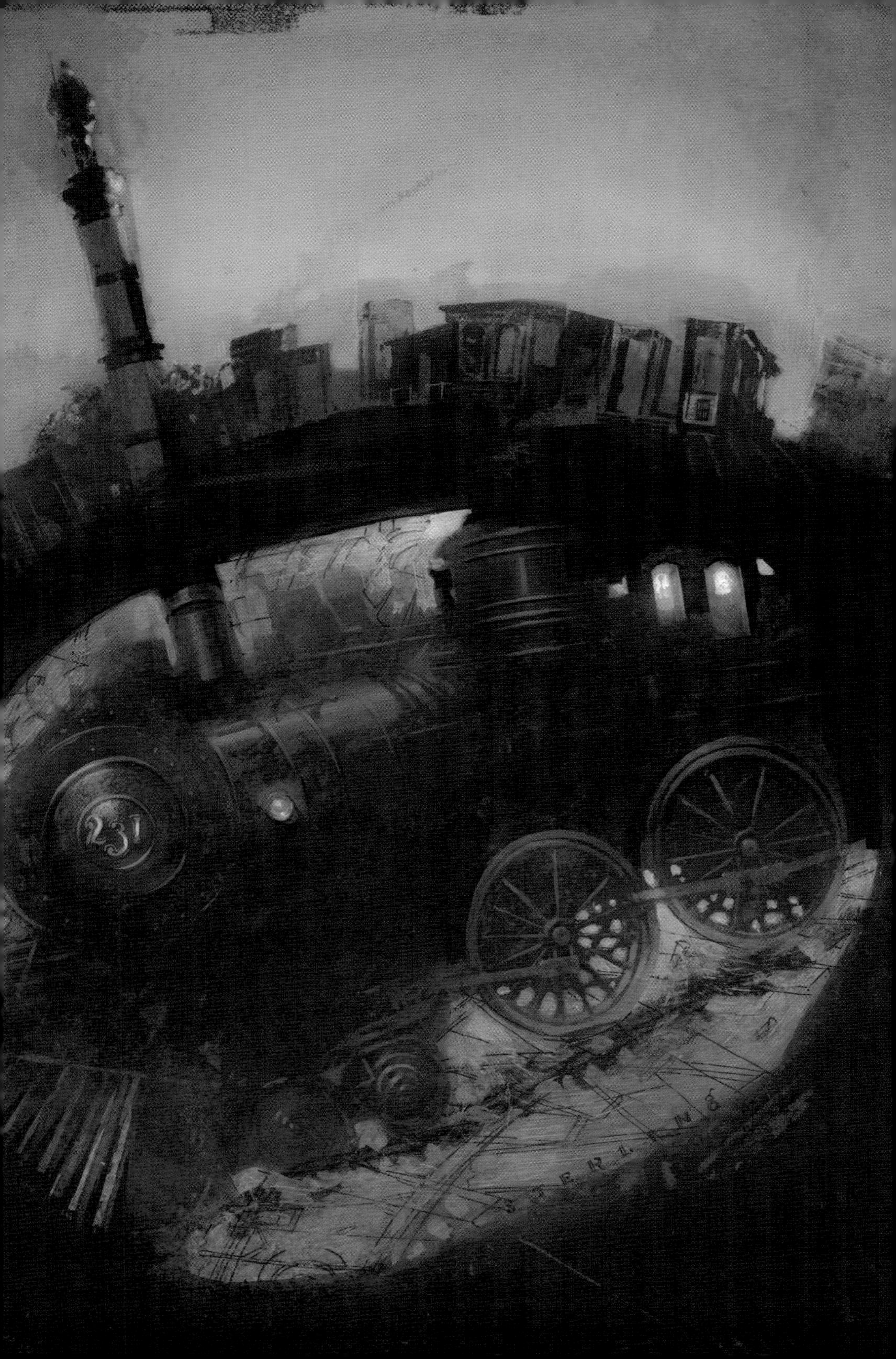
231

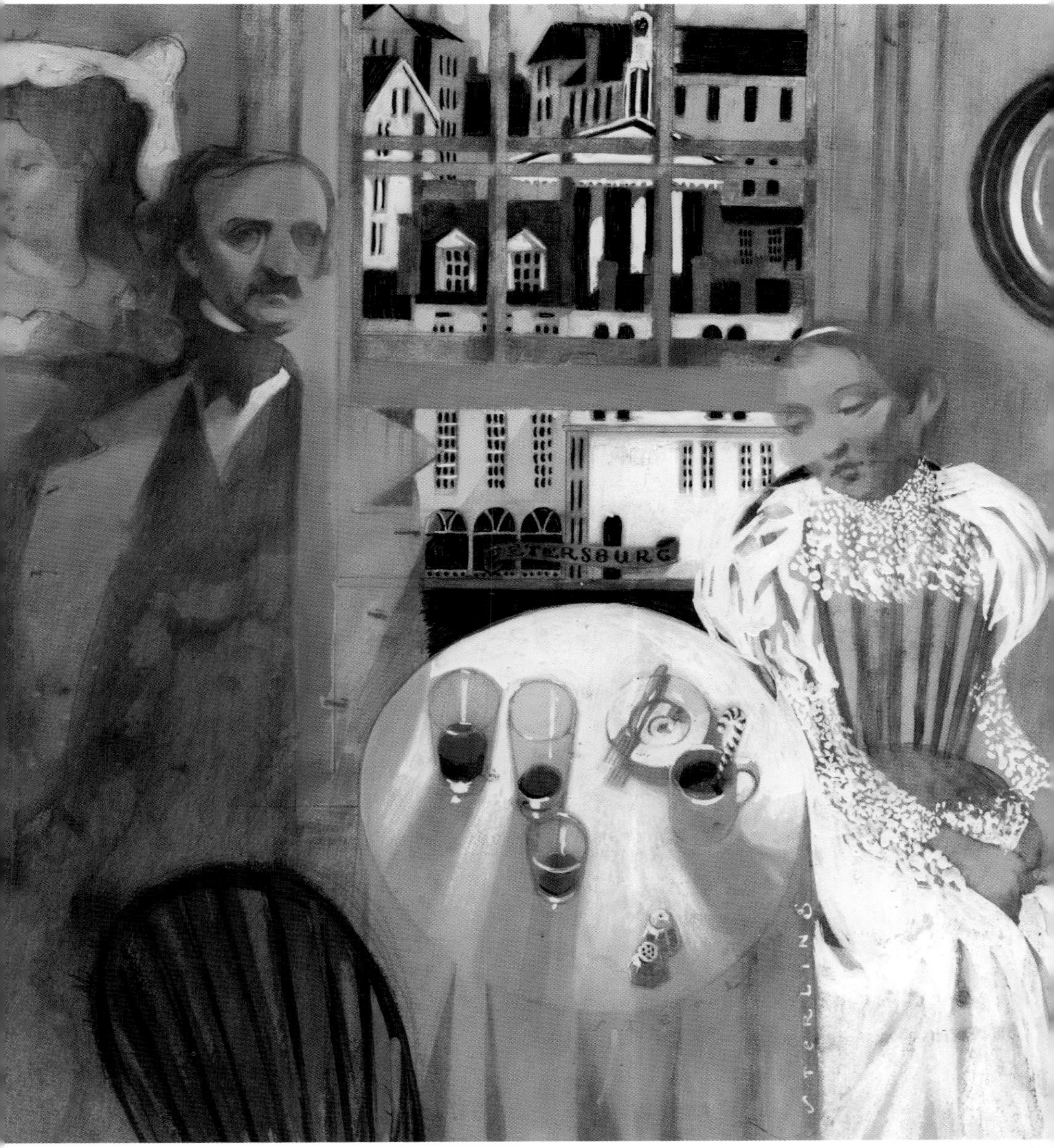
RSBURG
STERLING

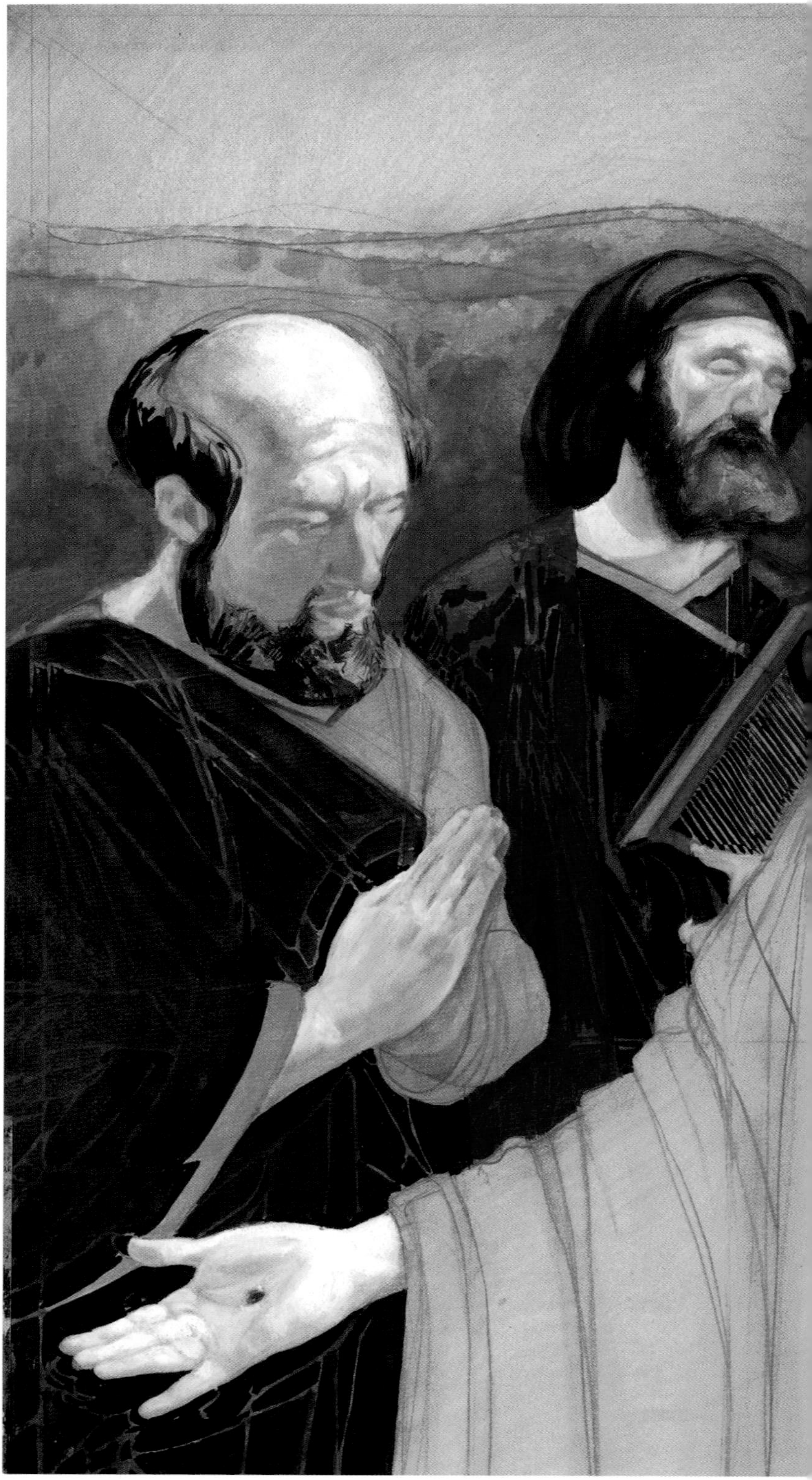

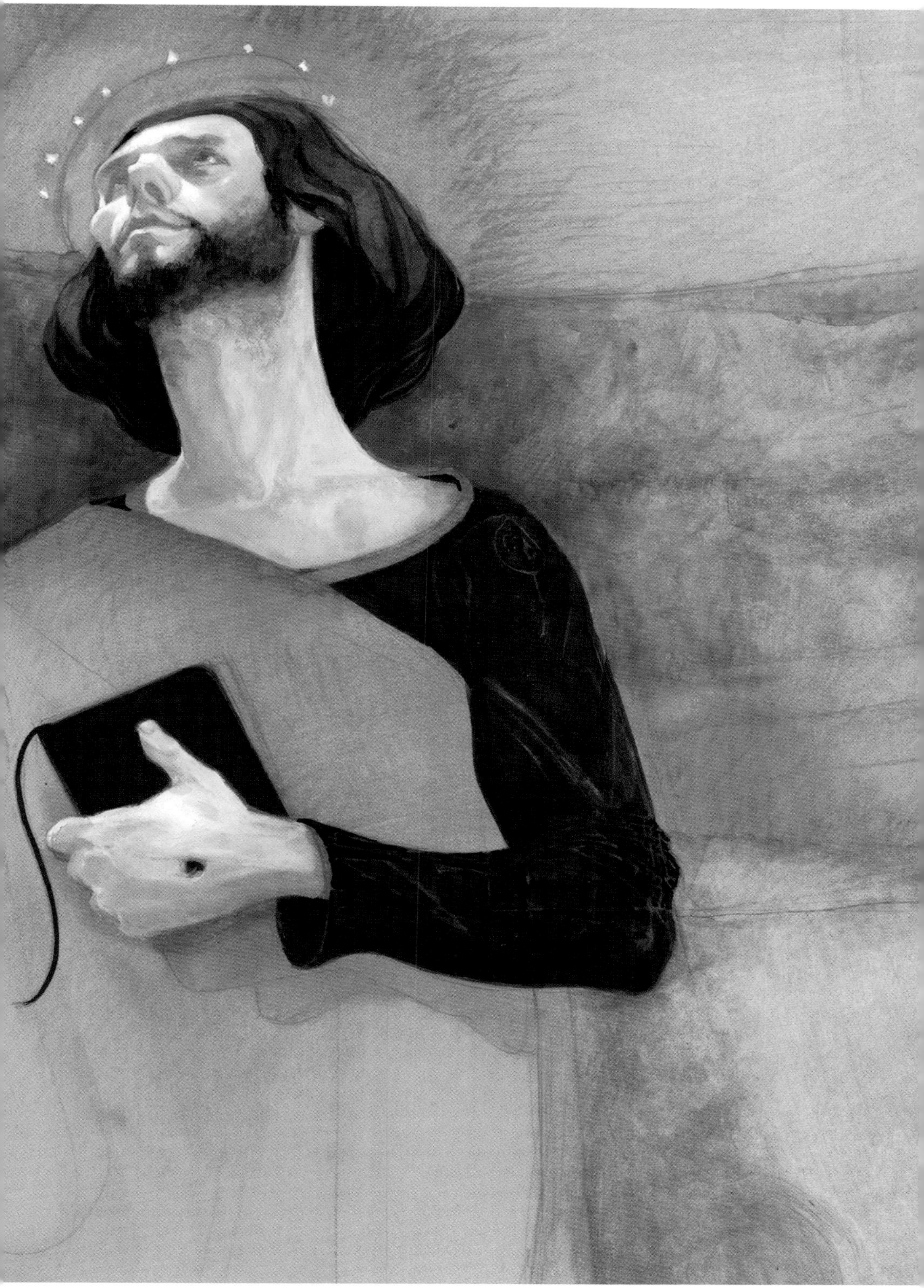

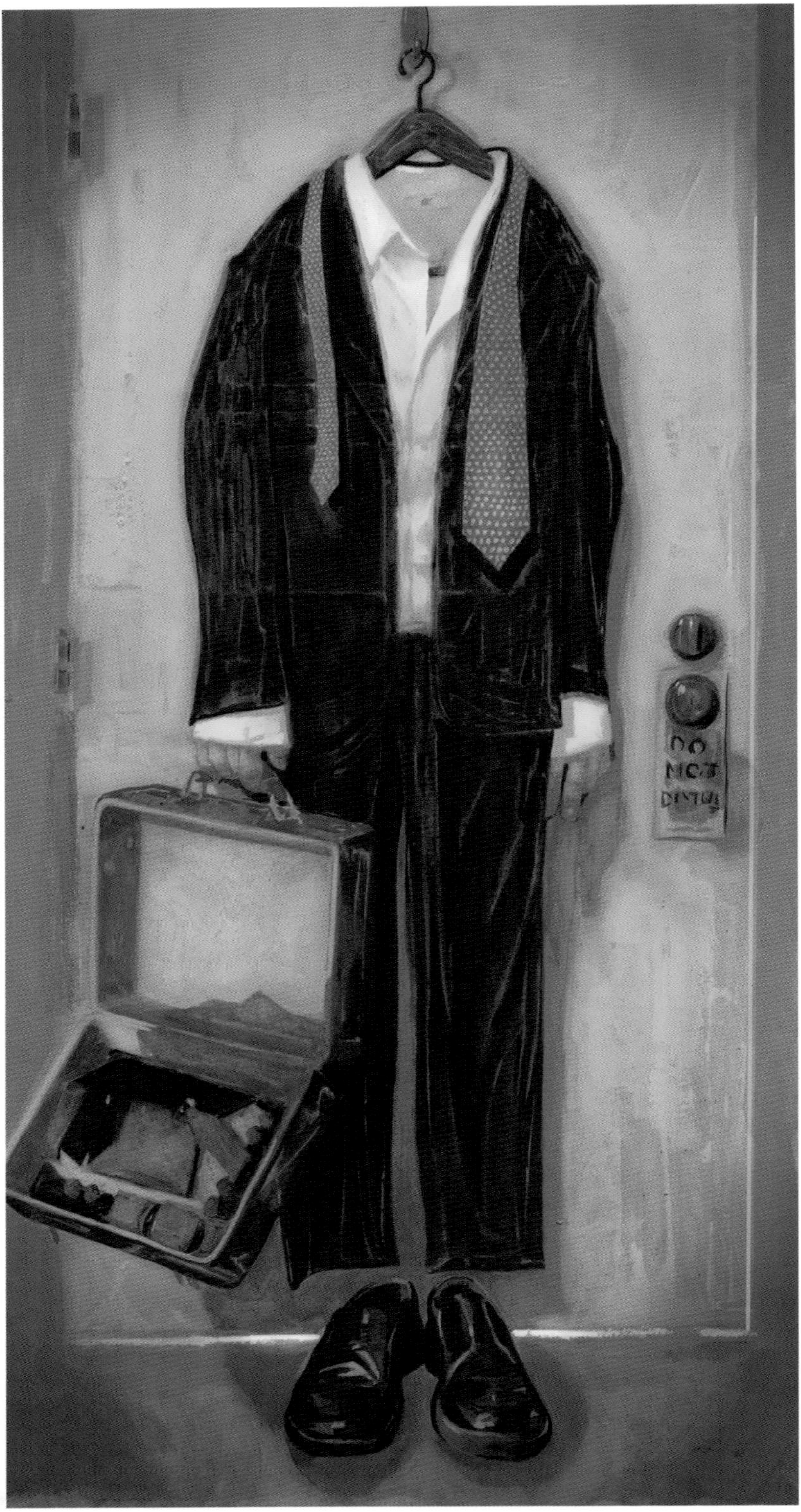
DO
NOT
DISTUR

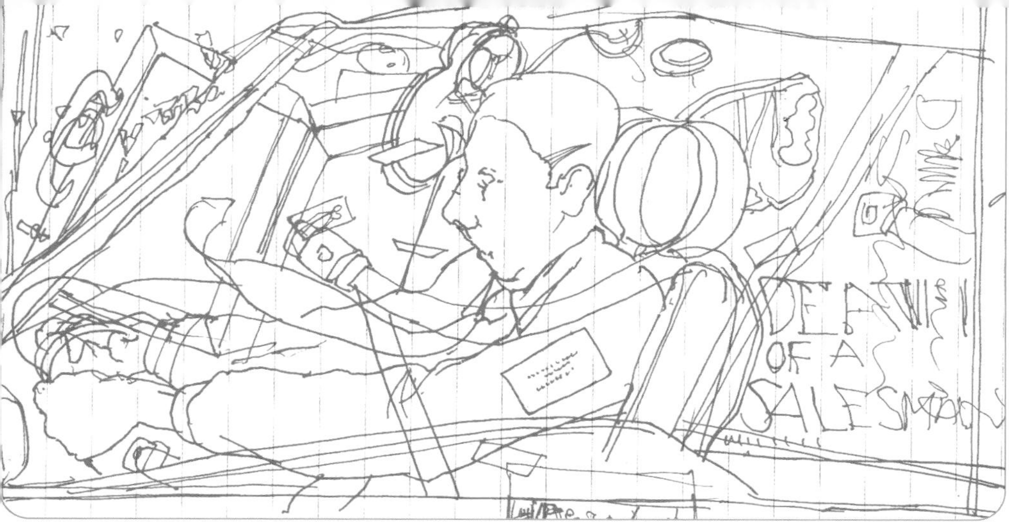
DEATH
OF A
SALESMAN

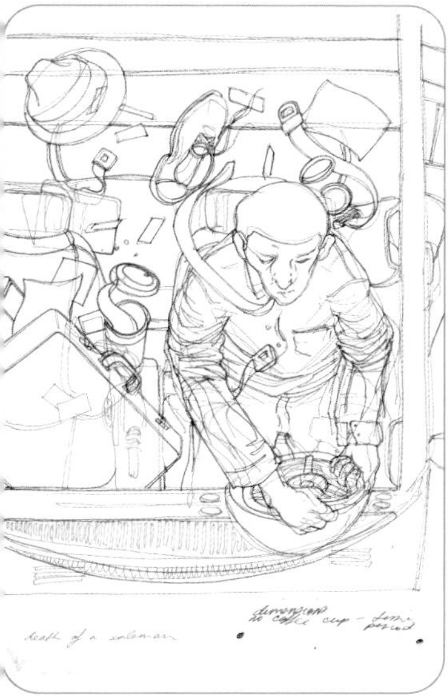
death of a salesman

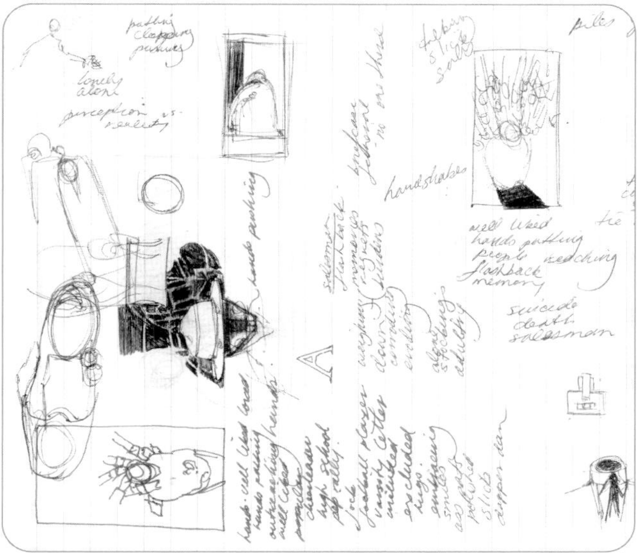
lonely
alone
perception vs.
reality
handshakes
hands pushing
suicide
death
salesman

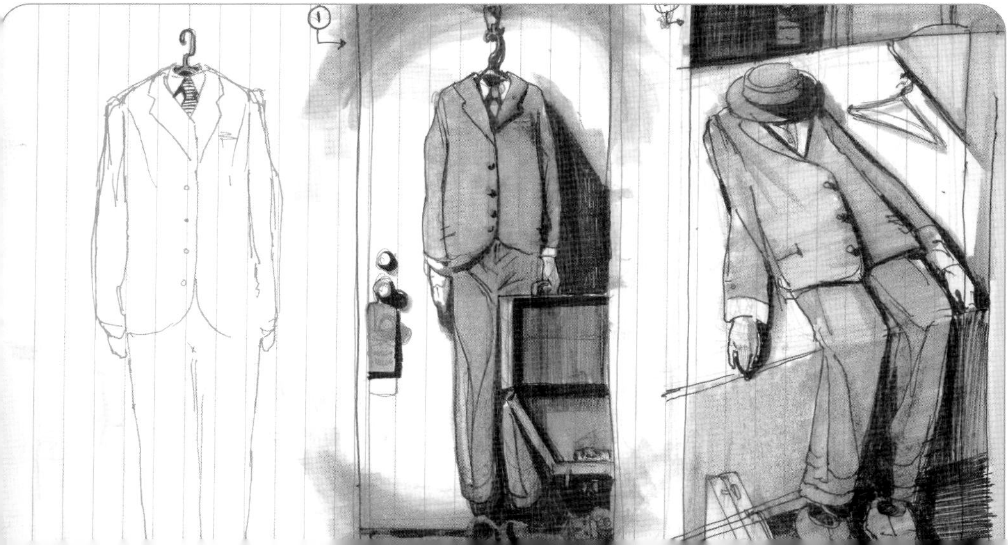

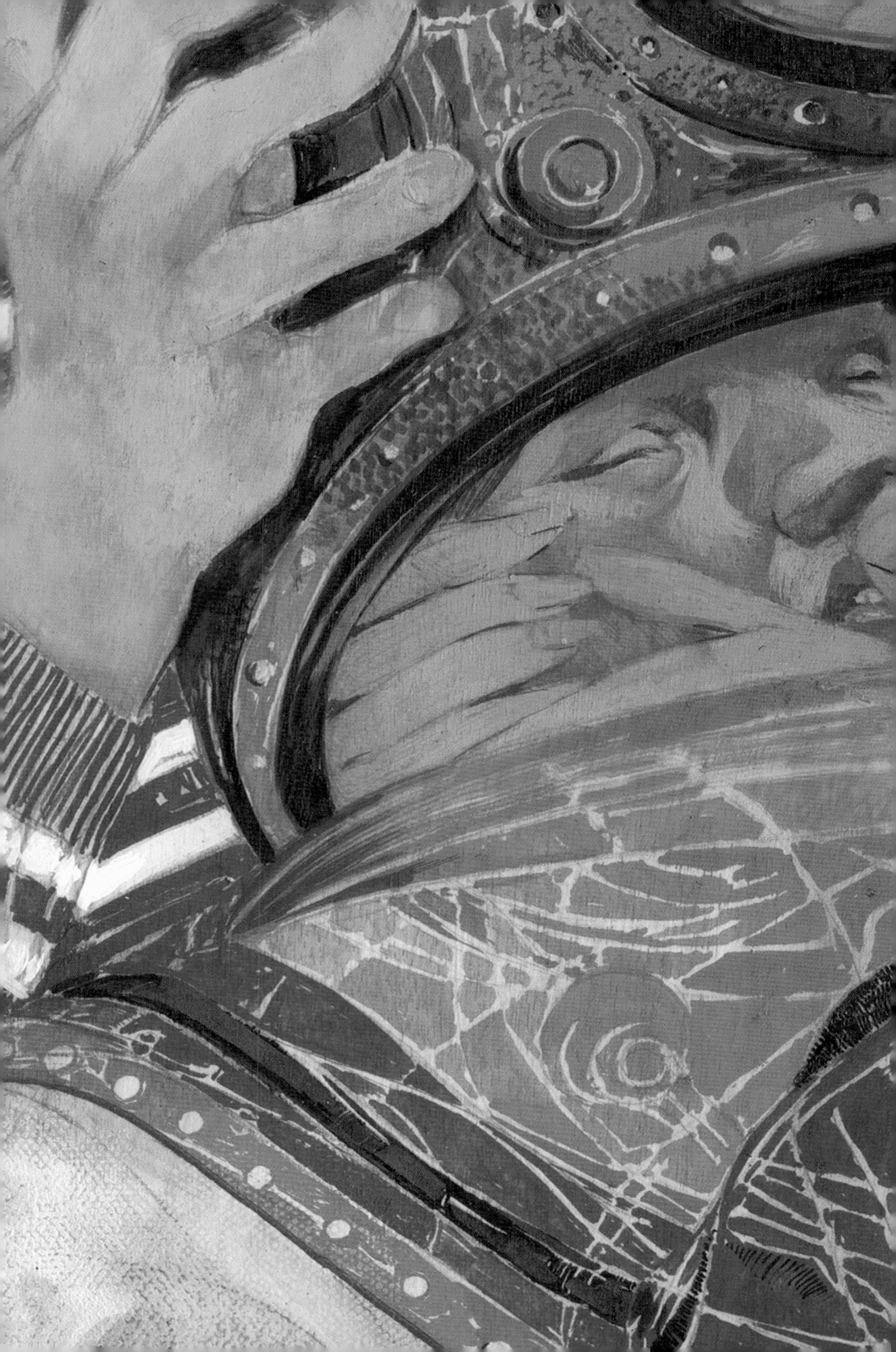

Illustration

There are signature images that have become benchmarks in my development as an artist. In identifying personal, overarching problems to solve, I have found that commercial parameters can be wrapped within personal philosophies. *I believe this to be the secret.*

"Shakespeare in the Park" (page 71) marked the successful pursuit and pairing of *line and tone.* "Audio Detective" (page 57) was inspired by the notion of showing *honesty* in my work. "Johnny Cash" (page 31) solved the problem of *time* as a concept. *Chaos vs. control* yielded the body of work for "Emergent" (pages 90-103). "Blessing of the Hounds" (page A, false title page) was painted in an attempt to combine *abstraction and realism.* "Mickey Mouse Club" (page 32) was the product of attempting to paint *soft edges with straight lines.* Each self-imposed challenge is the thread that links a period in my artistic growth. Once the question has been answered, a new problem is introduced.

Between the demands of a Blue Collar ethic and ambitions of a White Collar aesthetic, there is a channel uncluttered by bias and class. In this space, *commercial work is personal and personal work is handed the bullhorn.*

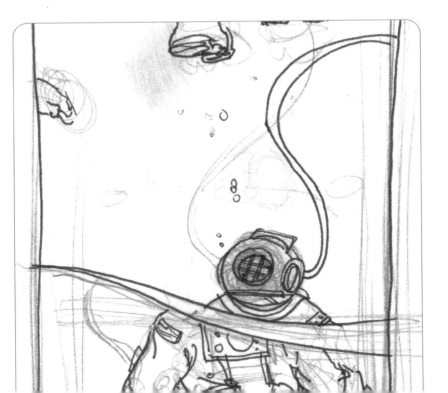

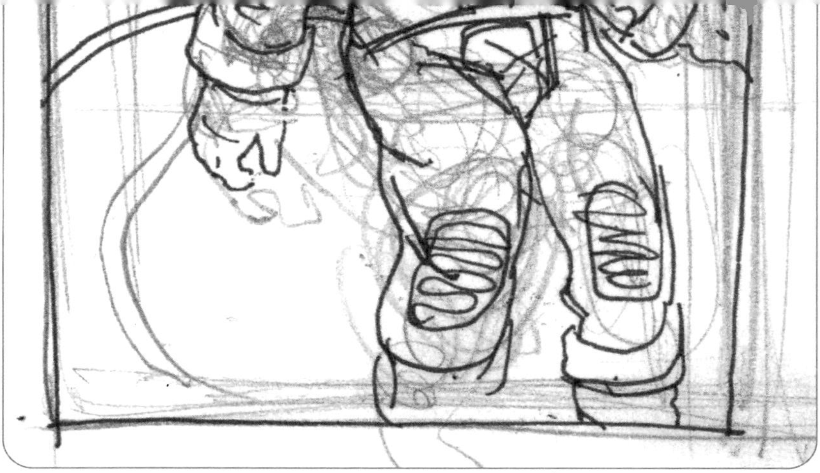

"The Bends"

Illustration tends to be about the idea or the story, rarely both. "The Bends" (front cover & pages 28-29) was my first successful realization of an image that lives comfortably between the *narrative* and the *concept.*

Commissioned as a chapter introduction for an illustration source book, I was provided only the theme – "pearls" as a catalyst. In my research of pearls, I discovered a distinction in quality between freshwater pearls that are farmed and those that are discovered in the sea.

In assignments without definitive parameters, the challenge is in identifying the problem to solve. Once clearly articulated, a solution can be found. In this instance, the client's product provided the missing information. Illustrators use source books to generate commissions. Stock illustration is the antithesis of commissioned work; the latter much more valuable than the former. The deep-sea diver surfaced as the logical allegory to communicate adventure and exploration.

And what is greater than wealth? *Love.* The diver returns to the surface with treasure in his hand and Venus in his heart as his shipmates frantically try to save his life.

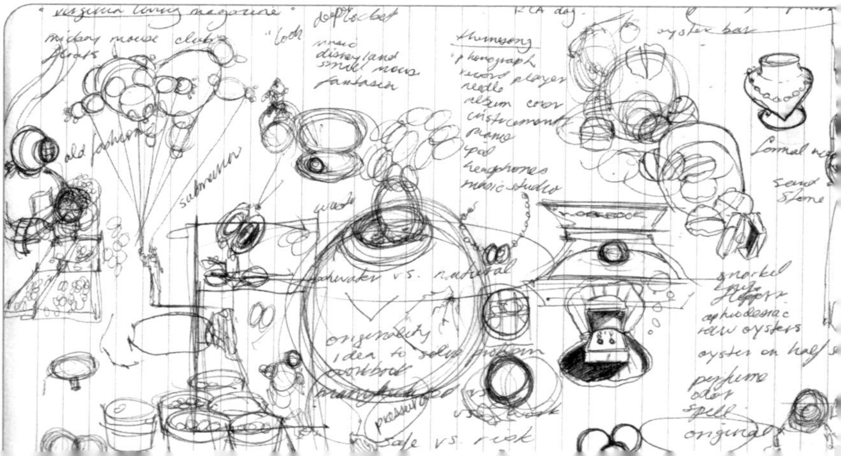
mickey mouse club
disneyland
phonograph
record player
needle
album cover
headphones
music studio
oyster bar
old fashioned
submarine
snorkel
raw oysters
oyster on half
perfume
odor
safe vs. risk

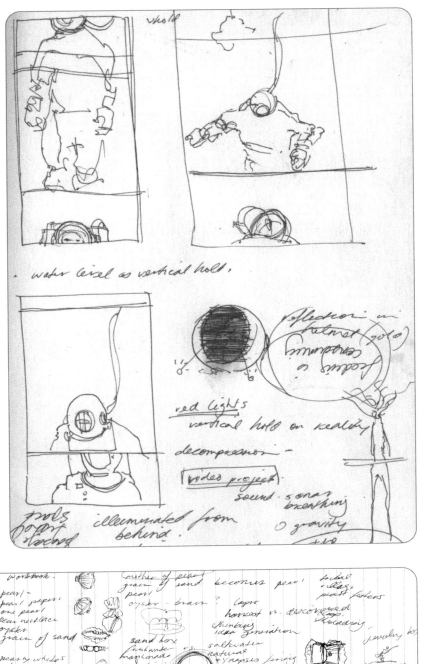

whole

water level as vertical hold.

Reflection in helmet (gold)

Product is ...

red lights
vertical hold on reality

decompression

[video project]

sound · sonar
breathing

illuminated from behind.

○ gravity

+10

workbook.

pearl —
pearl papers
one pearl
pearl necklace
oyster
grain of sand

pearly whites
teeth

snowball +

pearl collector
earring
ring
saltwater

mother of pearl
grain of sand becomes pearl
pearl
oyster - brain? layers
harvest vs. discovered

thinking
idea generation

sand box   saltwater
freshwater vs. natural
manmade   + synapse firing

string of ...
brainstorming
sharing ideas
thought bubble
clasp
hinge
down shell bra
pearl farmer

lime pressure
coal: diamond

social
village
pearl fishers

thinking

jewelry box

course
goddess of love

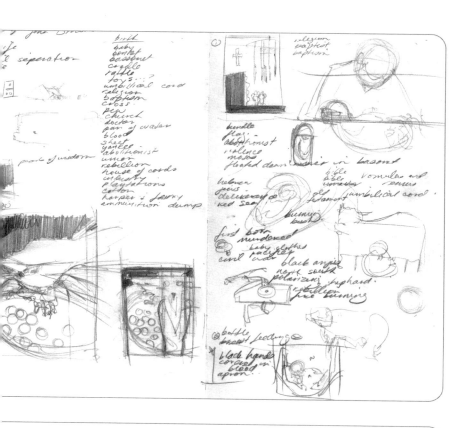

birth
baby
bonnet
bassinet
cradle
rattle
toys...?
umbilical cord
religion
baptism
cross
pen
church
pan of water
blood
sheep
yankee
abolitionist
union
rebellion
house of cards
industry
plantations
cotton
harper's ferry
ammunition dump

separation

part of wisdom

religion
baptist
baptism

bundle
flag
abolitionist
violence
mobs
flooded down river in basins

bible
vomulus and
uble
images
sewers

helmen
pens
delivery
red Sea
lamont
umbilical cord

human
bust

first born
murdered
baby clothes
civil war
pacifier
black angel

north south
polarizing shephard
artillery
fire burning

bottle
breast feeding

black hands
covered in
blood
apron

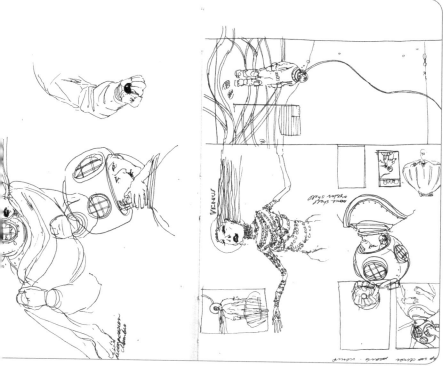

VENUS

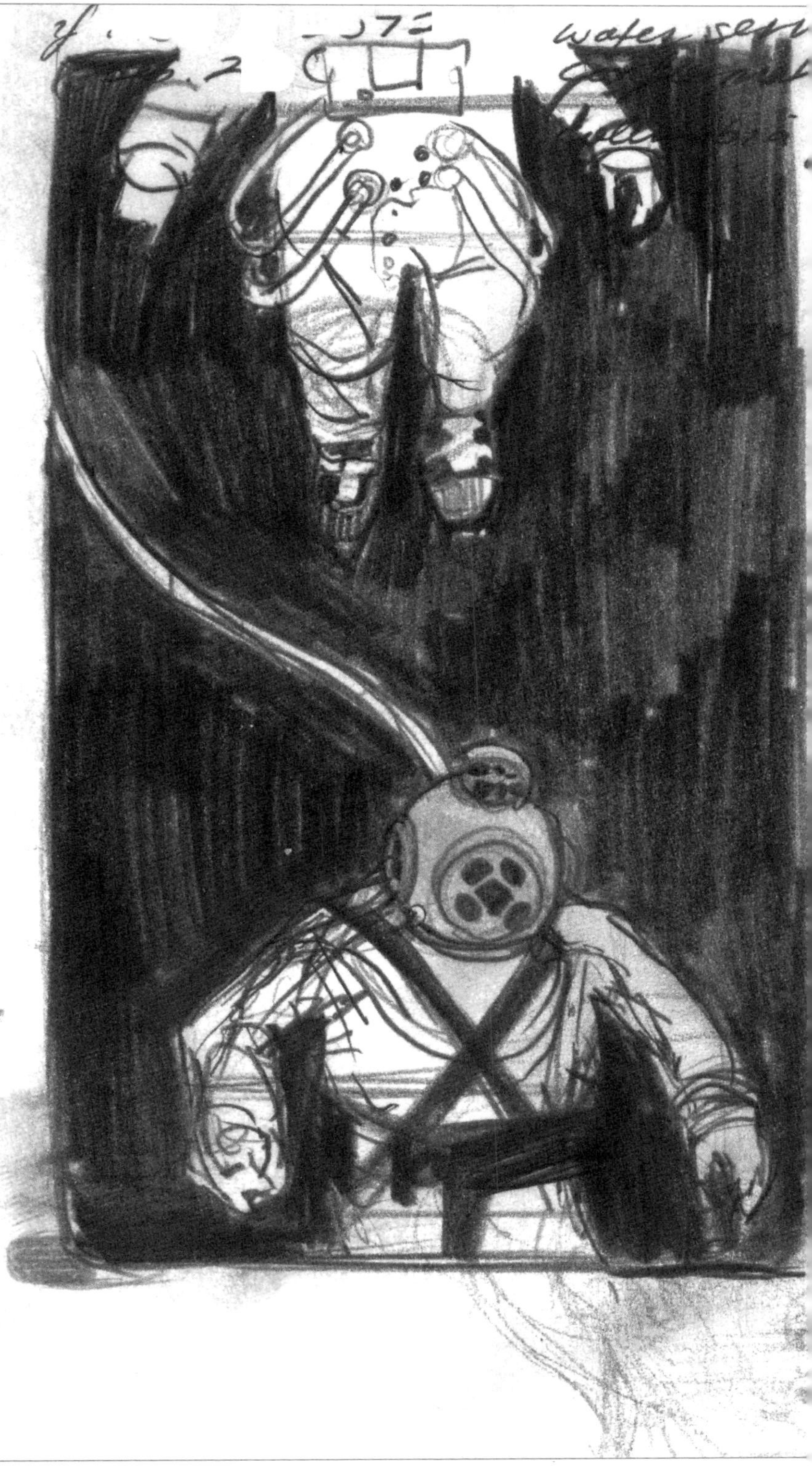

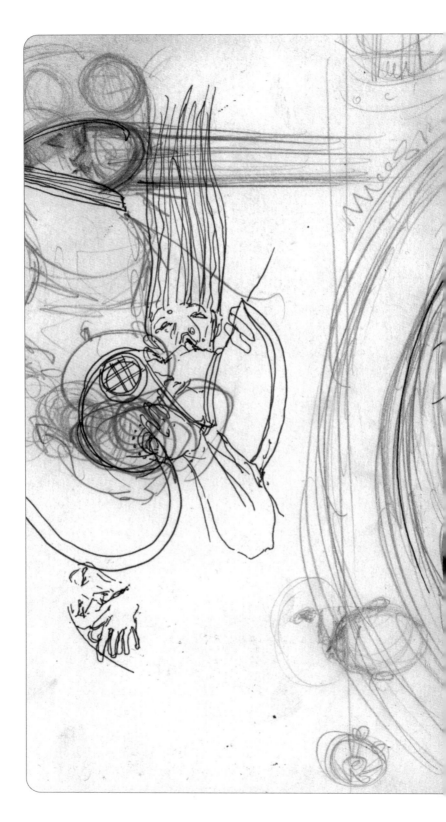

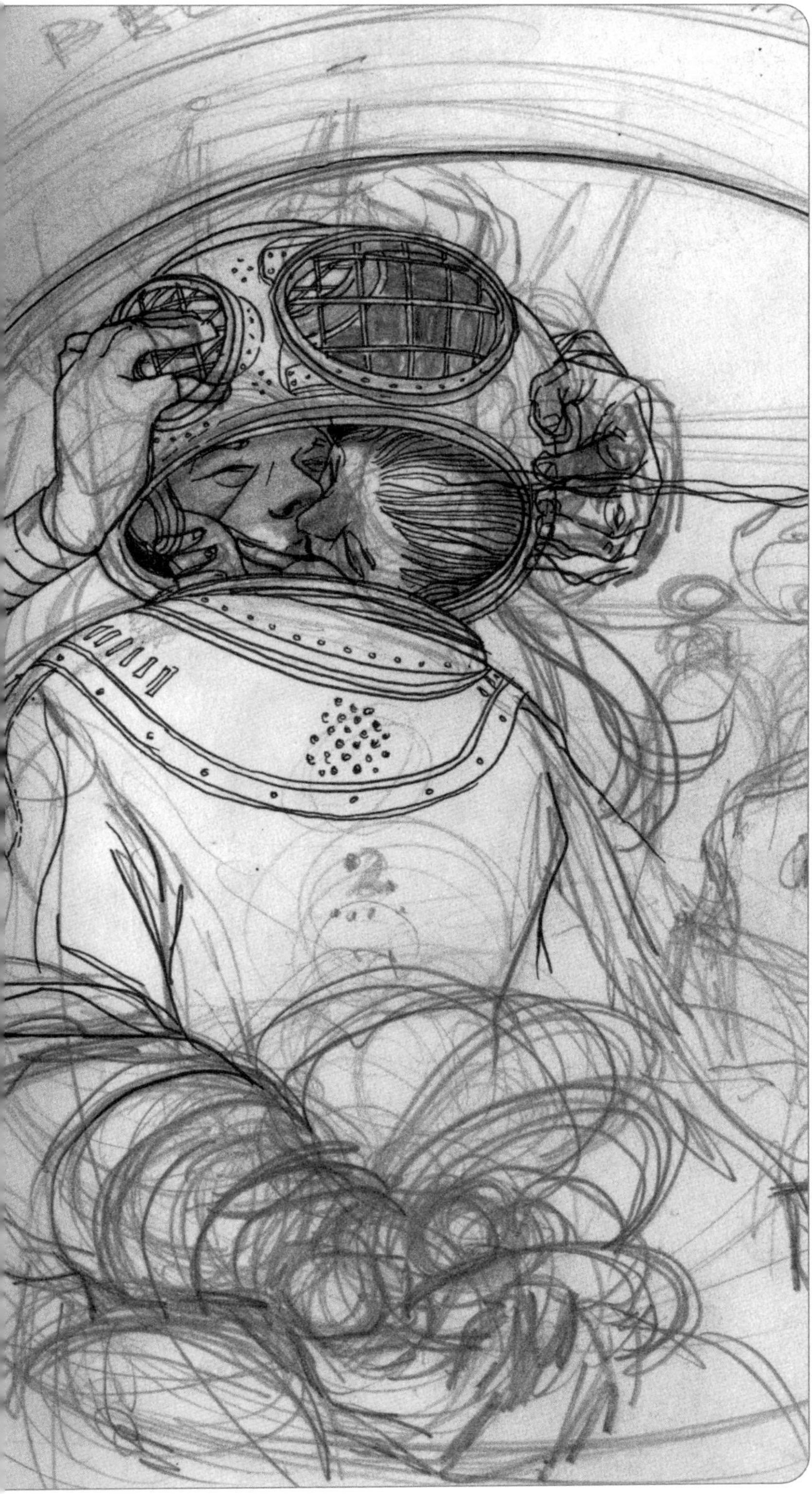

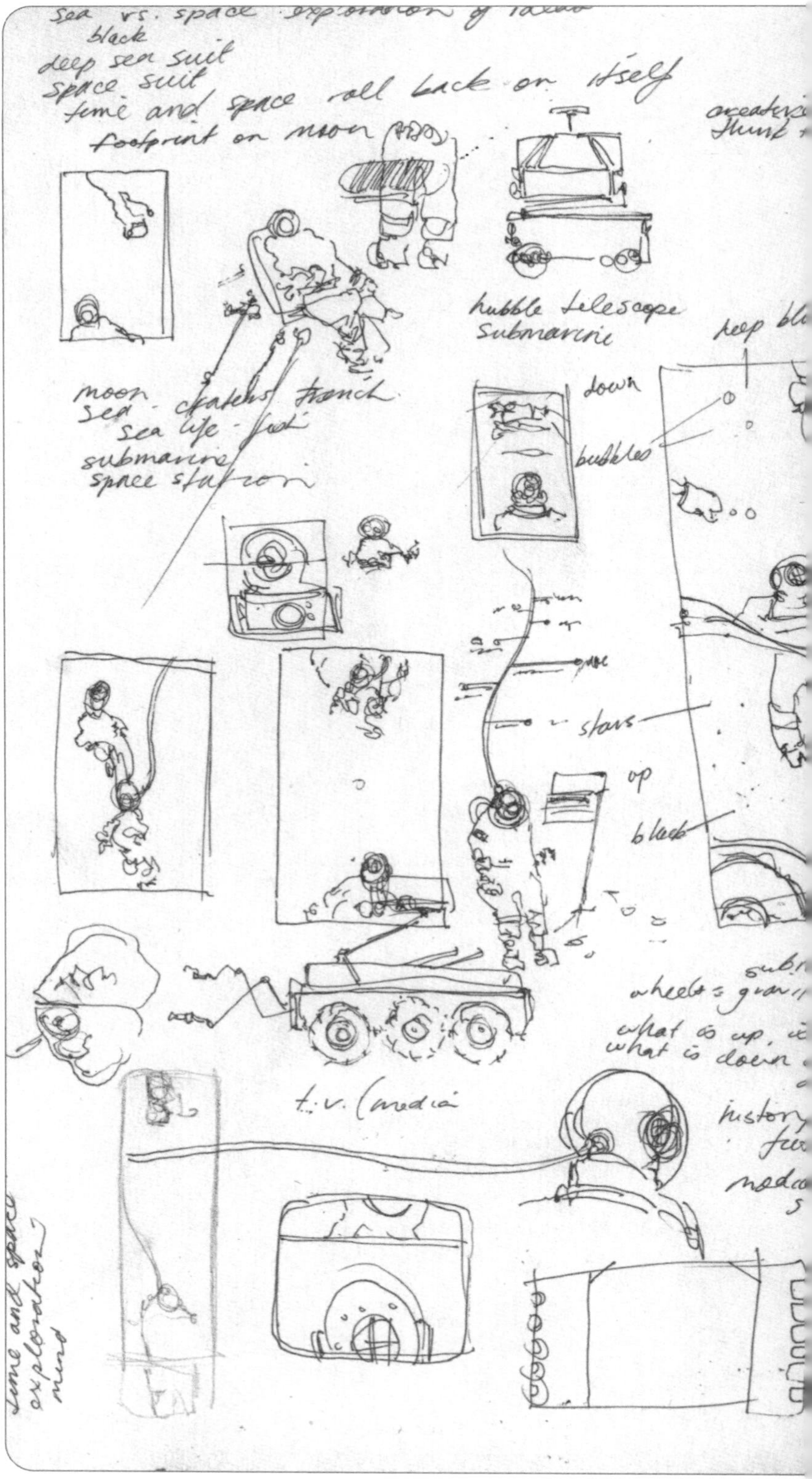

sea vs. space exploration of ideas
black
deep sea suit
space suit
time and space roll back on itself
footprint on moon

creatures
shine

hubble telescope
submarine

deep blue

moon craters trench
sea life-fish
submarine
space station

down

bubbles

stars

up

black

wheels gravity

submarine

what is up, i[s]
what is down

t.v. (media)

history
fir
media
s

time and space
exploration
mind

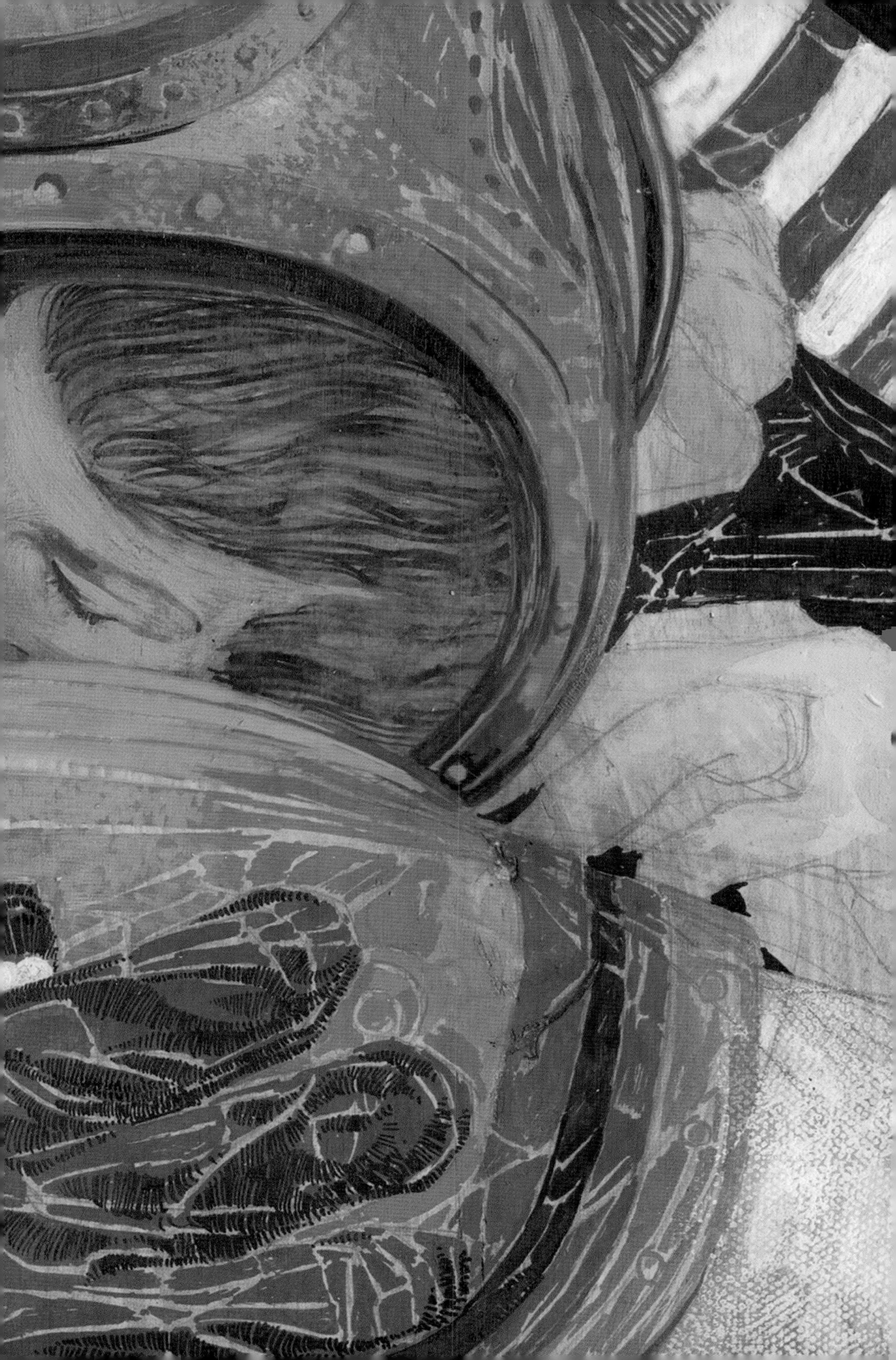

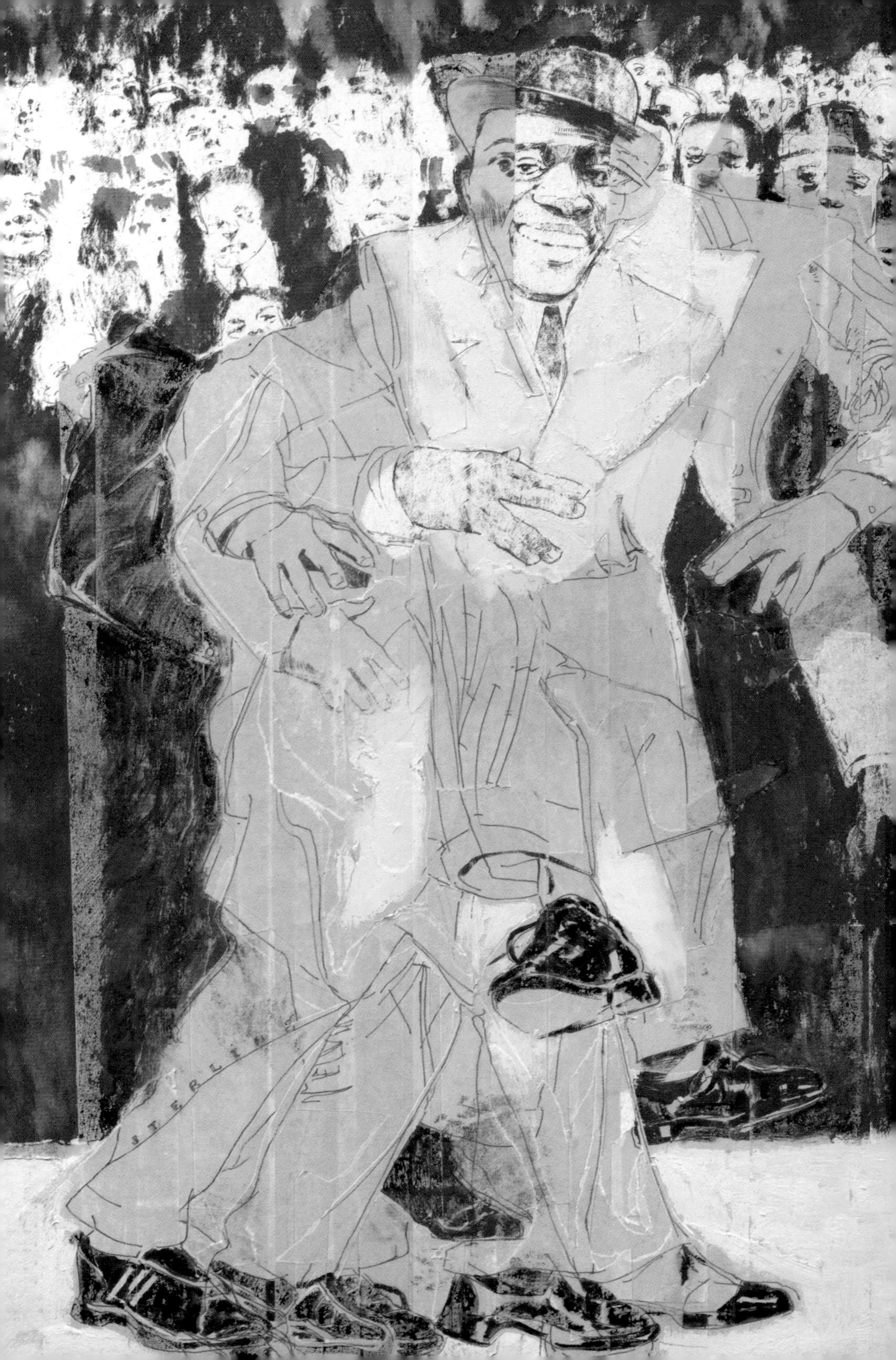
STERLIN

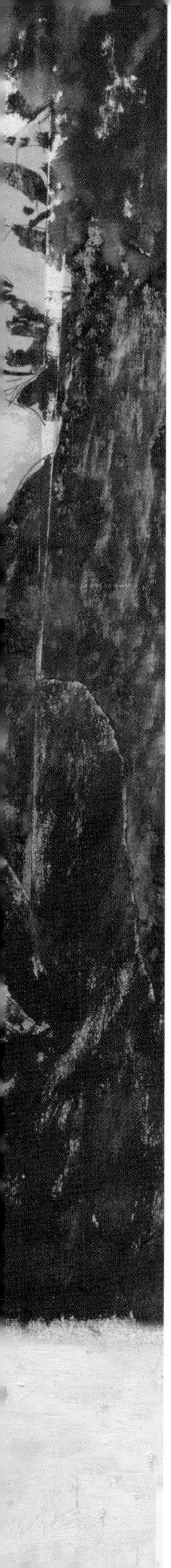

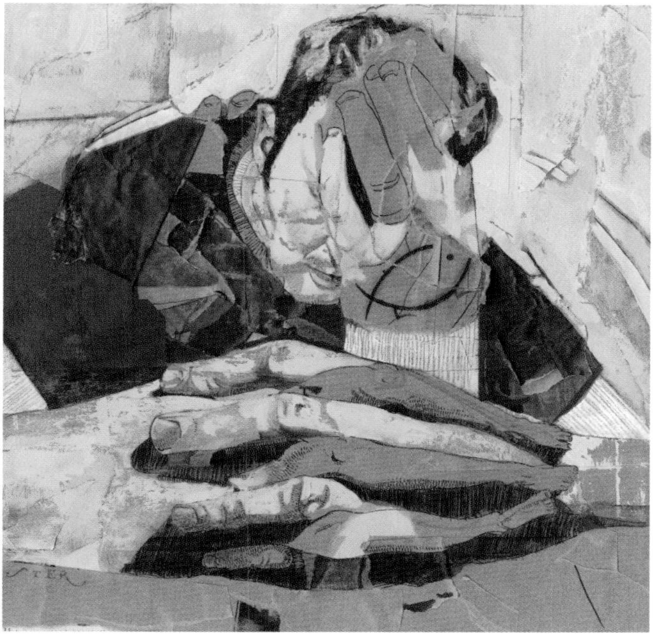

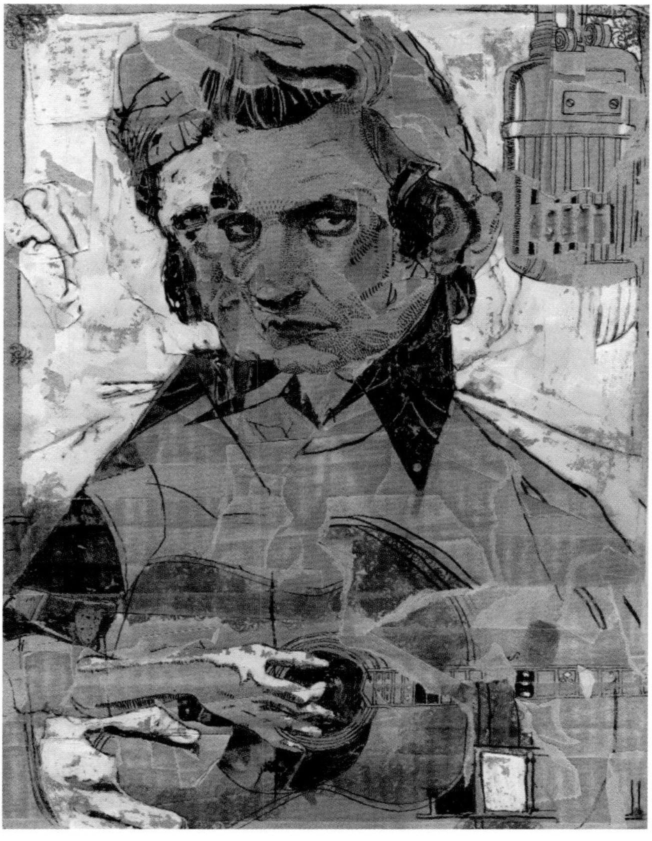

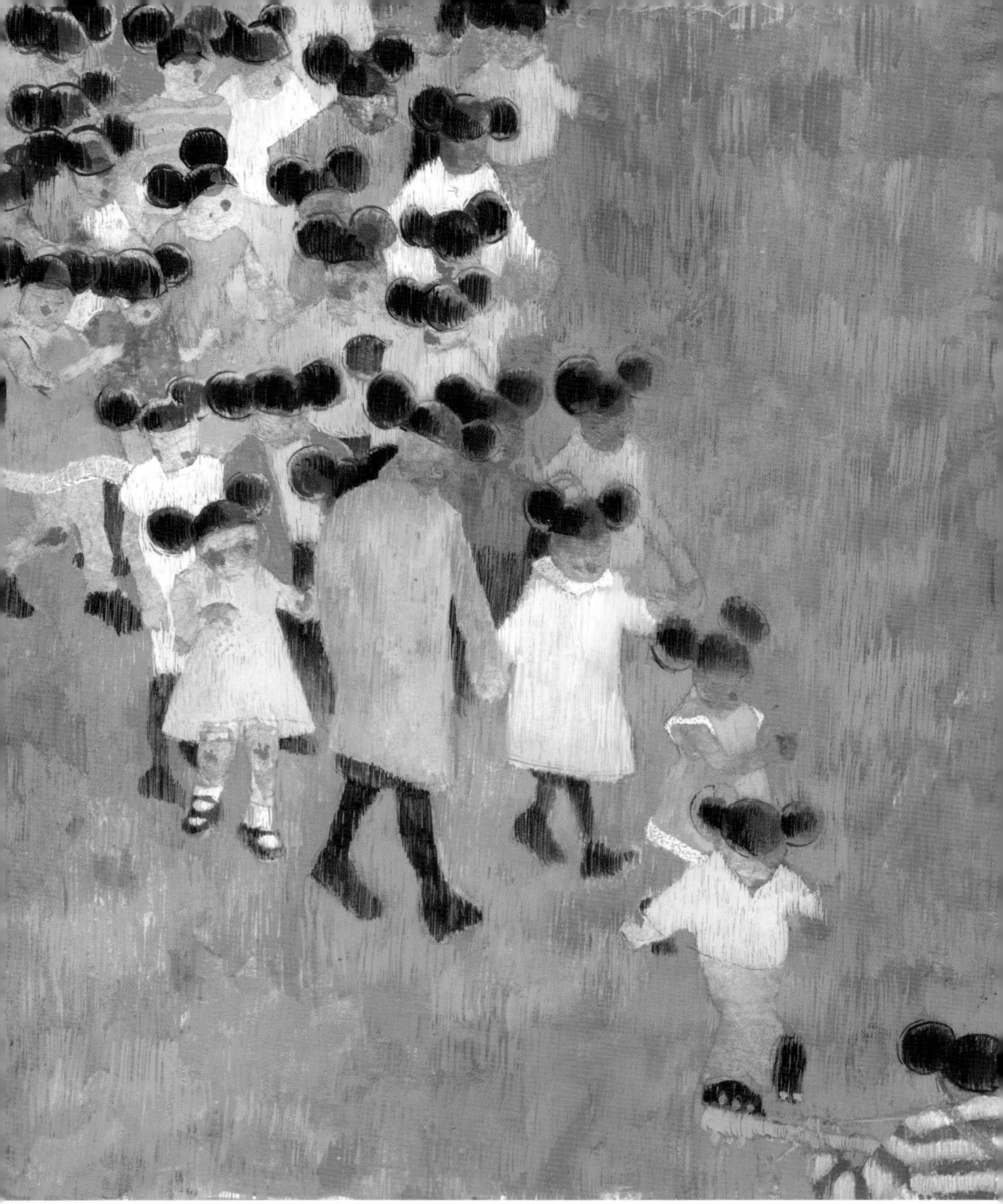

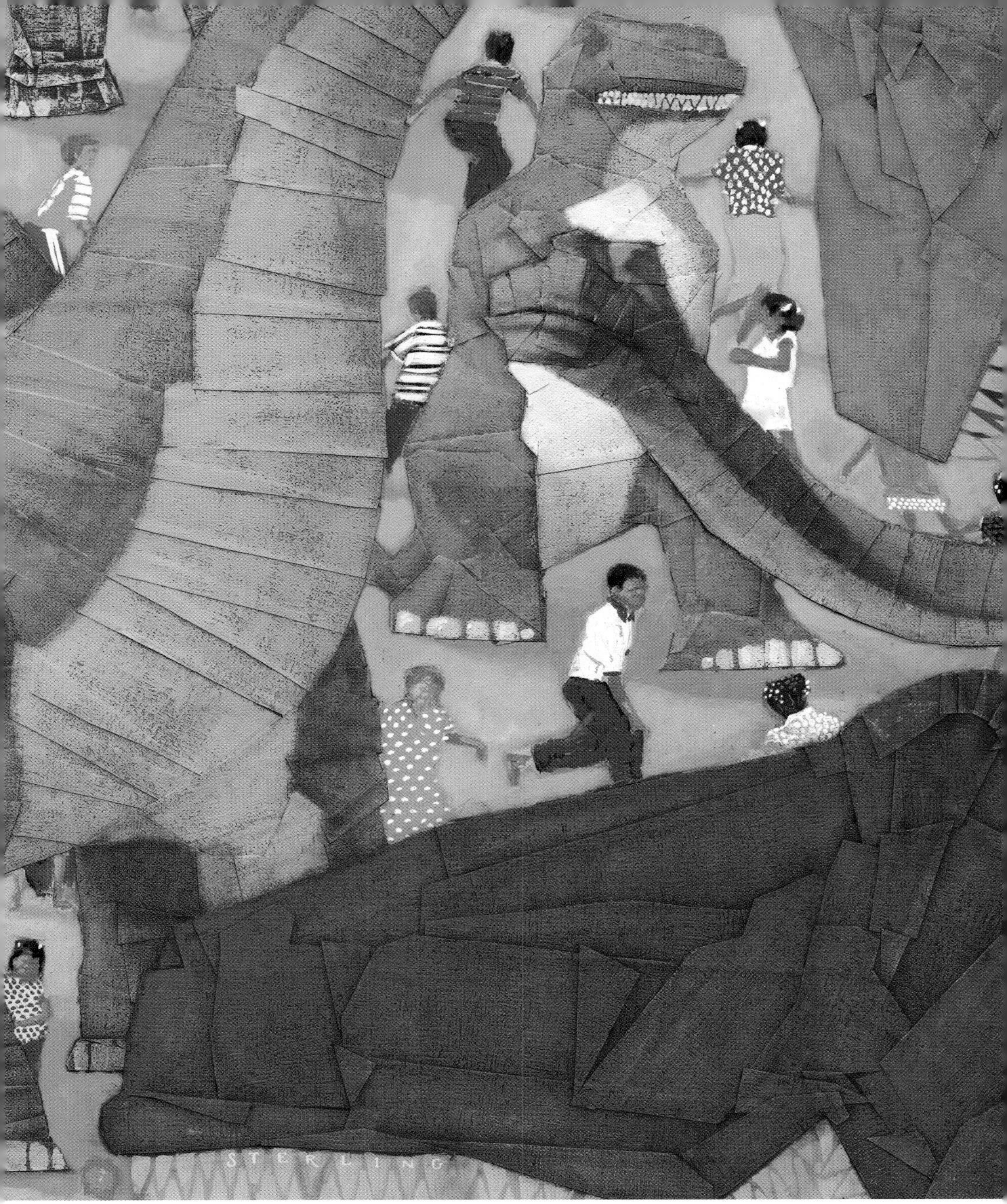
STERLING

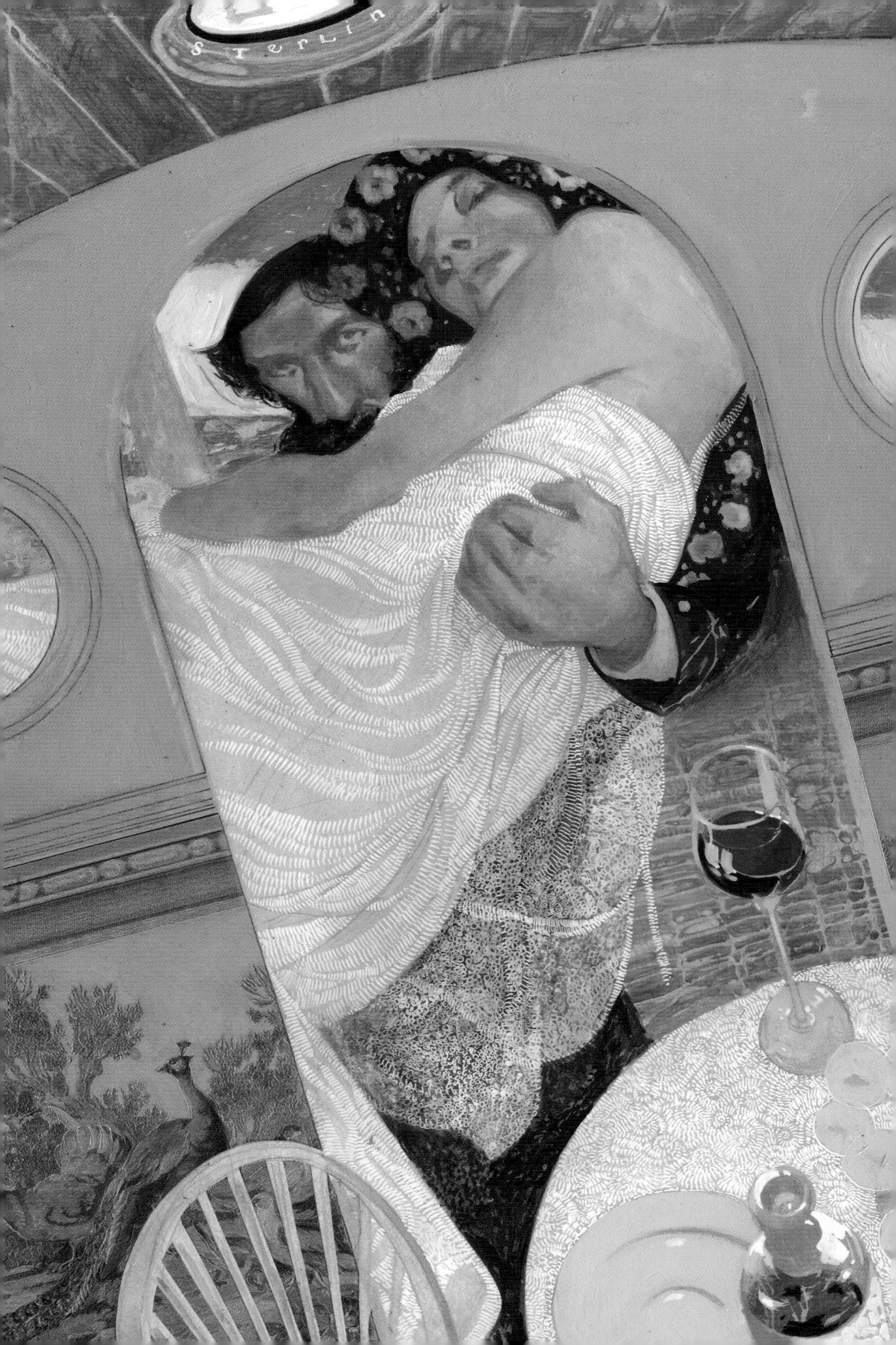

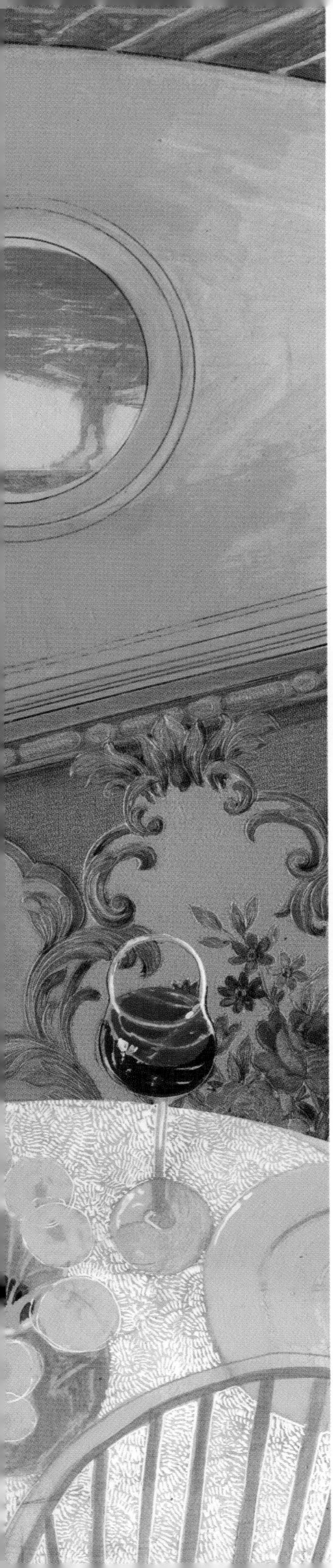

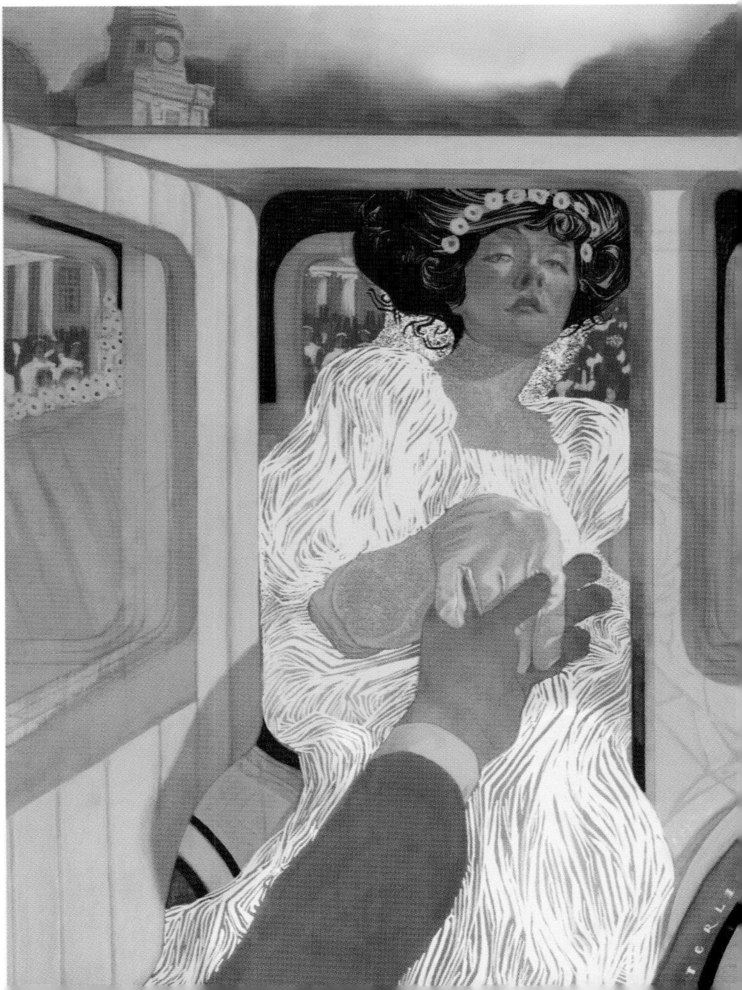

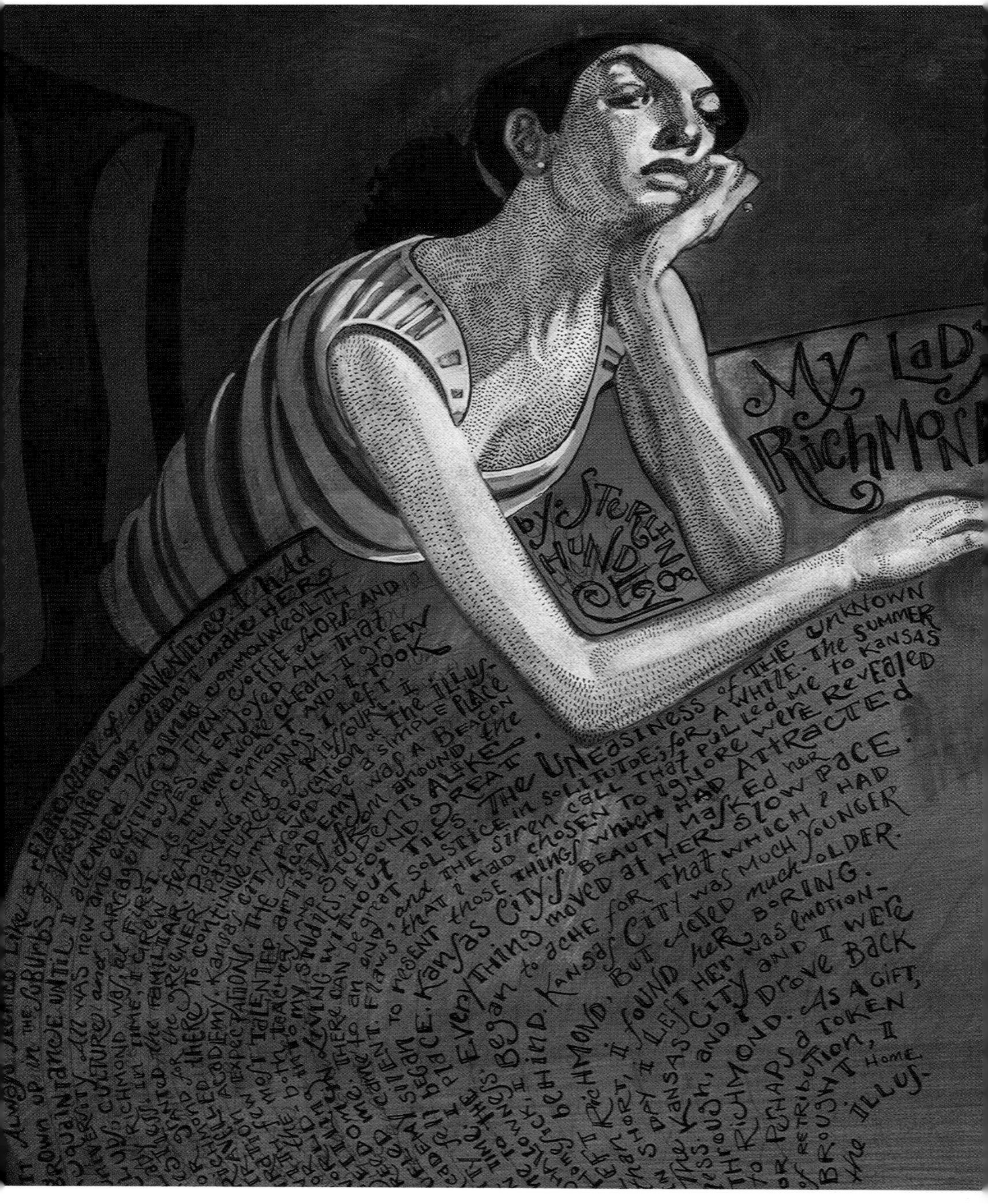

My Lady Richmond
by: Sterling Hundley ©2009
It always seemed like a celebration of convenience. I had
grown up in the suburbs of Virginia but didn't make her
acquaintance until I attended Virginia Commonwealth
University. All was new and exciting then. Coffee shops and
culture, and carriage houses. I enjoyed all that
the new wore clean. I grew
comfort and I took
my things I left. I
Missouri. I
education at the Illus-
be a simple place
was a beacon
from around the
students alike.
The uneasiness of the unknown
solstice in solitude; for a while. The summer
the siren call that pulled me to Kansas
that I had chosen to ignore were revealed
those things which had attracted
Kansas City's beauty masked her
everything moved at her slow pace.
began to ache for that which I had
behind. Kansas City was much younger
Richmond, but acted much older.
I found her boring.
I left her was emotion-
Kansas City and I were
and I drove back
Richmond. As a gift,
perhaps a token
of retribution, I
brought home
the Illus-

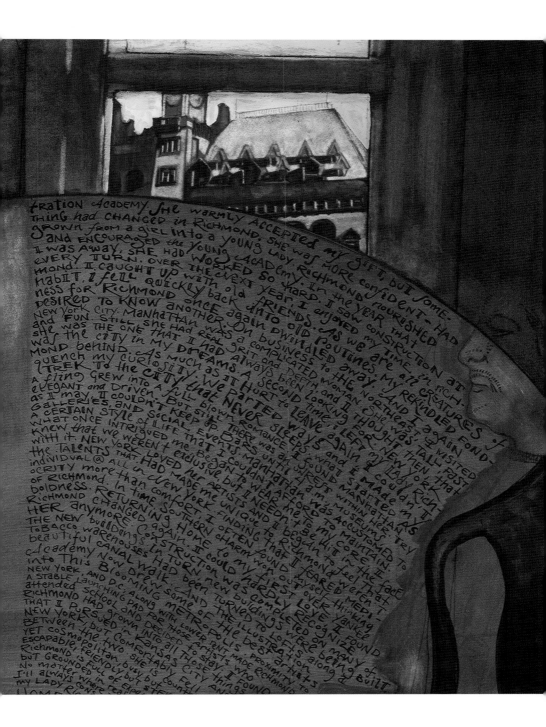

tration academy. She warmly accepted my gift, but something had changed in Richmond. She was more confident - had
grown from a girl into a young lady. Richmond nourished
and encouraged the young academy. In the year that
I was away, she had worked so hard. I saw construction at
every turn. Over the next year I enjoyed my time in Richmond. I caught up with old friends. As we are all creatures of
habit, I fell quickly back into old routines. My rekindled fond-
ness for Richmond once again dwindled away. I thought again
desired to know another. On business to the northeast I visited
New York City. Manhattan was a complicated woman. She was tall fast
and fun. Still she had real grit and depth and I could see
she was the one that I had always been looking. New York
was the city in my dreams. A second time I left my lady Richmond behind. As much as it hurt to leave again I made my
trek to the city that never sleeps and I started. Manhattan's
elegant and driven. But still there was a street within her
as I may. I couldn't keep up. Bars until I found myself within her
galleries, and social events that I am accustomed to
a certain style of life that I found hard to maintain.
what once intrigued me began to wear me to my core. I
knew that we weren't exclusive but I needed to feel that
with it. New York loved her artists and I am in the face
the talents that had made me unique and I began to feel that
individual at all in New York. Finding that Richmond wasn't
ocrity more than comfort. I often found myself over thinking
of Richmond. In time southern charm won out. I feared
boldness. Returning home to my first love, I recognized
Richmond changed again. I could hardly recognize many of
her anymore. Construction was completed. I found
the new buildings in turn had been turned to lofts along a
Tobacco warehouses. And some of the illustration being built
beautiful canal walk now drew some of the best artists to
Academy now blooming. And D.C. along with lower metropolis, proximity to
into this blooming launching pad for those artists who
New York, and D.C. along with the best artists
a stable school and decided to stay. I found Richmond to
attended Richmond had grown into all those things
Richmond
that I pursued in Kansas City things
New York, but comfortably fell between the two
yet cosmopolitan, busy but country
escapable, friendly but but
Richmond is full of expected an
but grounded in respect
No matter where I roam
I'll always consider
my lady Rich
Homer

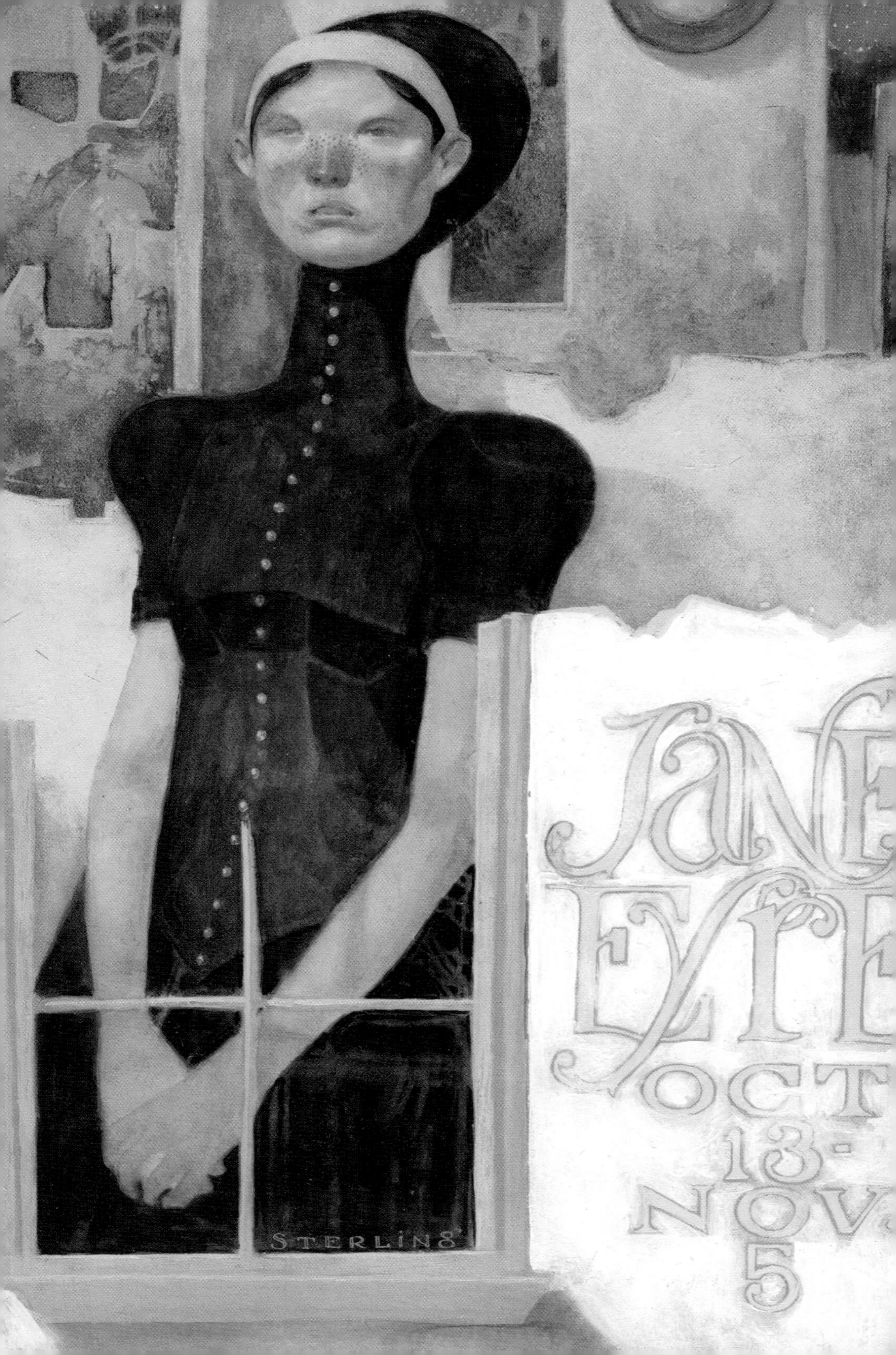
STERLING
JANE
EYRE
OCT
13-
NOV
5

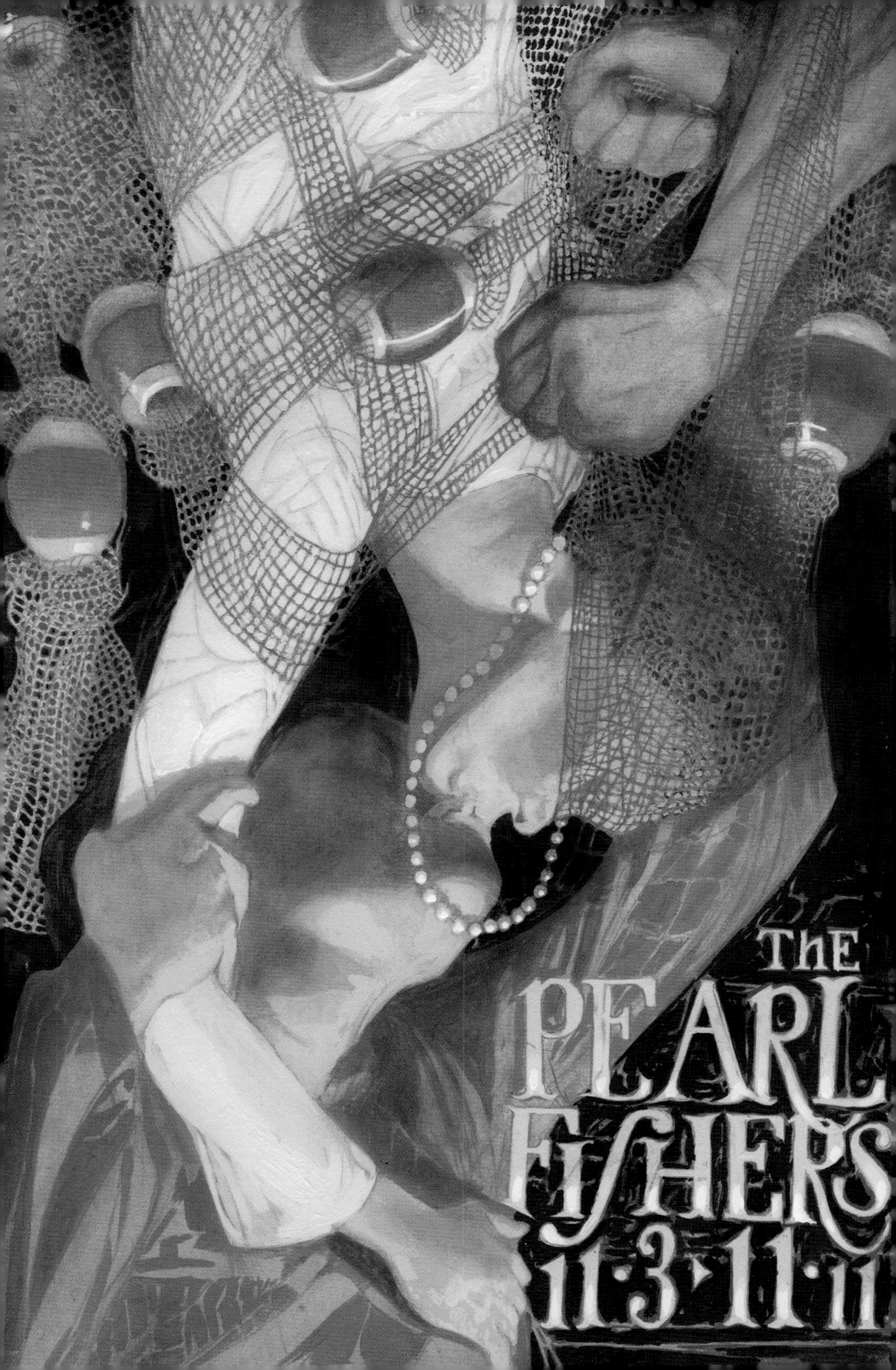
The
PEARL
FISHERS
11·3·11·11

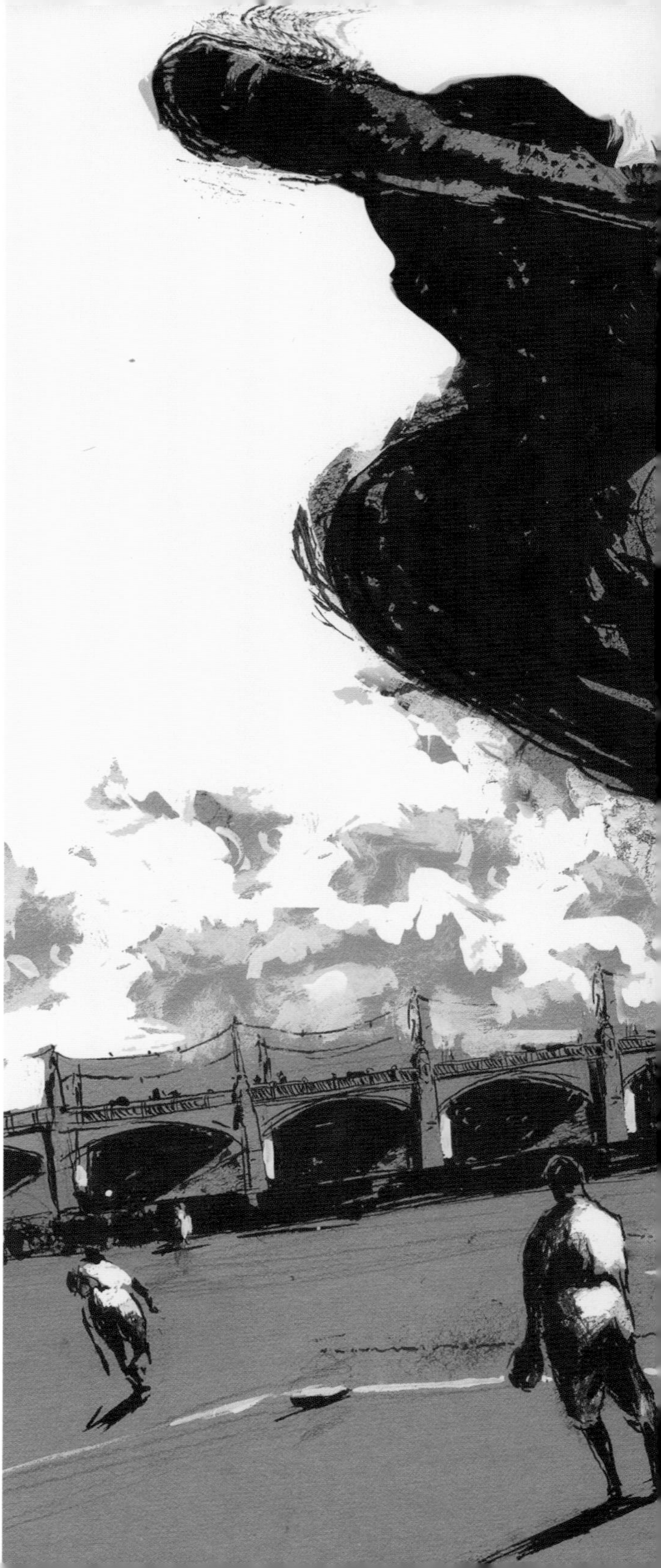

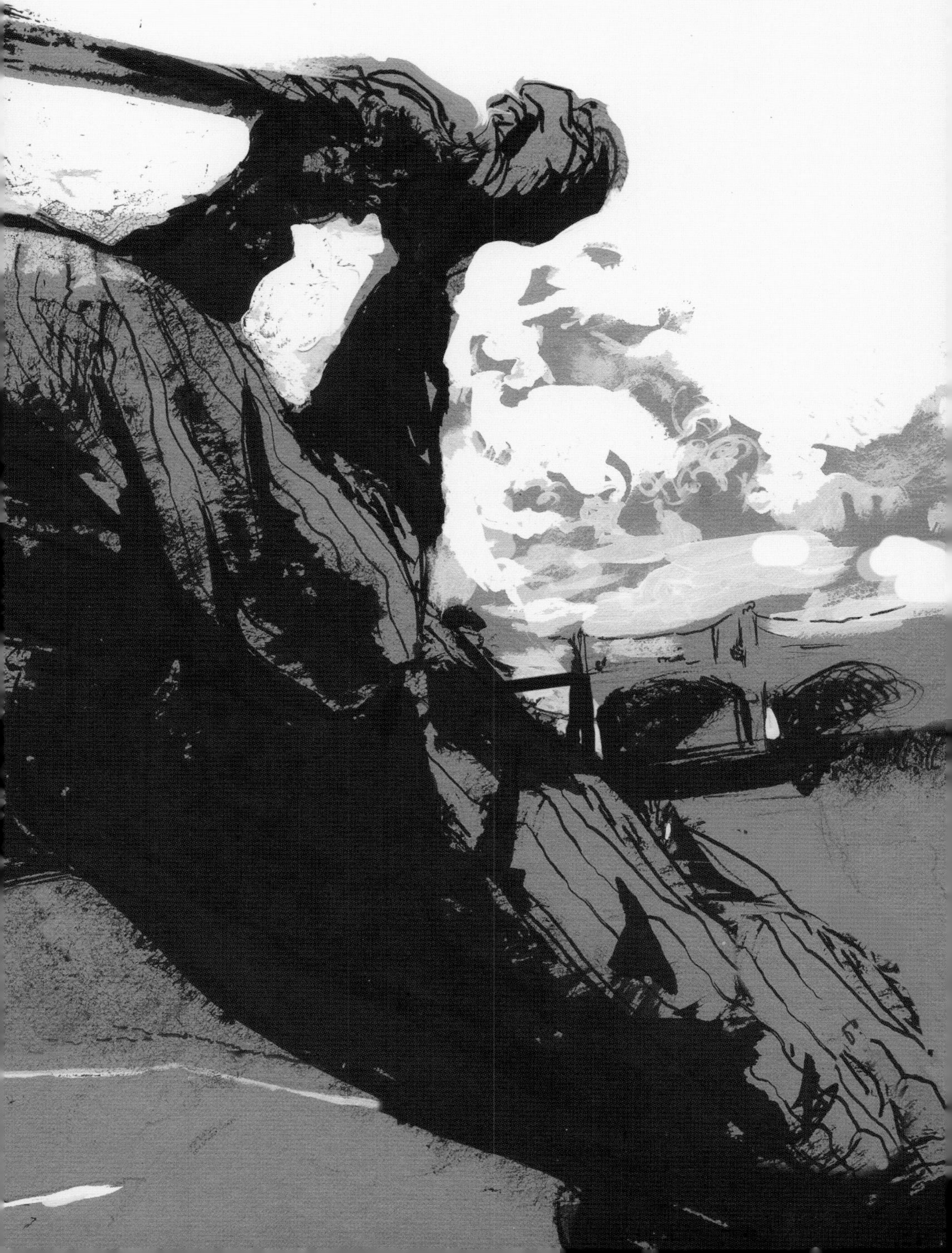

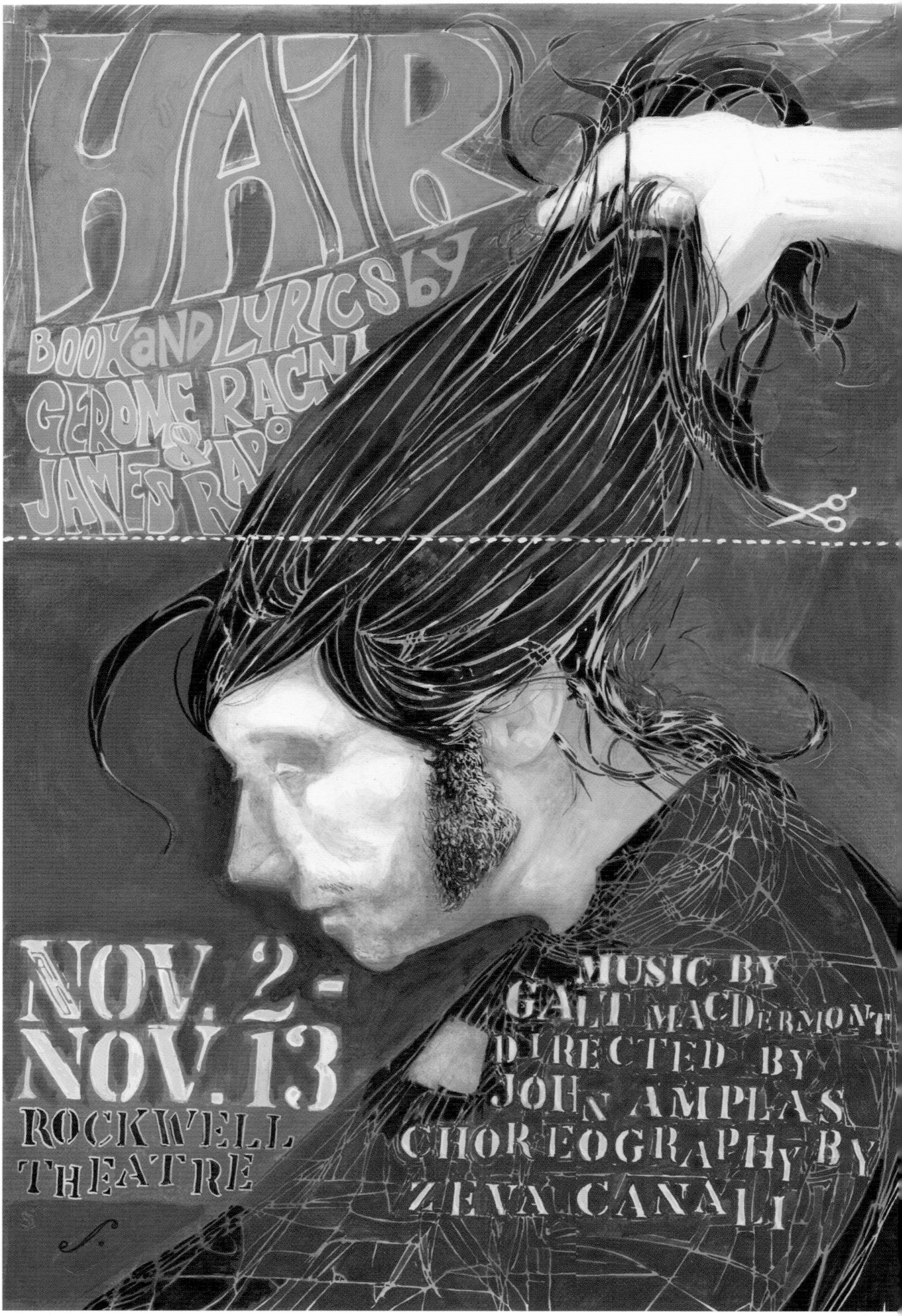
HAIR
BOOK AND LYRICS BY
GEROME RAGNI
& JAMES RADO
NOV. 2 -
NOV. 13
ROCKWELL
THEATRE
MUSIC BY
GALT MACDERMONT
DIRECTED BY
JOHN AMPLAS
CHOREOGRAPHY BY
ZEVA CANALI

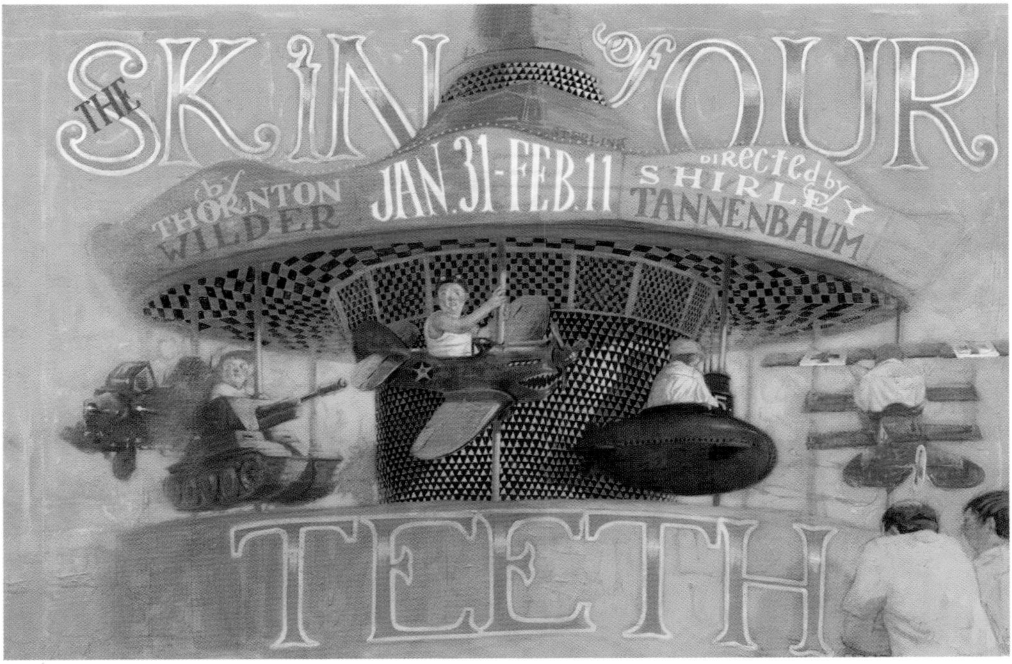
THE SKIN of OUR
by THORNTON WILDER
JAN. 31-FEB. 11
Directed by SHIRLEY TANNENBAUM
TEETH

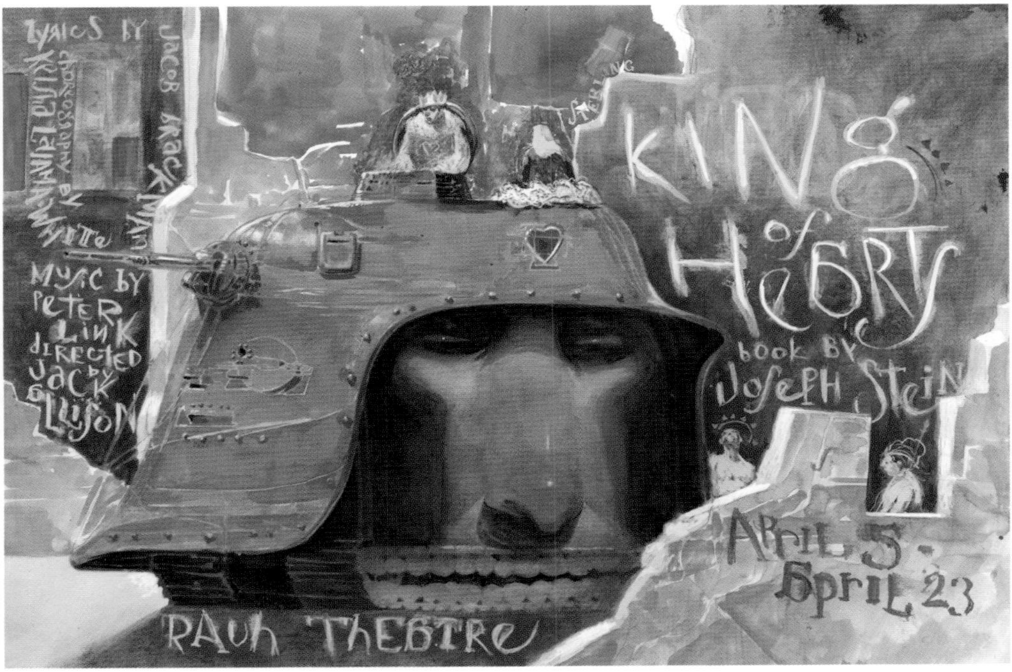
Lyrics by Jacob Brackman
Music by Peter Link
King of Hearts
book by Joseph Stein
April 5 - April 23
Rauh Theatre

DIRECTED BY John Sheppard

Musical Producing

Producing DIRECTOR Ronald

February 18-29

MARAT SADE

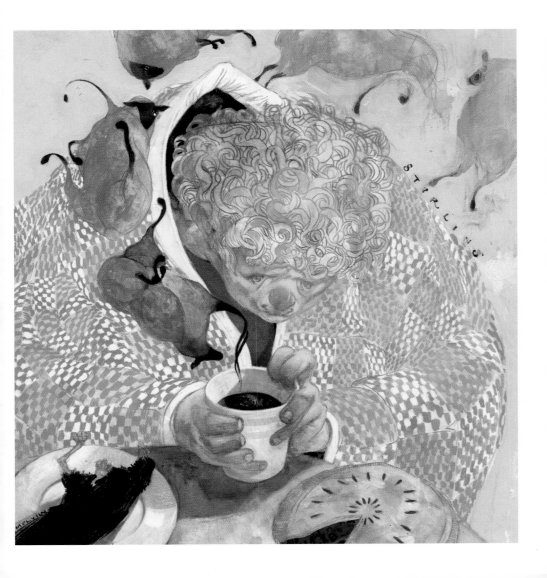

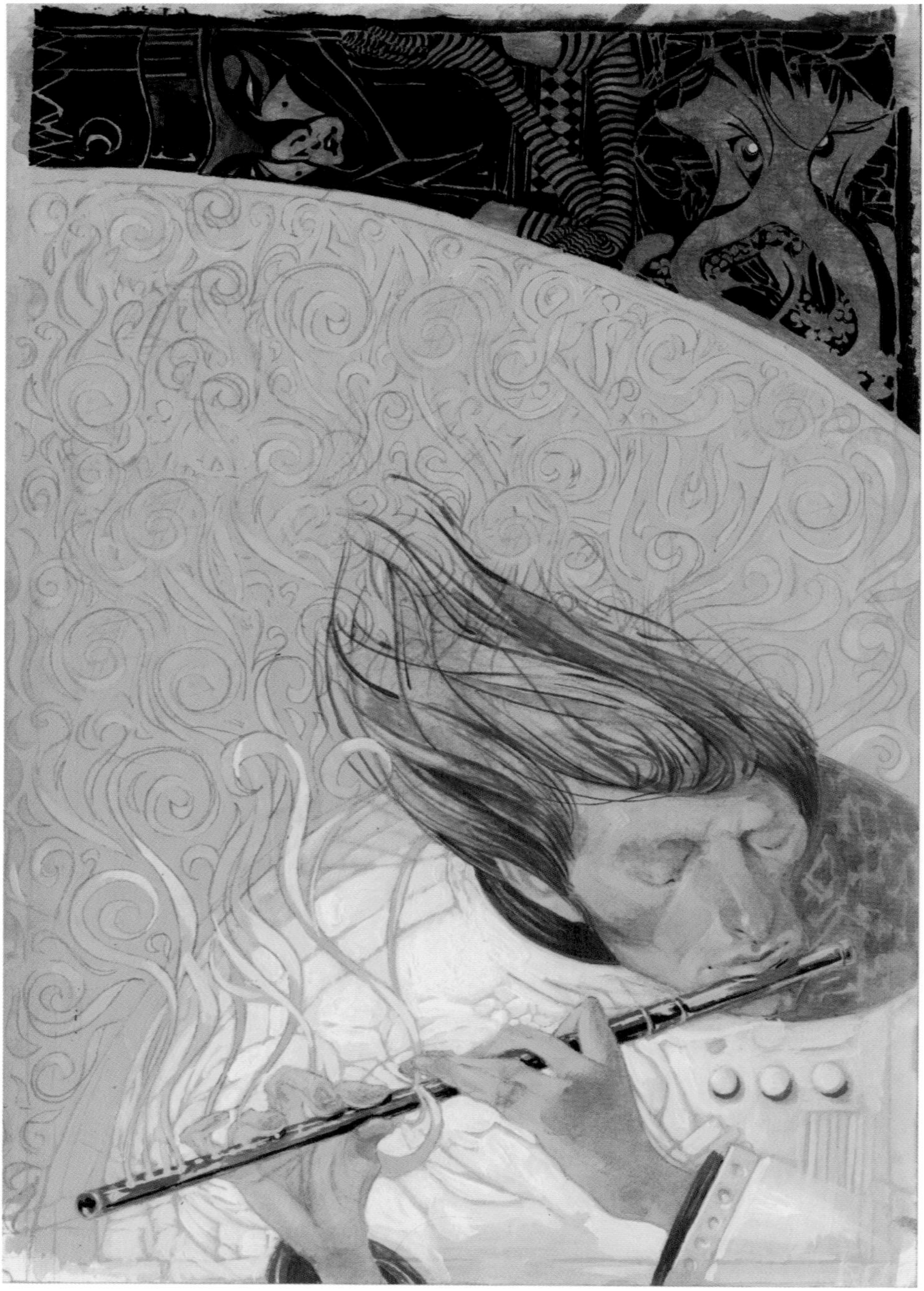

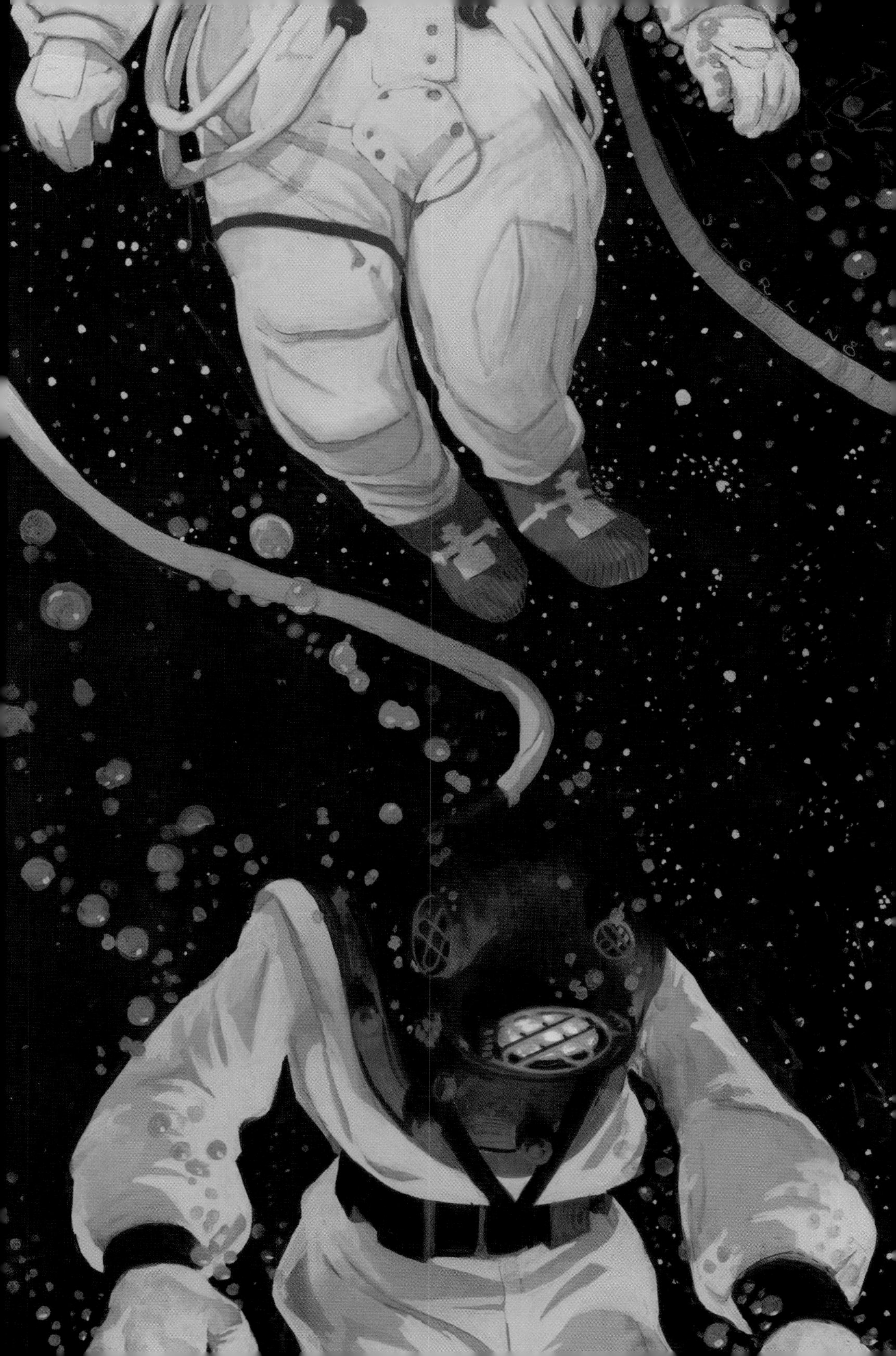

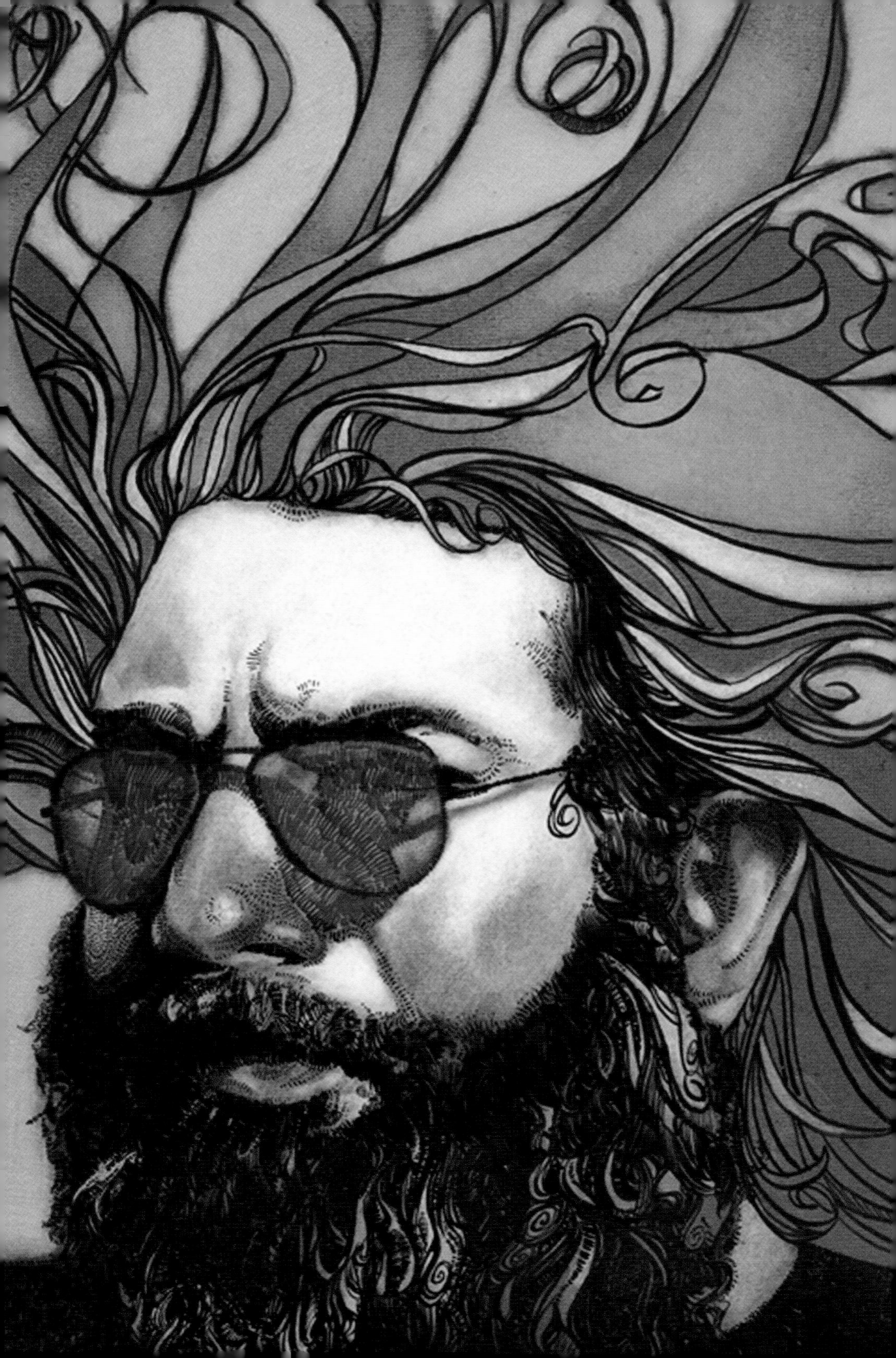

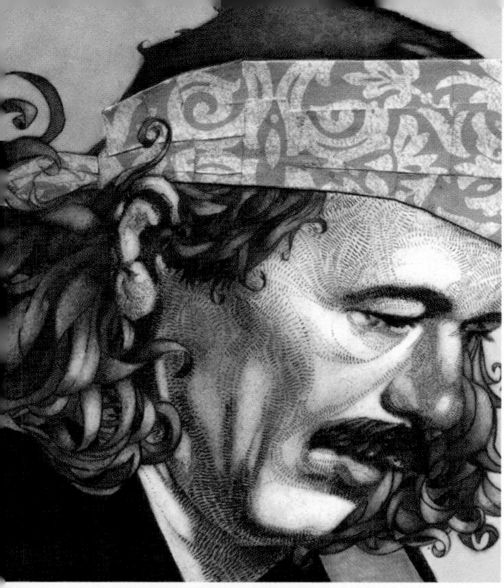

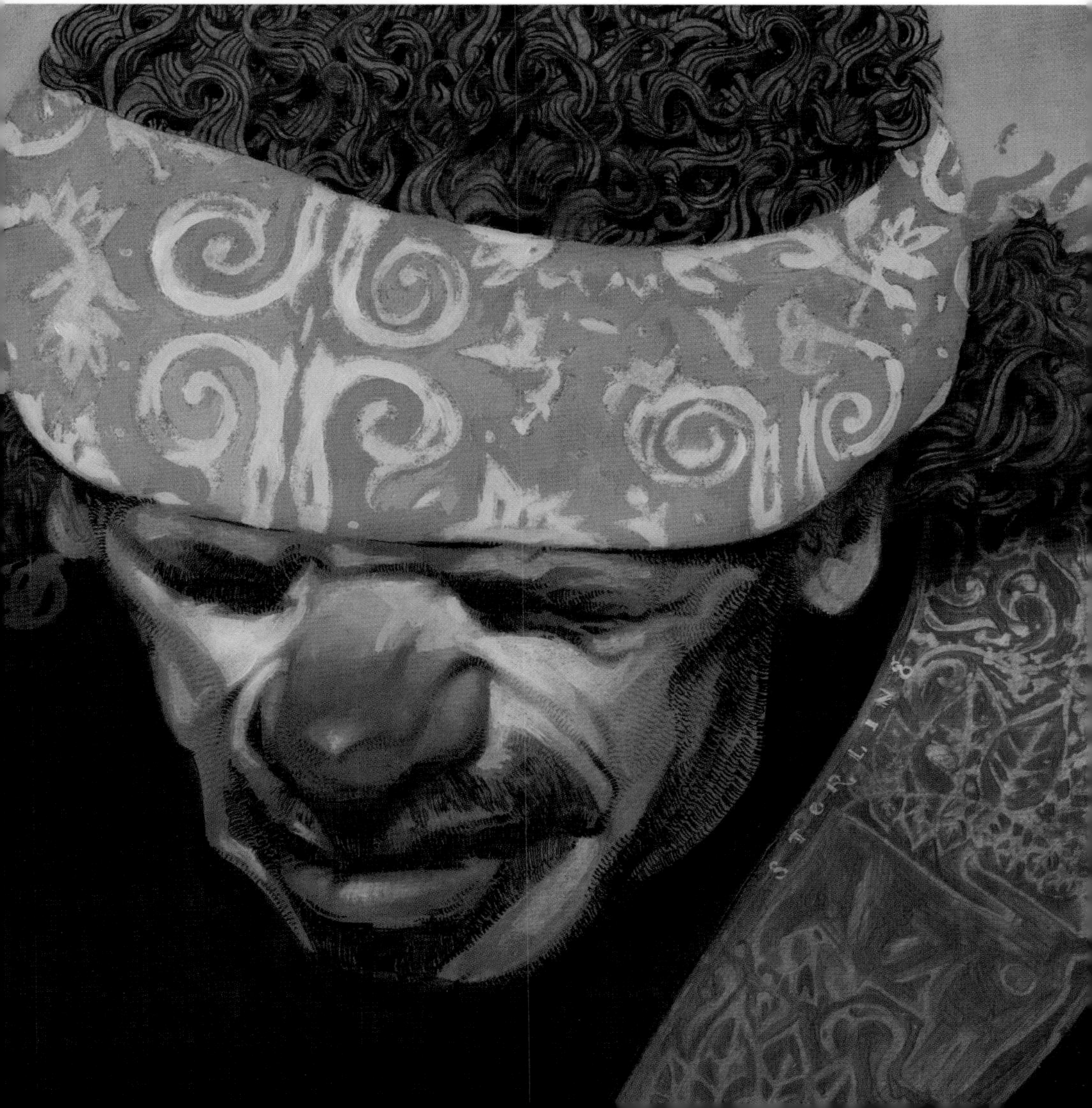
STERLING

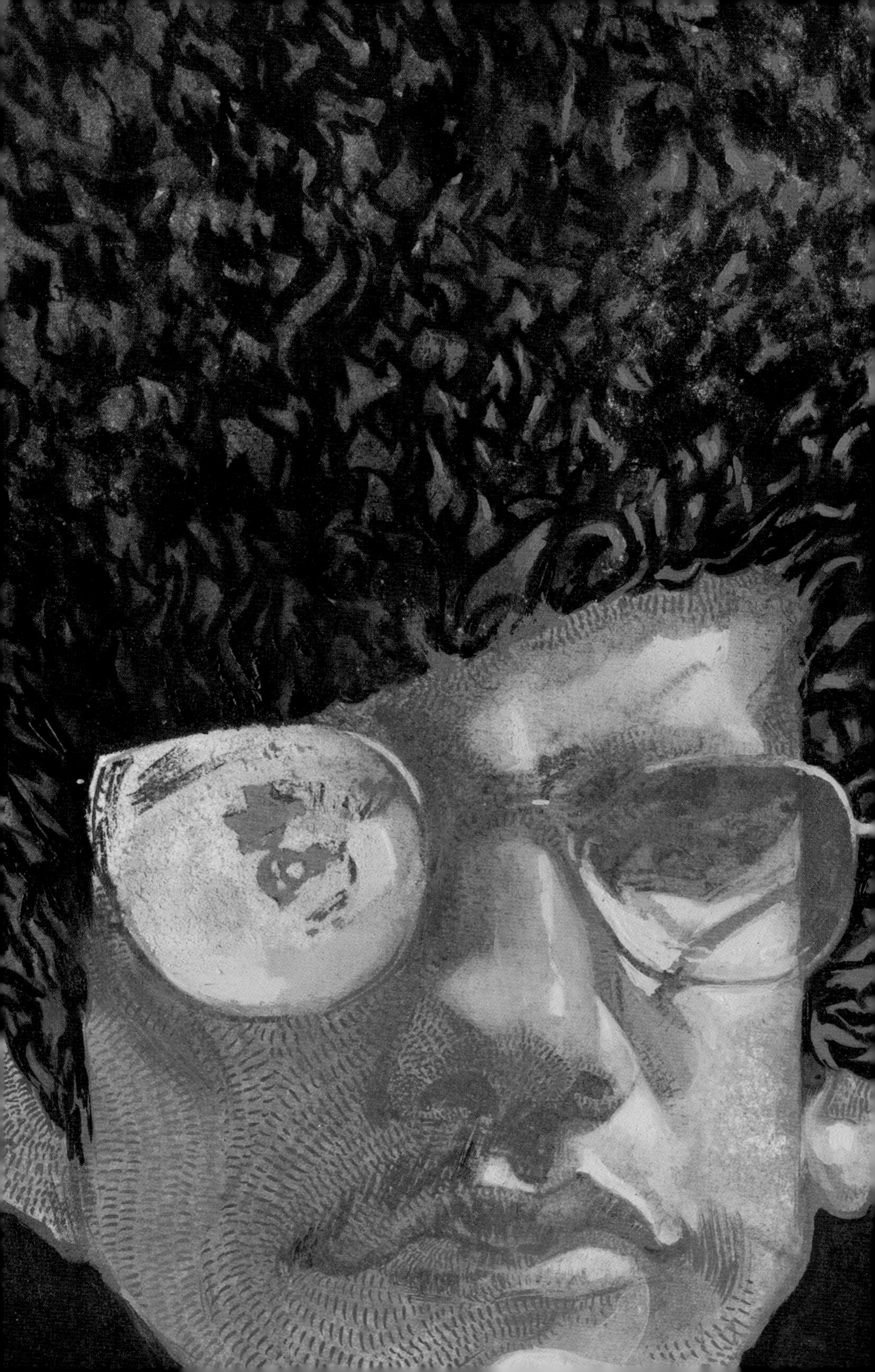

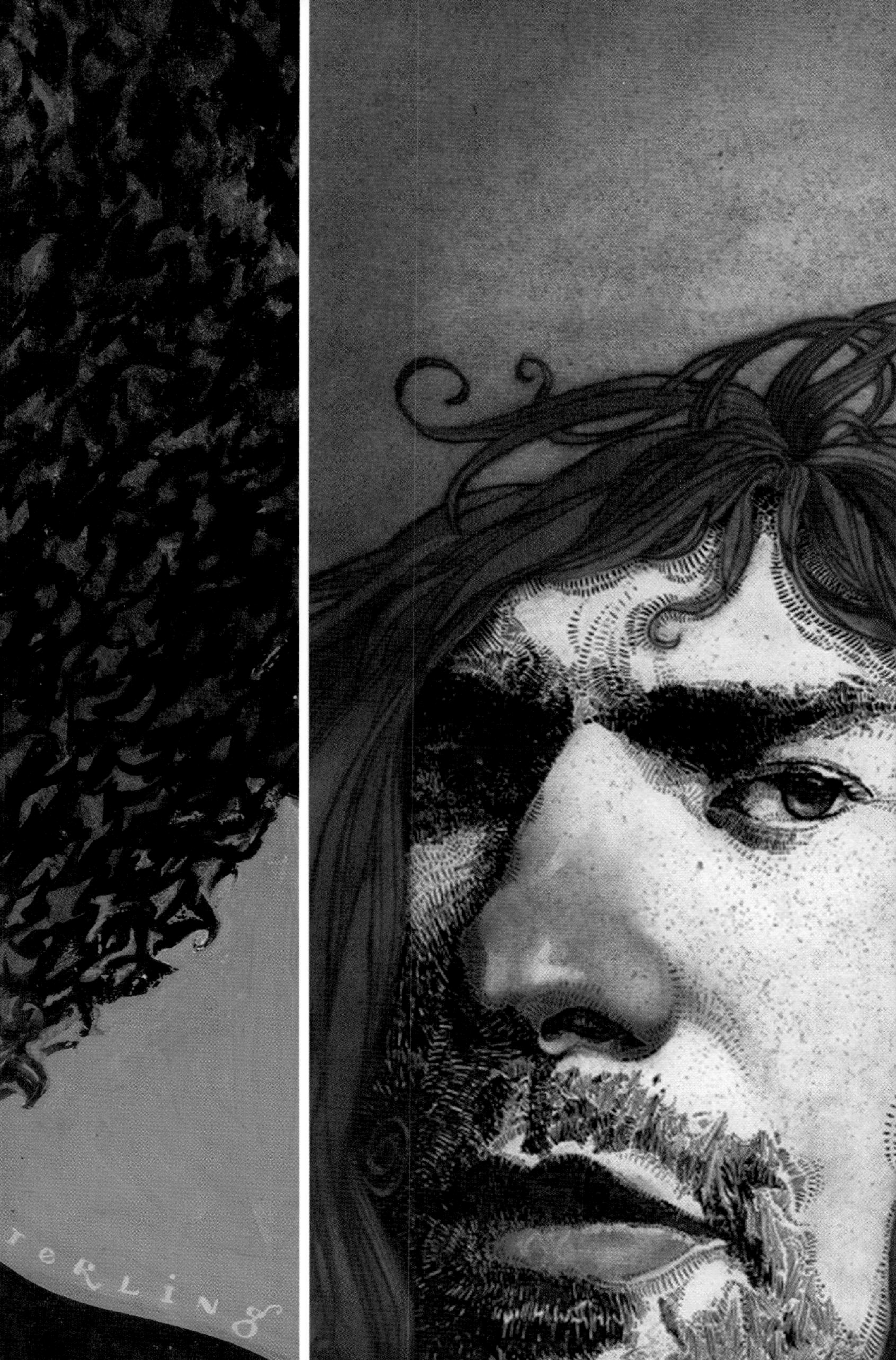
TERLING

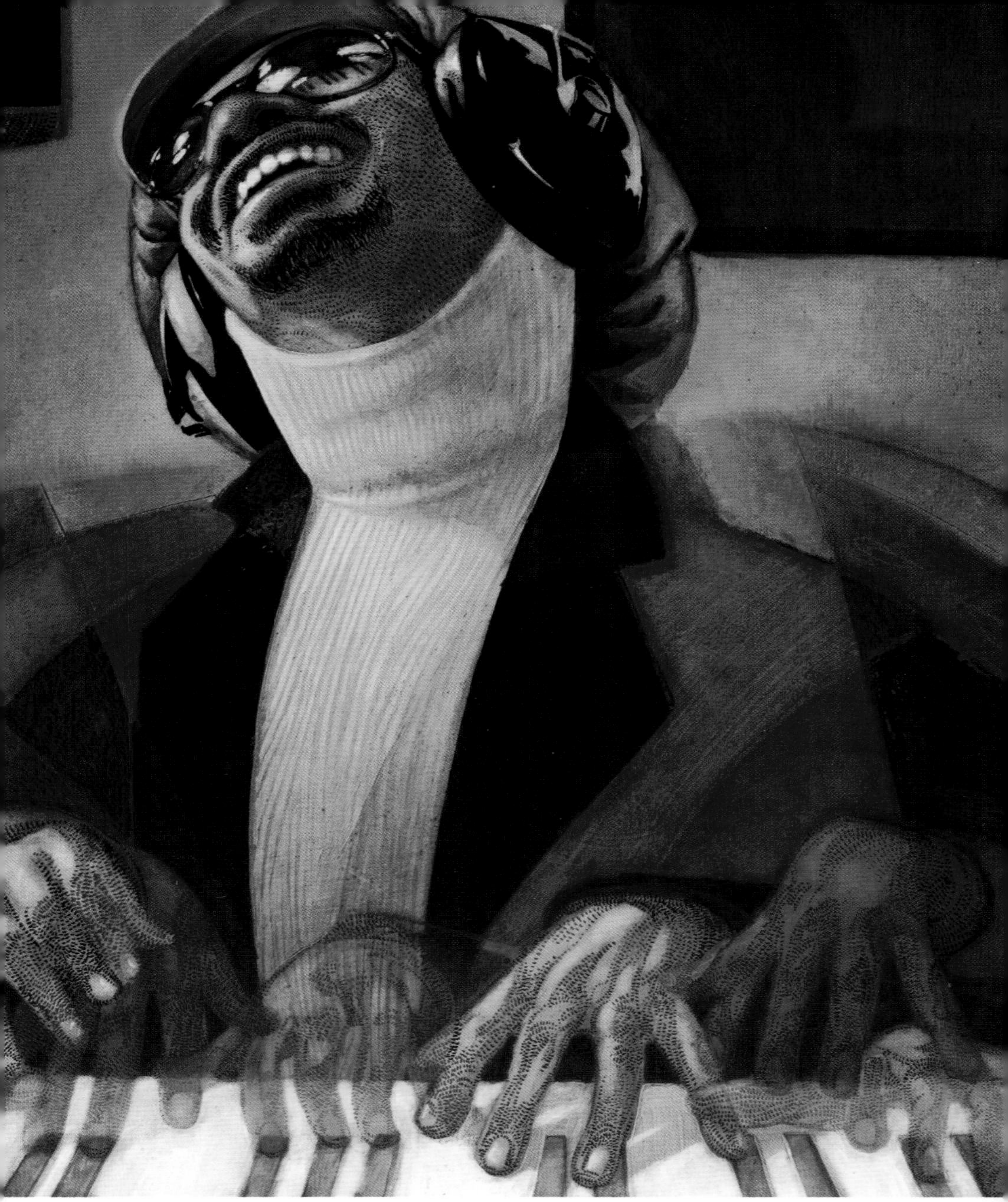

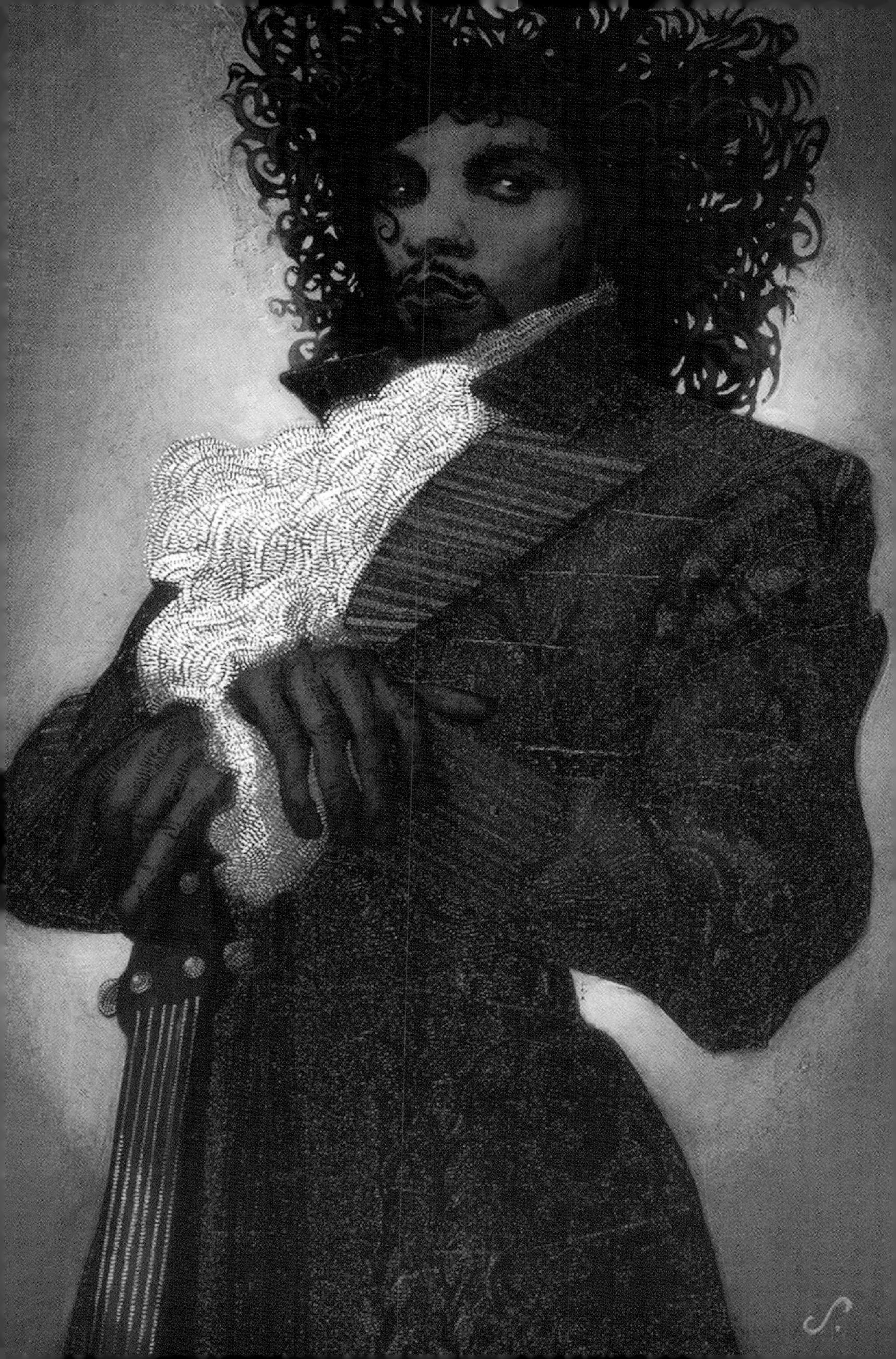

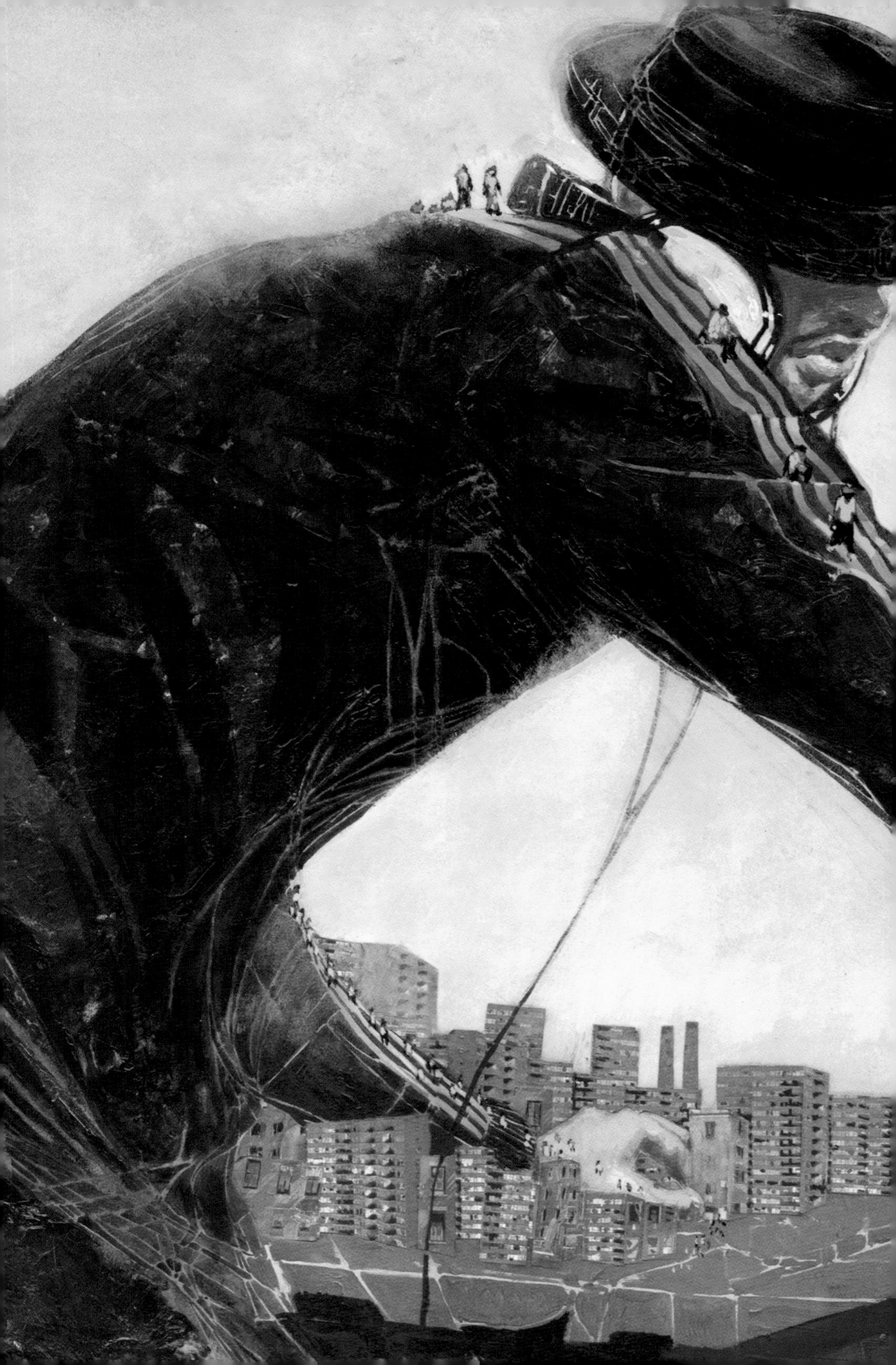

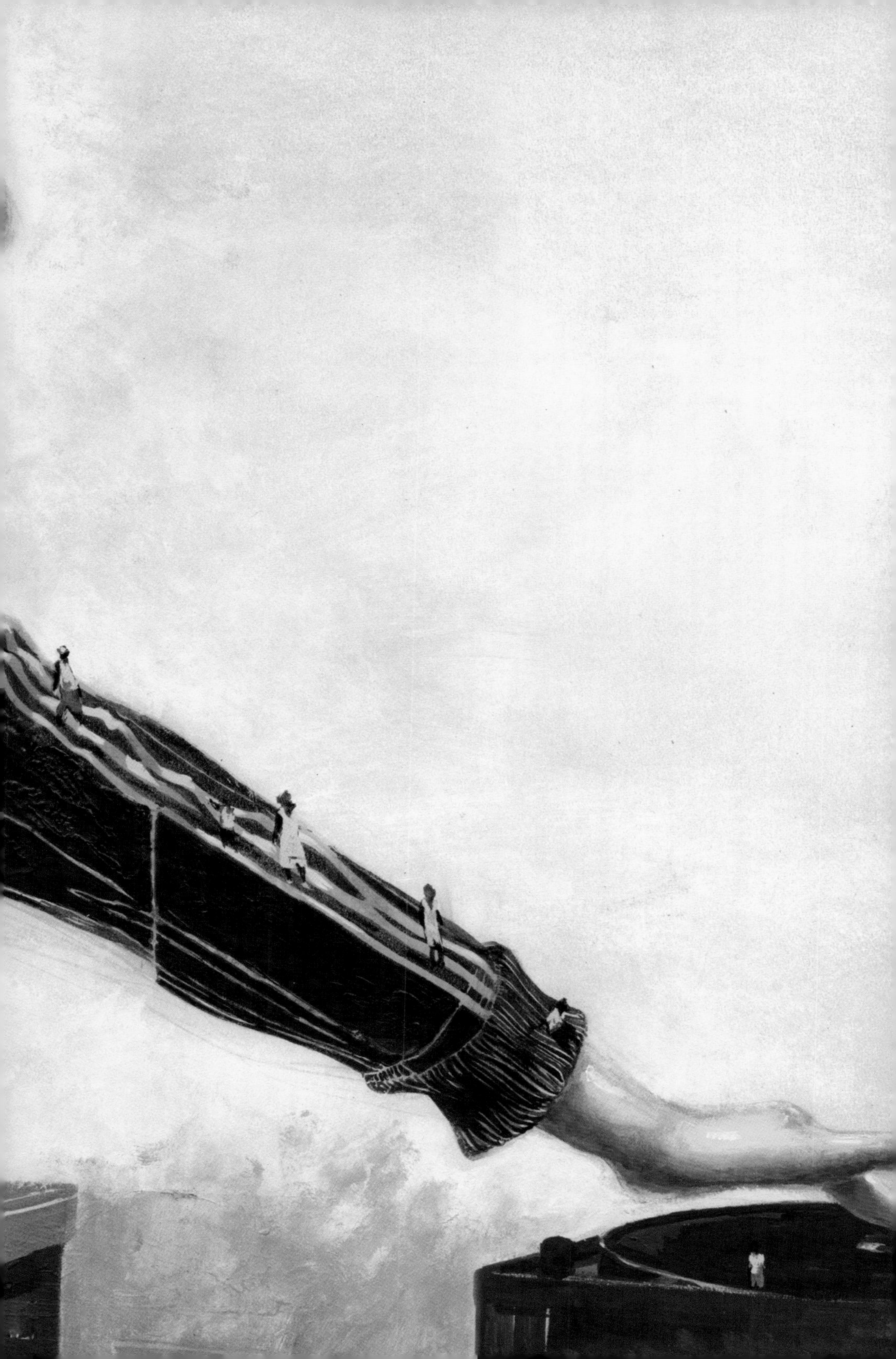

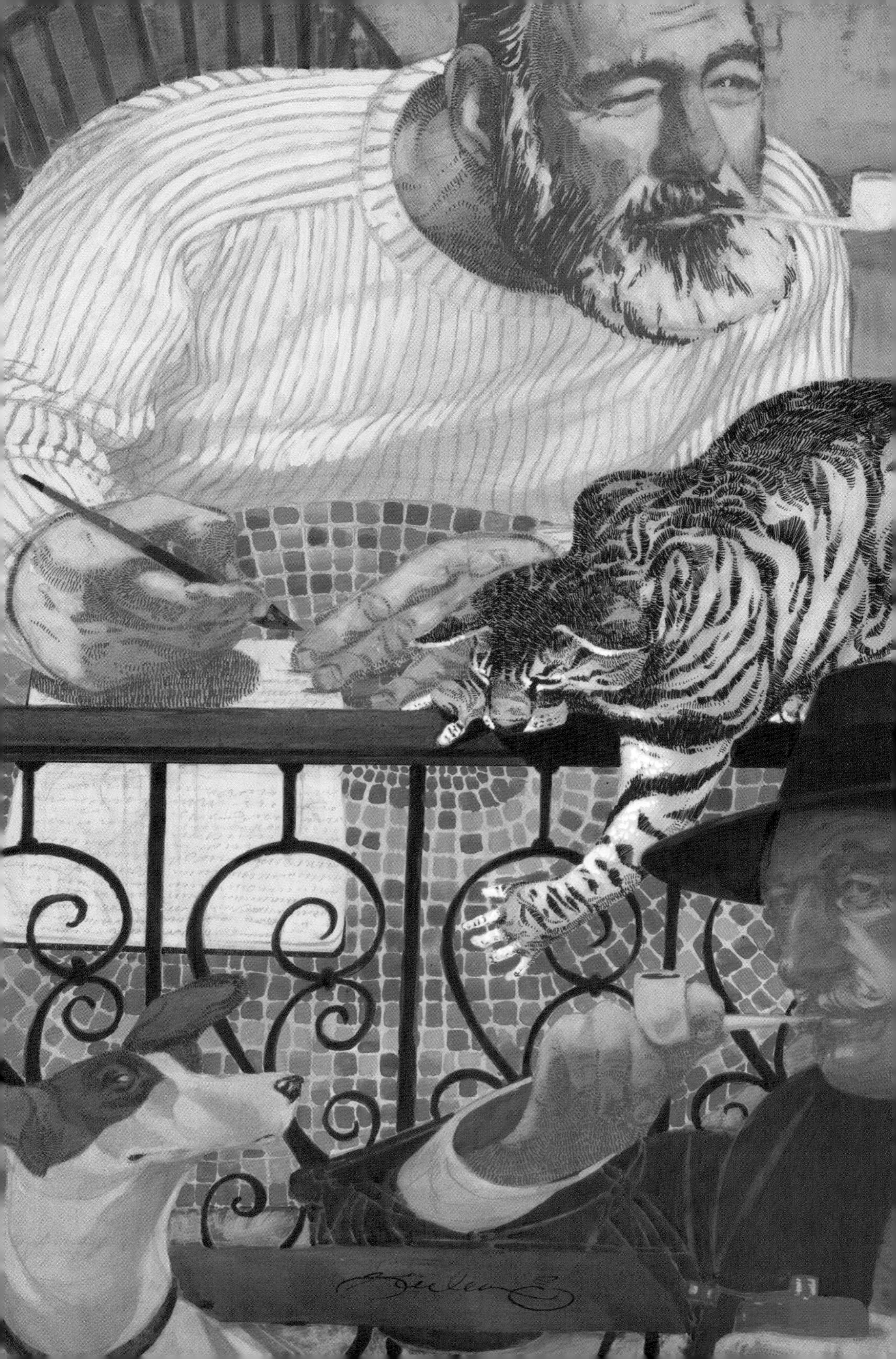

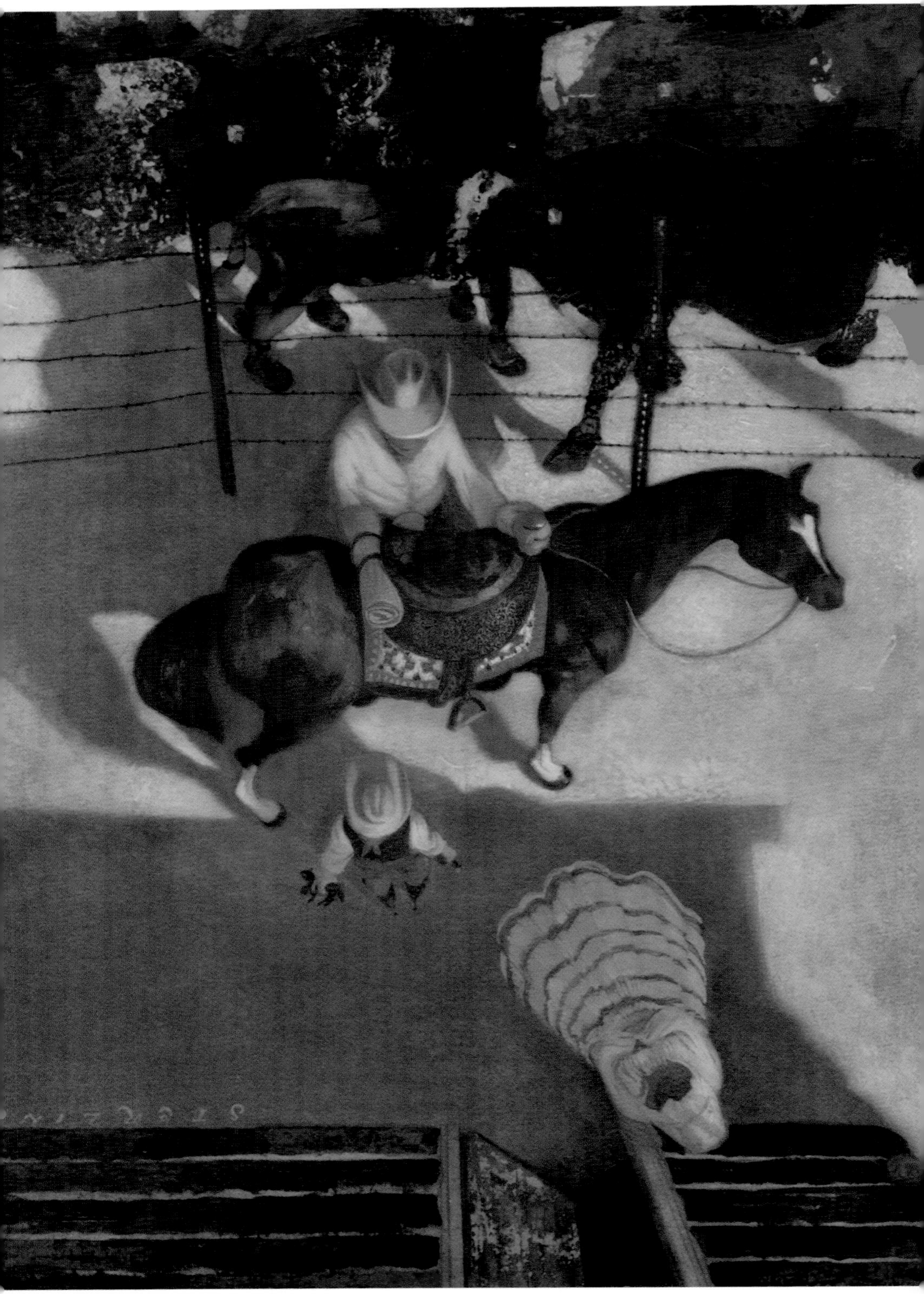

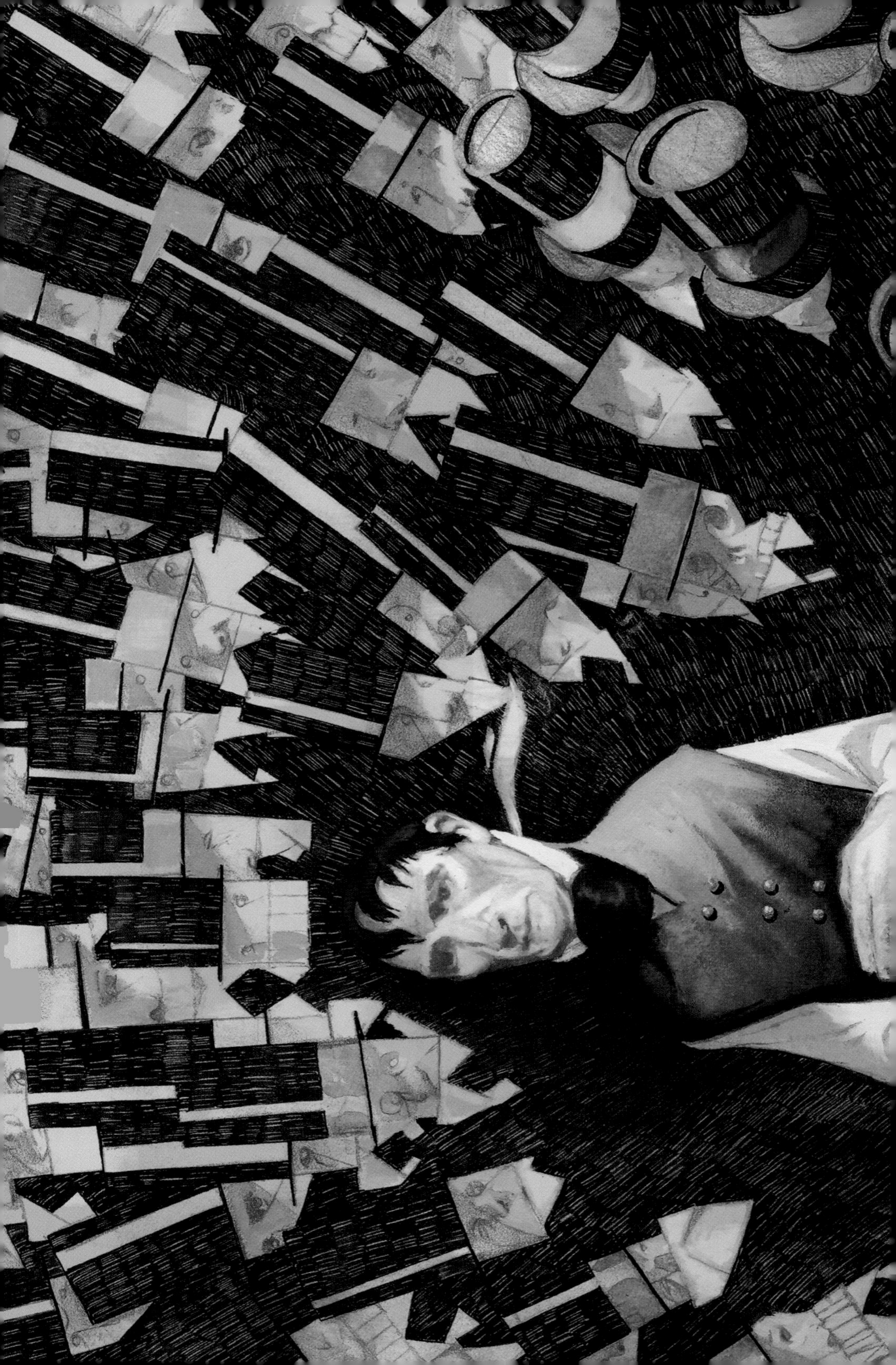

Confusion

In my career, I have assumed a great deal of the viewer. I have assumed a visual intelligence and a collective curiosity. When illustration transcends its function and the commerce that instigates it, imagery has the potential to move the masses.

Illustration is oft defined as *Illuminating Text.* This definition can relegate the image as secondary to text and the artist as servant to the author. To be commissioned does not

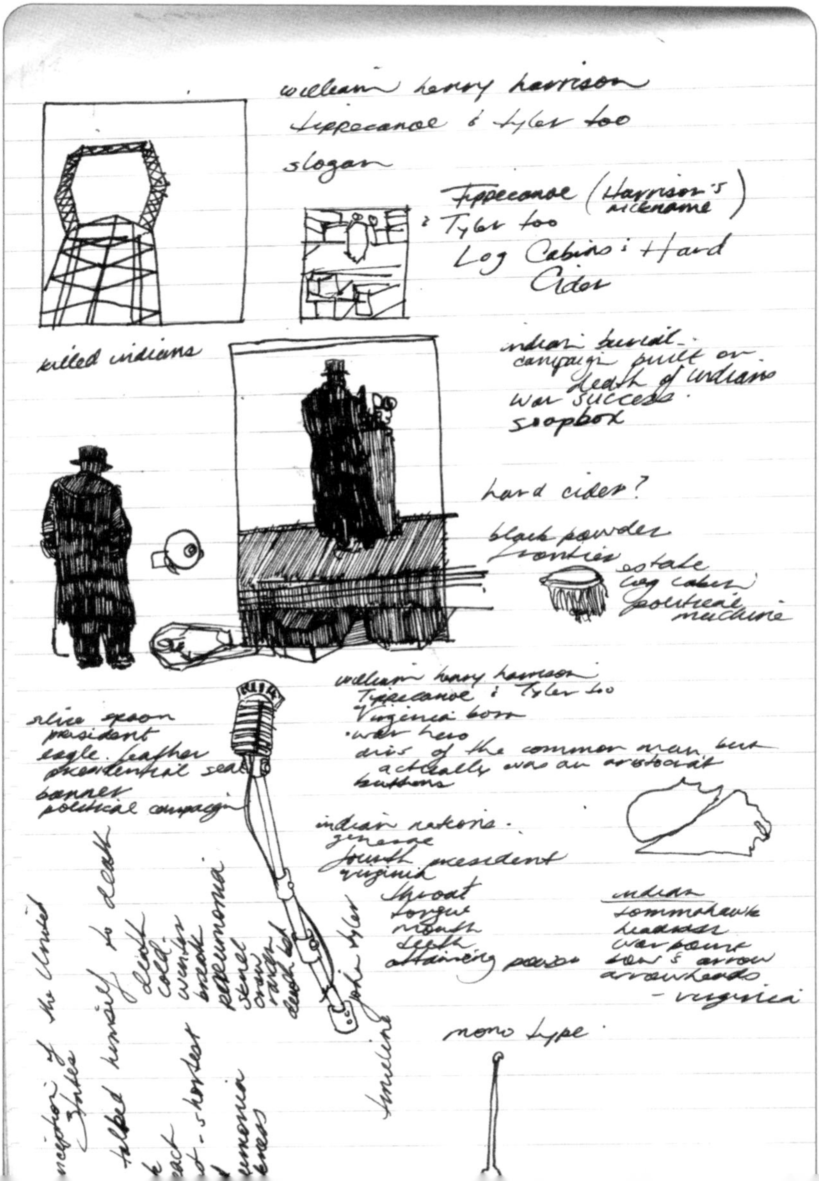
william henry harrison
tippecanoe & tyler too
slogan
Tippecanoe (Harrison's nickname)
& Tyler too
Log Cabins & Hard Cider
killed indians
soapbox
hard cider?
black powder
frontier
political campaign
mono type

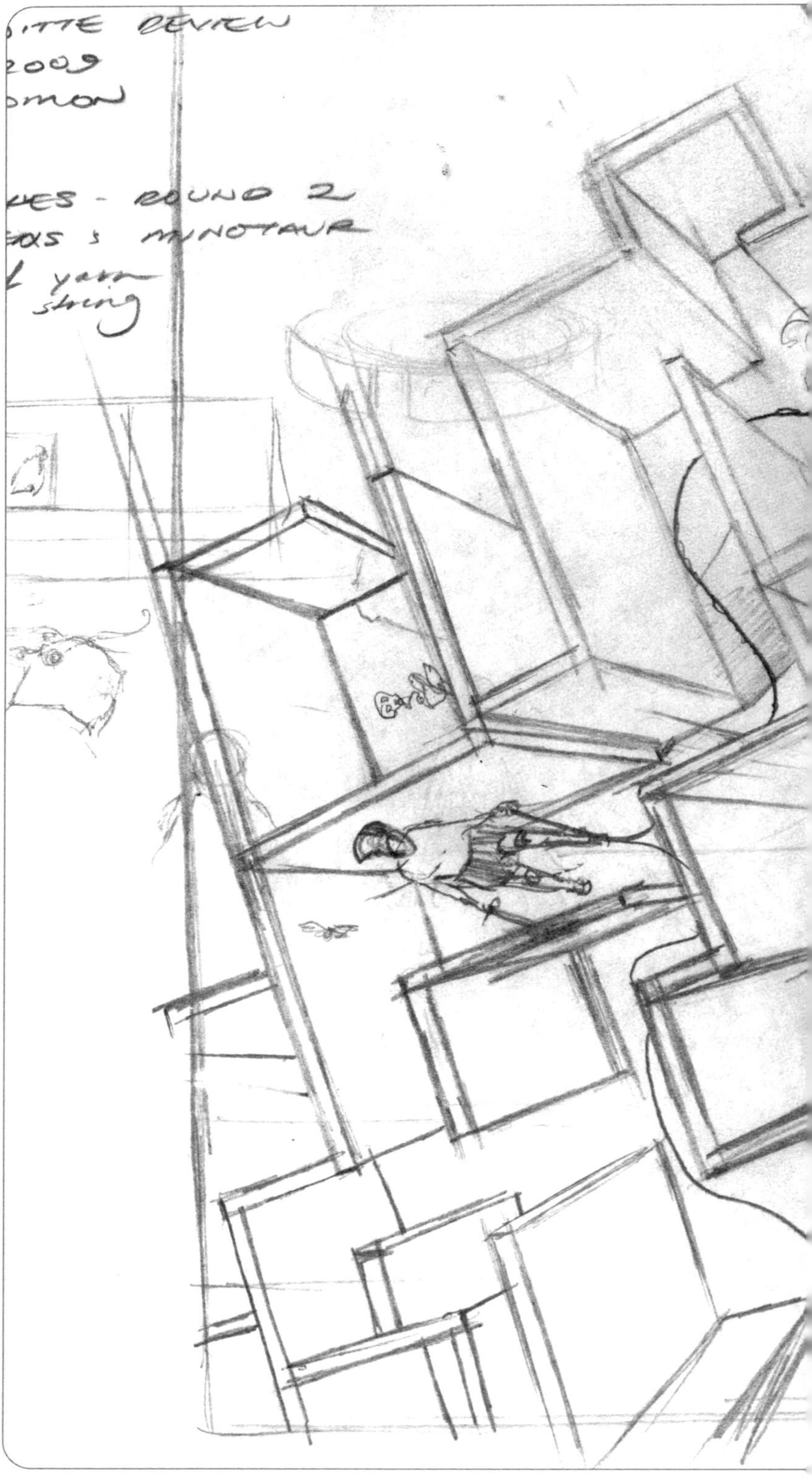
…ITTE REVIEW
…2009
…OMON
…KES - ROUND 2
…EUS [?] & MINOTAUR
…of yarn
string

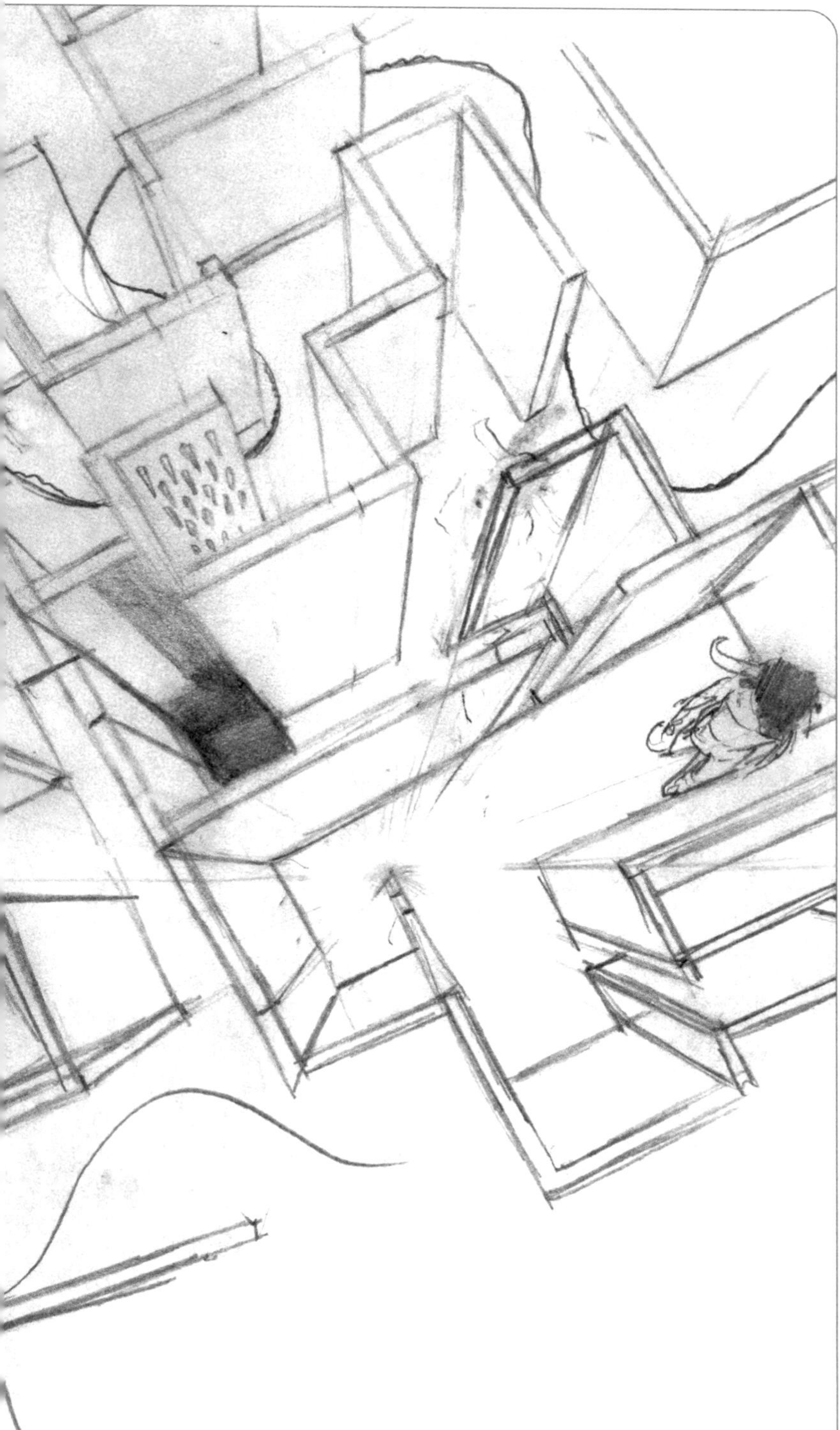

dismiss accountability. Illustration is art that must survive in spite of commerce and purpose.

The work in this section challenges that widely accepted description of applied art by asking: *must illustration articulate?*

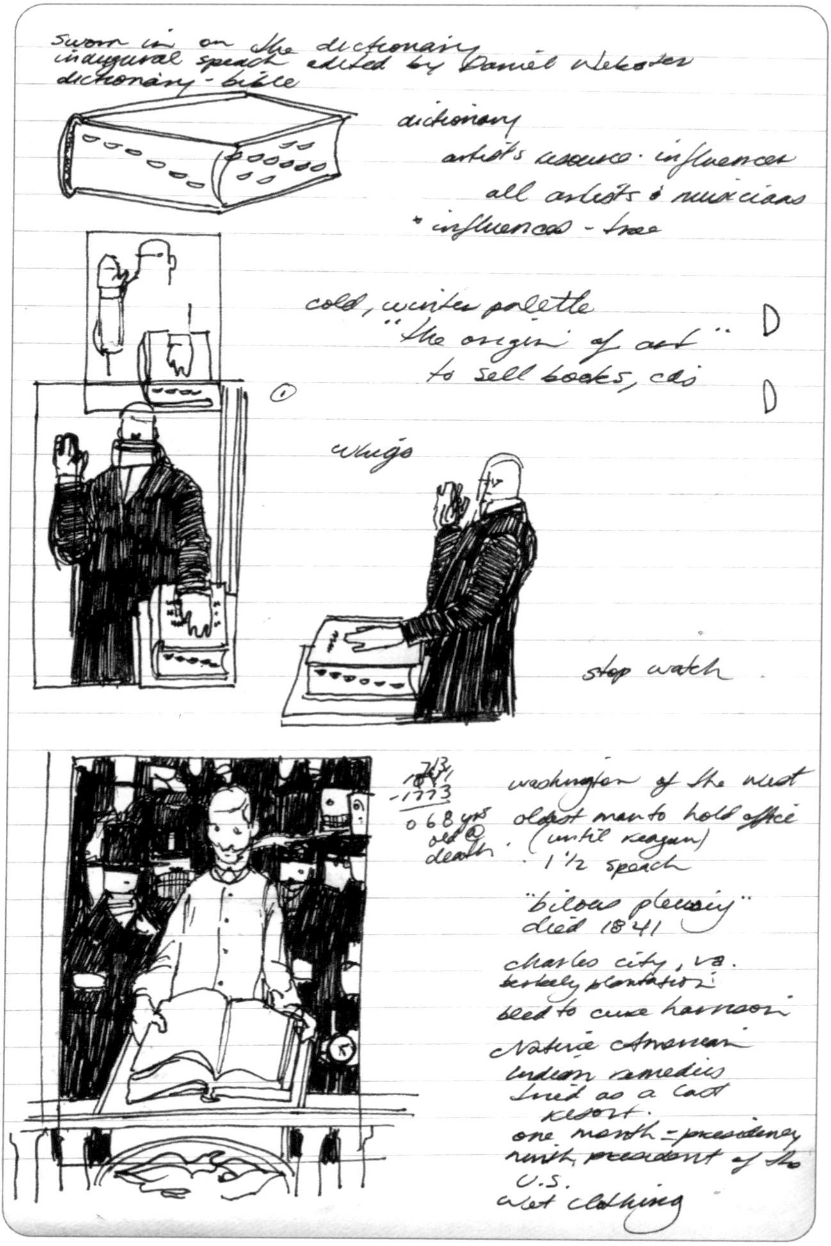
sworn in on the dictionary
inaugural speech edited by Daniel Webster
dictionary - bible
dictionary
artist's resource · influences
all artists & musicians
+ influences - tree
cold, winter palette
"the origin of art"
to sell books, cds
stop watch
1841
-1773
68 yrs old @ death
washington of the west
oldest man to hold office
(until Reagan)
1½ speech
"bilious pleurisy"
died 1841
charles city, va.
berkeley plantation
bleed to cure harrison
Native American
indian remedies
used as a last resort.
one month - presidency
ninth president of the U.S.
wet clothing

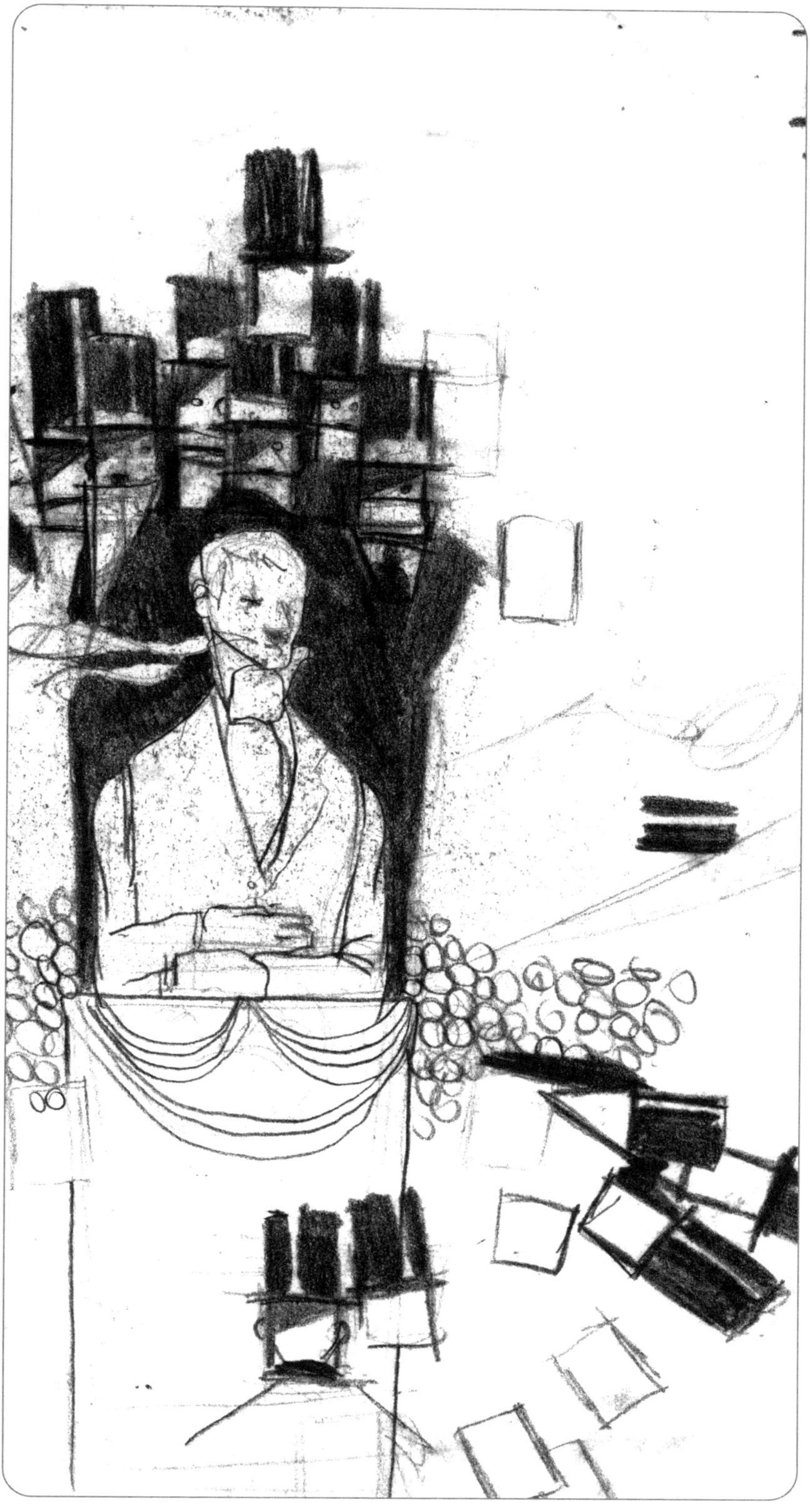

On March 4, 1841, William Henry Harrison, the newly elected President of the United States delivered the longest inauguration speech in history. Forgoing hat, scarf and gloves on that cold, rainy day, Harrison was soon stricken with pneumonia. Within a month, Harrison was dead – his Presidential term the shortest on record.

The duality of Harrison's life and death presented a unique problem requiring an unorthodox solution. Harrison's inspiring rise and unsettling demise are echoed in an image with no definitive top or bottom. Employing perspective allowed for a solution that depicts Harrison's inaugural address when viewed vertically, while showing his wake when read horizontally. "William Henry Harrison" (pages 59-61).

+ + +

A father and son duck-hunting trip goes horribly wrong when they are quickly submerged by a flooding river. Near drowning, they are pulled into the pea green boat by a stranger. The father soon discovers that the man who owned the boat has long since been dead. Using a point of view under the water's surface to provide an element of violence and confusion, the isolated duck decoy and the sole of the boys boot are introduced as keys in interpreting the image in "Pea Green Boat" (pages 66-67).

+ + +

"Labyrinth" (pages 62-63) accompanied an article about the need to implement inherent structures that would assist company leaders in avoiding known pitfalls. Assuming the reader's knowledge of the well-known mythos of Theseus and the Minotaur, the labyrinth was used to provide a context writ with known dangers and inherent structures. A cubist approach to perspective allows the viewer to see future dangers that Theseus cannot, while the thread indicates a clear point of entry and exit.

+ + +

Peter Francisco, the Virginia Giant, was a Revolutionary icon. At 6'5" and over 260 pounds, he was a giant in his day. Legend begins where history ends and the truth lies somewhere between. Witness accounts tell of an unstoppable man who could carry a cannon, lift a horse and best eleven men. Massing of color and shape were used to introduce action and violence to the illustration. The British soldiers become the key in deciphering "Virginia Giant" (page 64).

+ + +

"Monolith" (detail, pages 74-75) for Stanley Kubrick's anthology, was a guttural reaction to a haunting image from *Full Metal Jacket* depicting a mass grave. As a reflection of the chaos of war, grouping was used to create a mass grave in the shape of Kubrick's iconic monolith from *2001: A Space Odyssey*.

+ + +

Choosing life on the range over a life with his family, a young cowboy saddles up to leave home in "Lone Ranger" (page 58). A horse was used to separate the composition between the symbols of life at home: the cowboy's wife, child and cabin, from the symbols of life on the range: the cowboy and his cattle. "Lone Ranger" employs a rolling perspective to present a 180 degree flattening of space from the top of the composition to the bottom.

+ + +

"Curse Tree" (page 17), set in Jamestown, Virginia, depicts the story of a young girl, forbidden to wed an elderly statesman by her mother. Damned for their irreverence, in life and in death, the mother's curse manifests as a sycamore tree that grows between the lover's tombs, pushing the daughter's casket within inches of her mother's. Using the break in the earth as a division between reality and horror, the tree's subterranean roots are used to impede the cursed couple's perpetual search for one another in the afterlife.

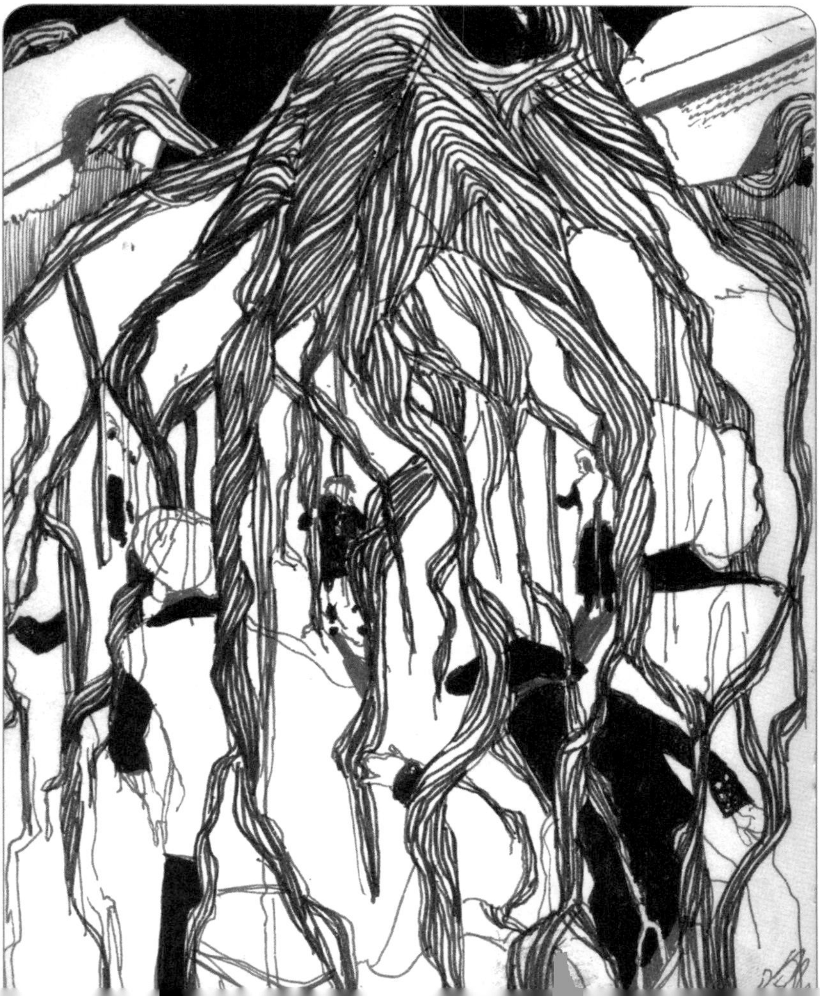

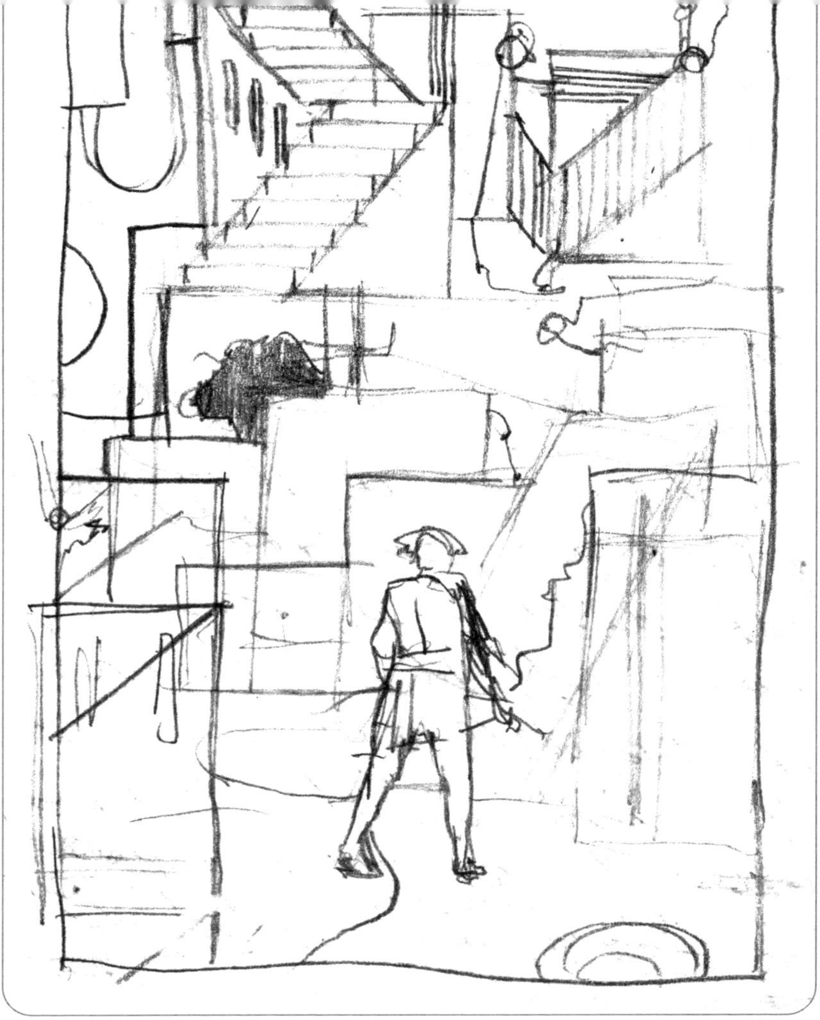

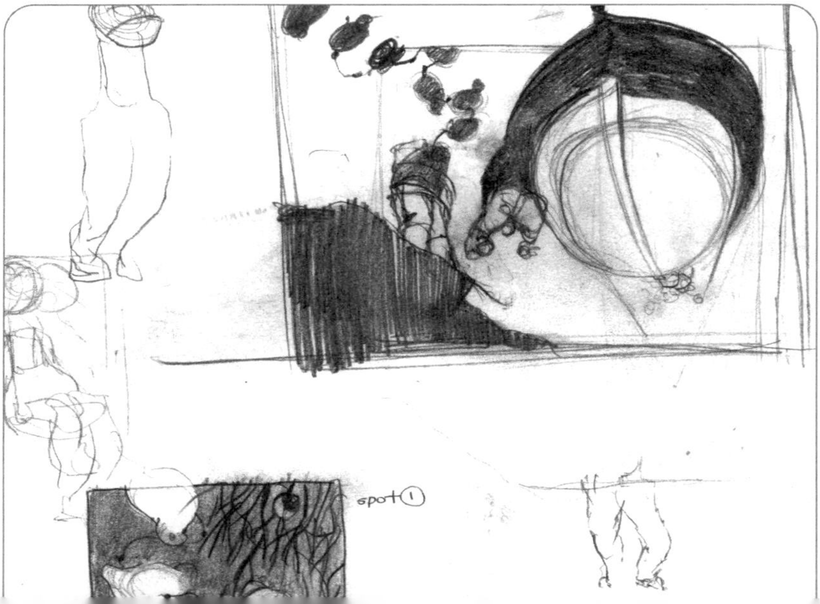
spot ①

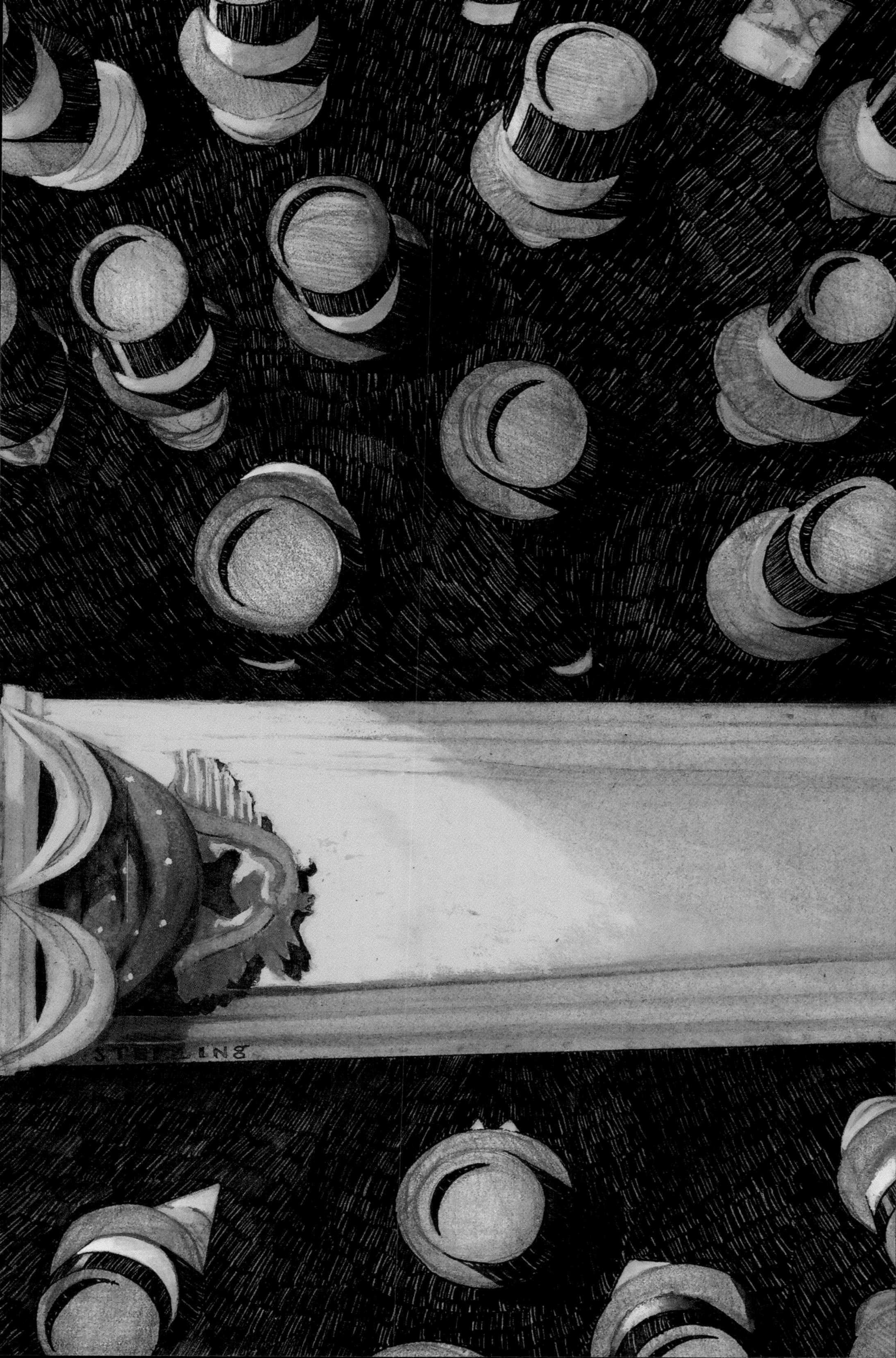

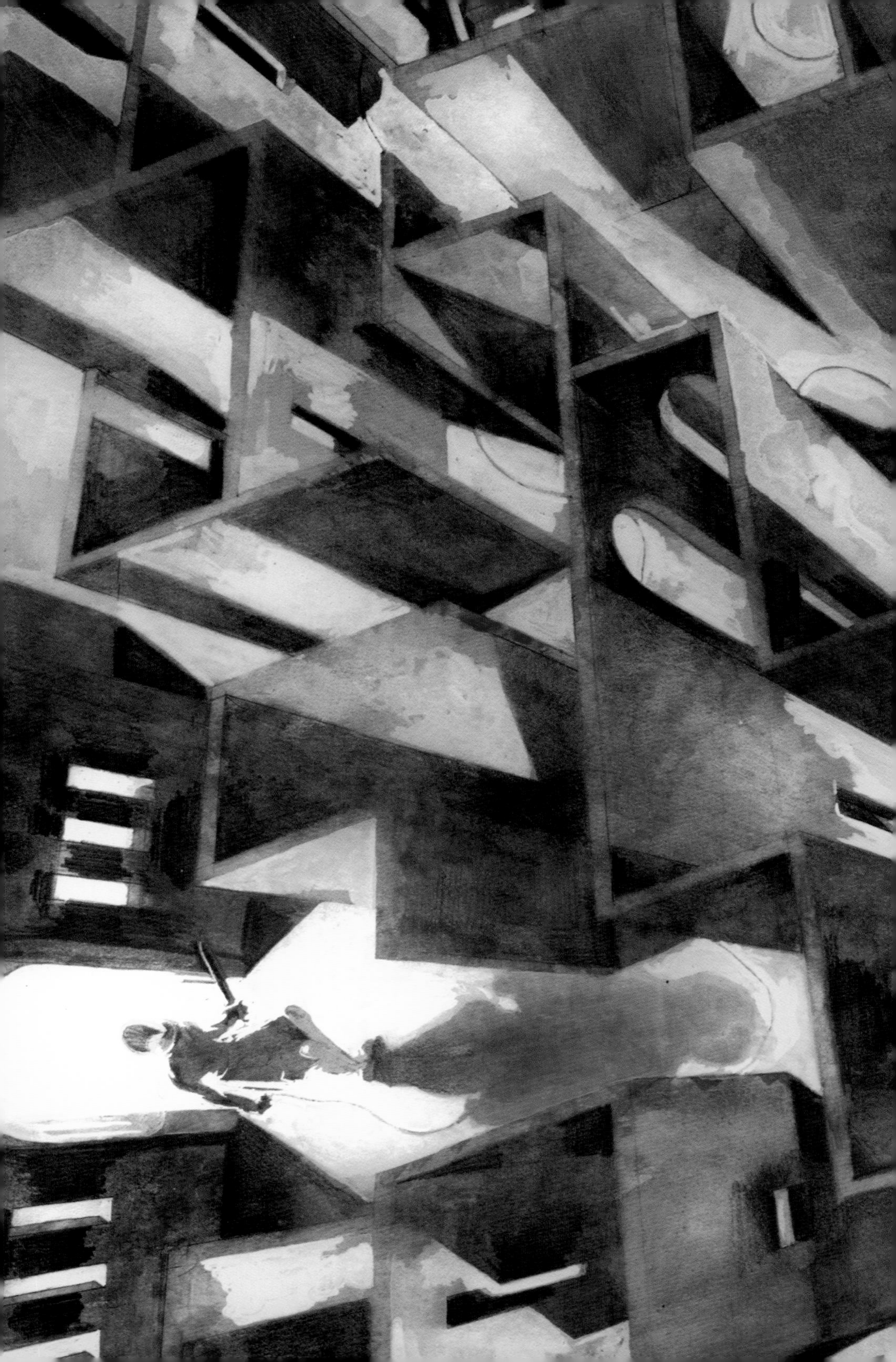

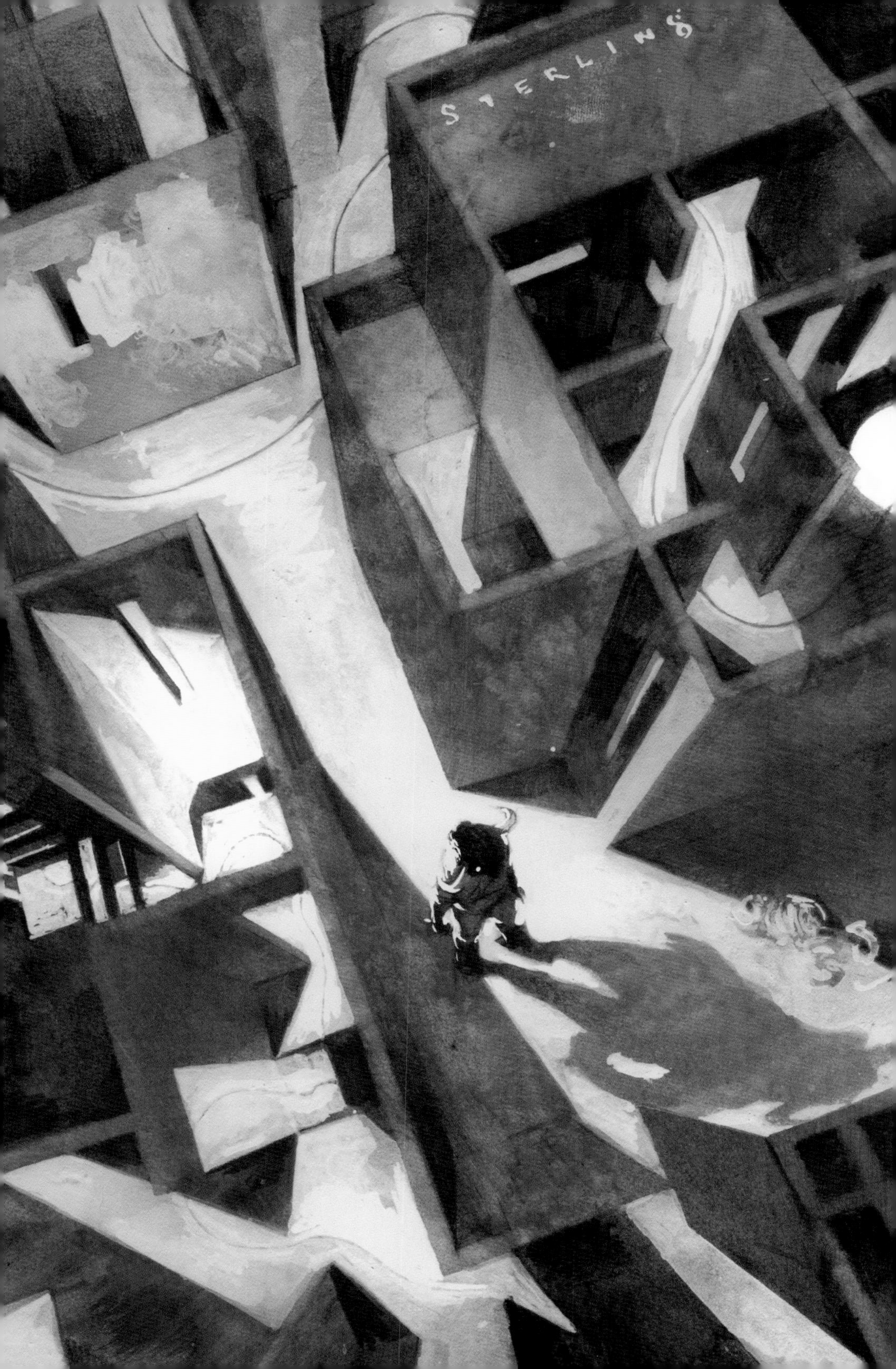
STERLING

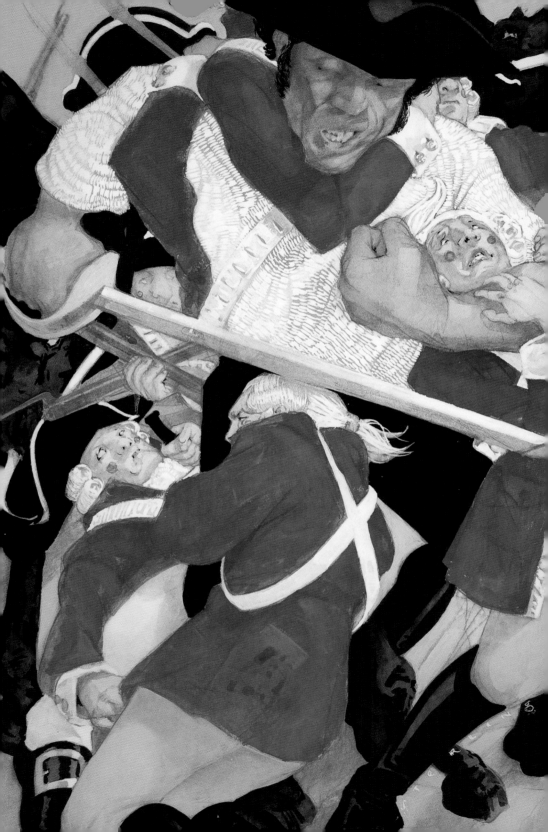

Virginia Billy Tyler Francisco Revolutionary
one... man...
needed an extraordinary hero than
Francisco was just such a hero. At 6'7" and 260
pounds, Francisco was a giant in stature and
a regiment... well Francisco is credited
with inhuman feats of heroism, bravery and
strength during the Revolutionary War

once as well known as Davy Crockett or Daniel Boone
"Hercules of the Revolution"
"Giant of Virginia"

first Pedro Fr. Then Peter Fr.
kidnapped for ransom?
banged two dueling men together which ended their argument.

FOLK HERO - LEGEND.
TALL TALES -
        giant
    Pedro Francisco   revolutionary war   conquistadors
    5 foot blade, 6' sword   British
    cavalry
    infantry
    soldier
    Paul Bunyan
    6'6 - 260 lbs.
    infantryman
    countless feats
    ...

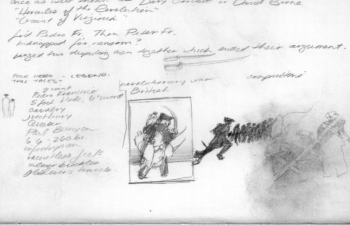

FOLK

Page 65

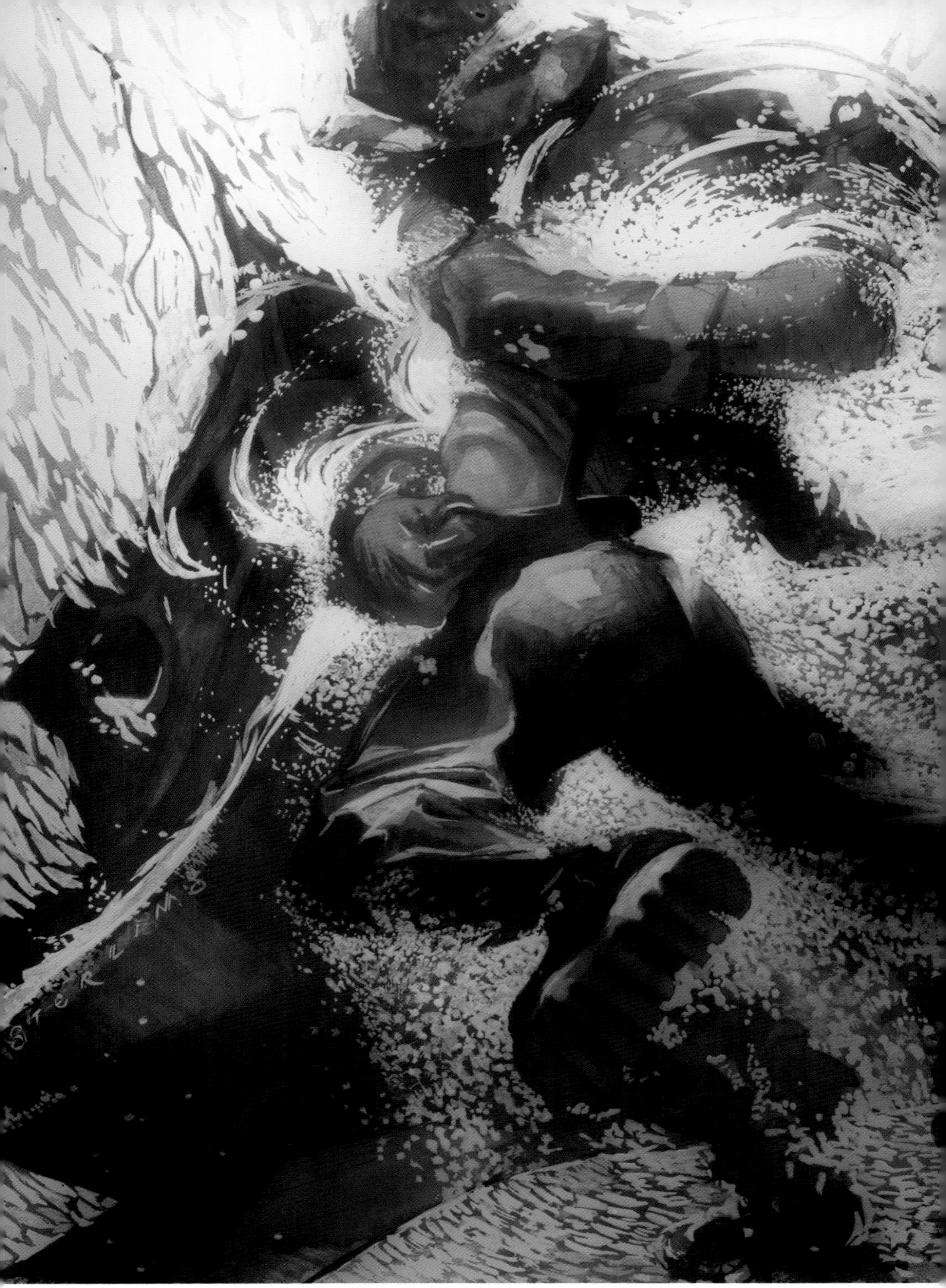

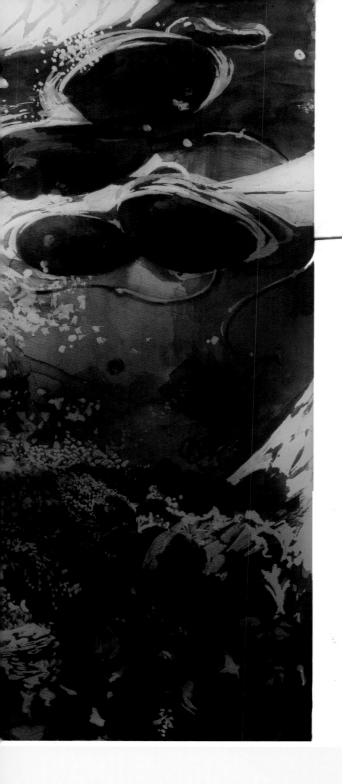

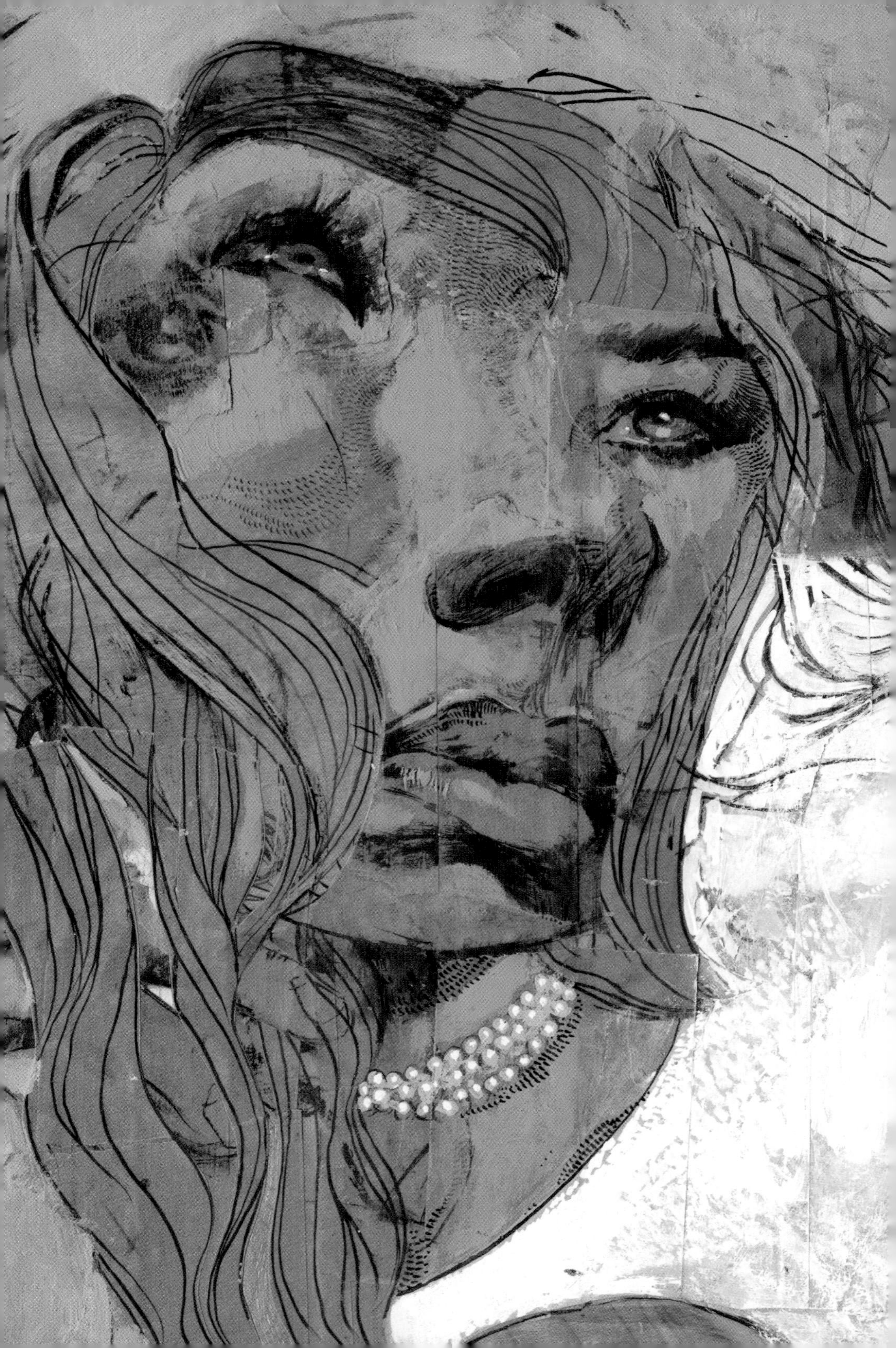

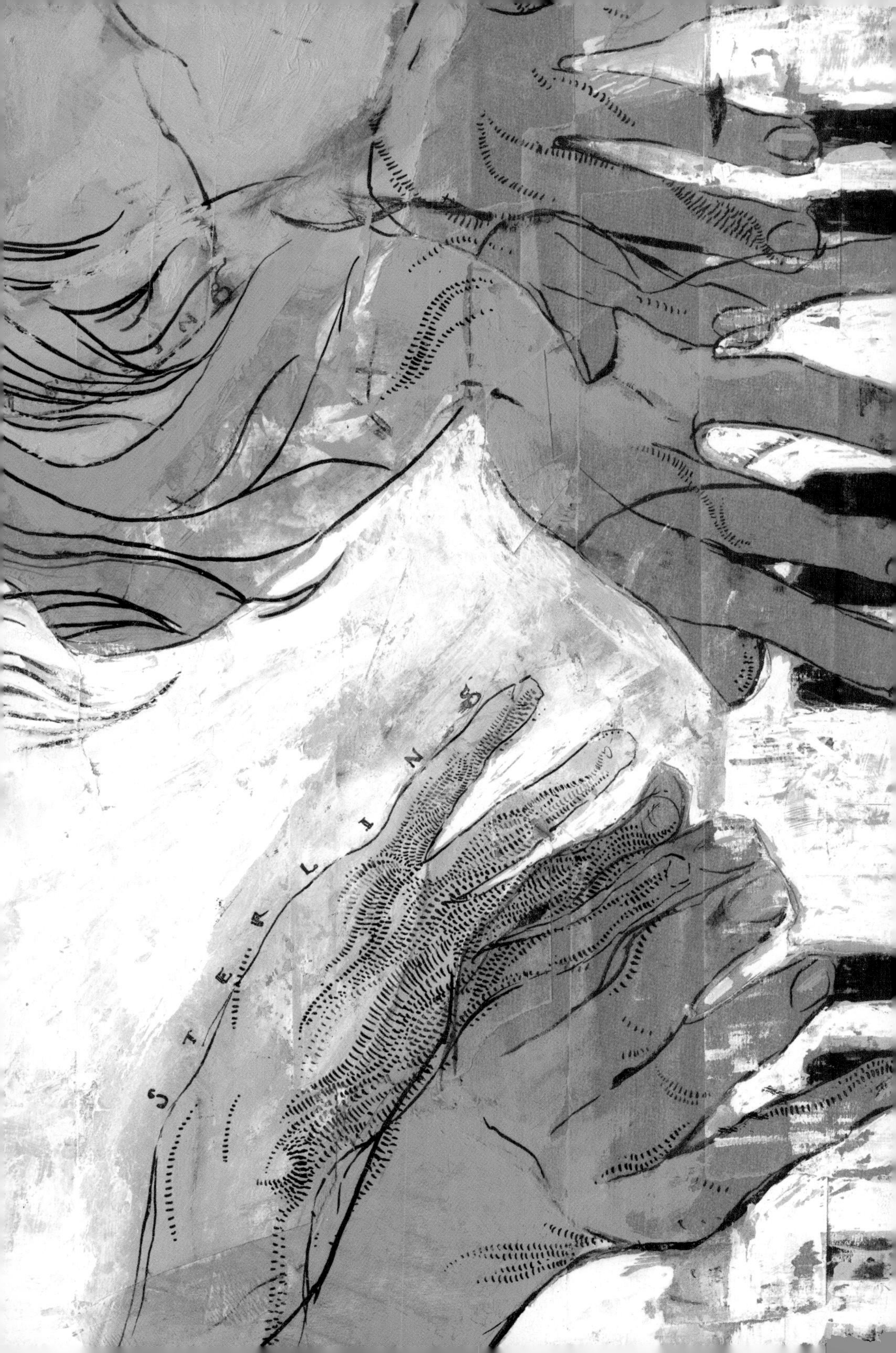

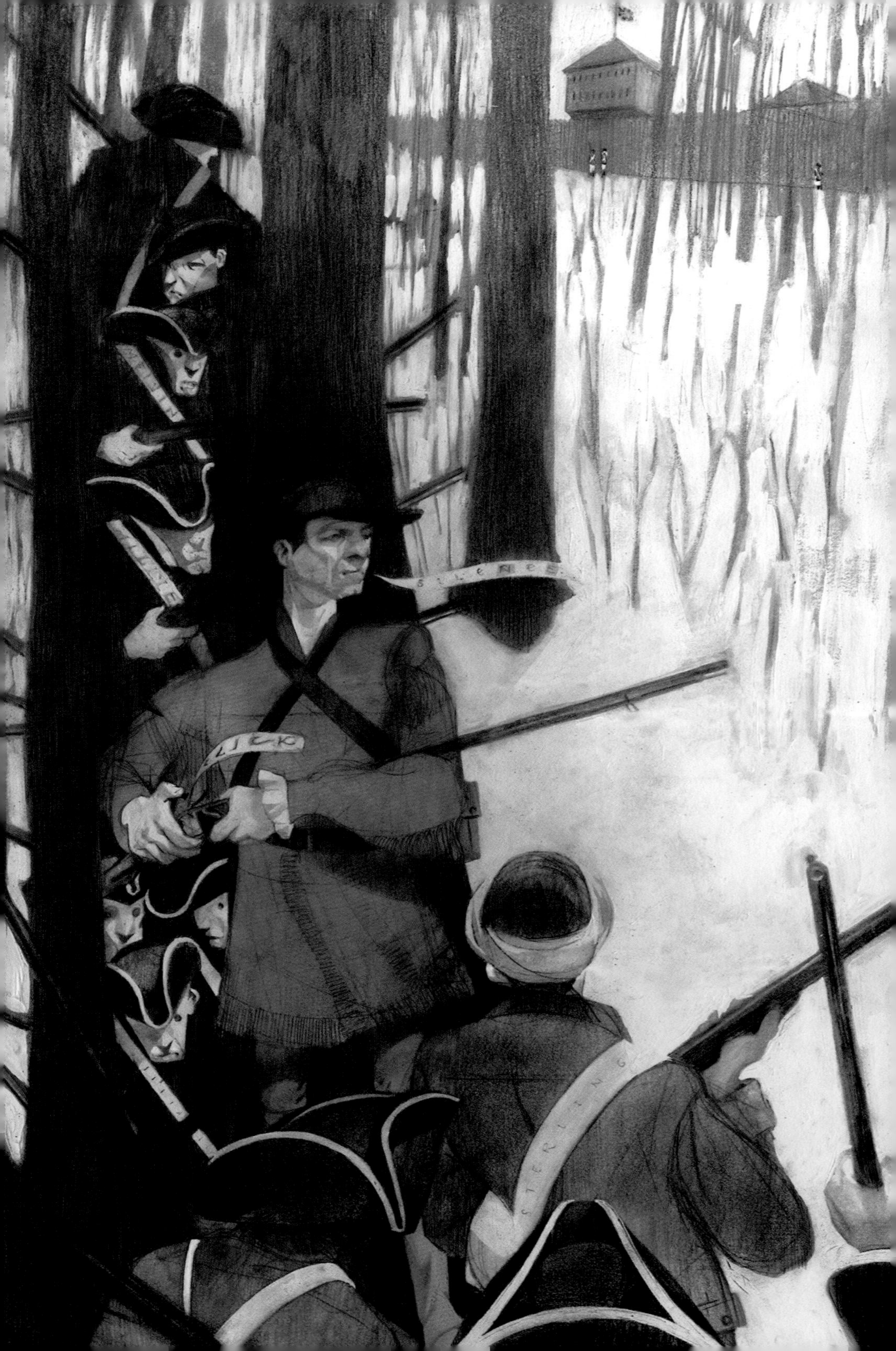
SILENCE
STERLING

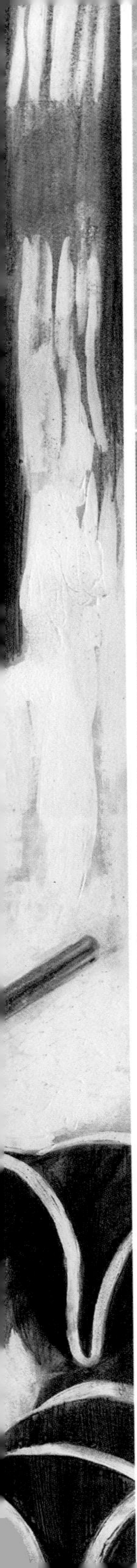
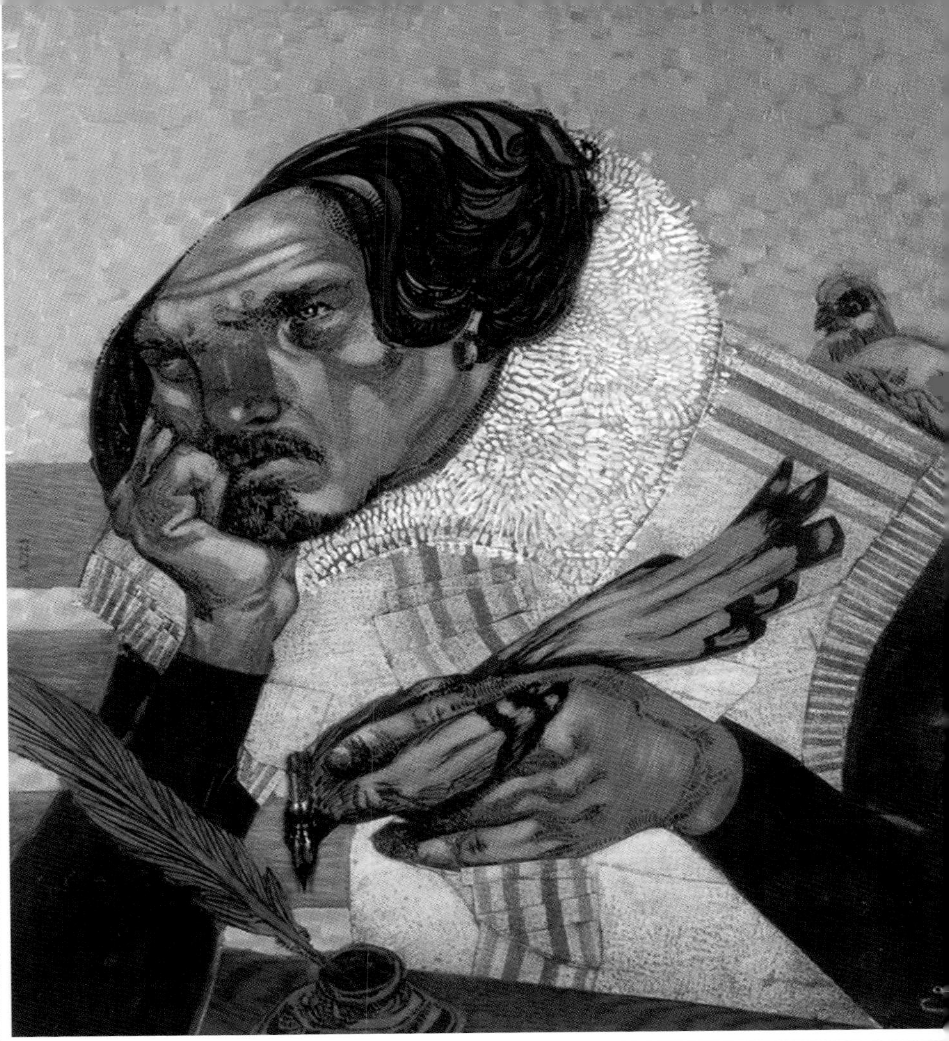

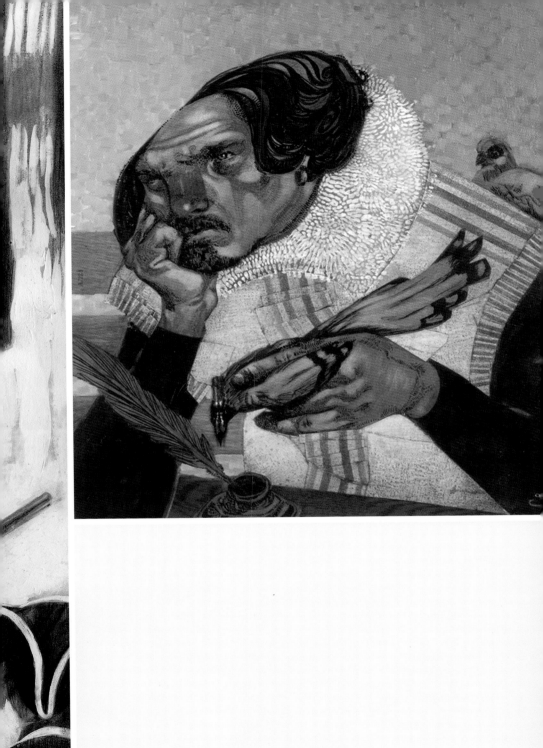

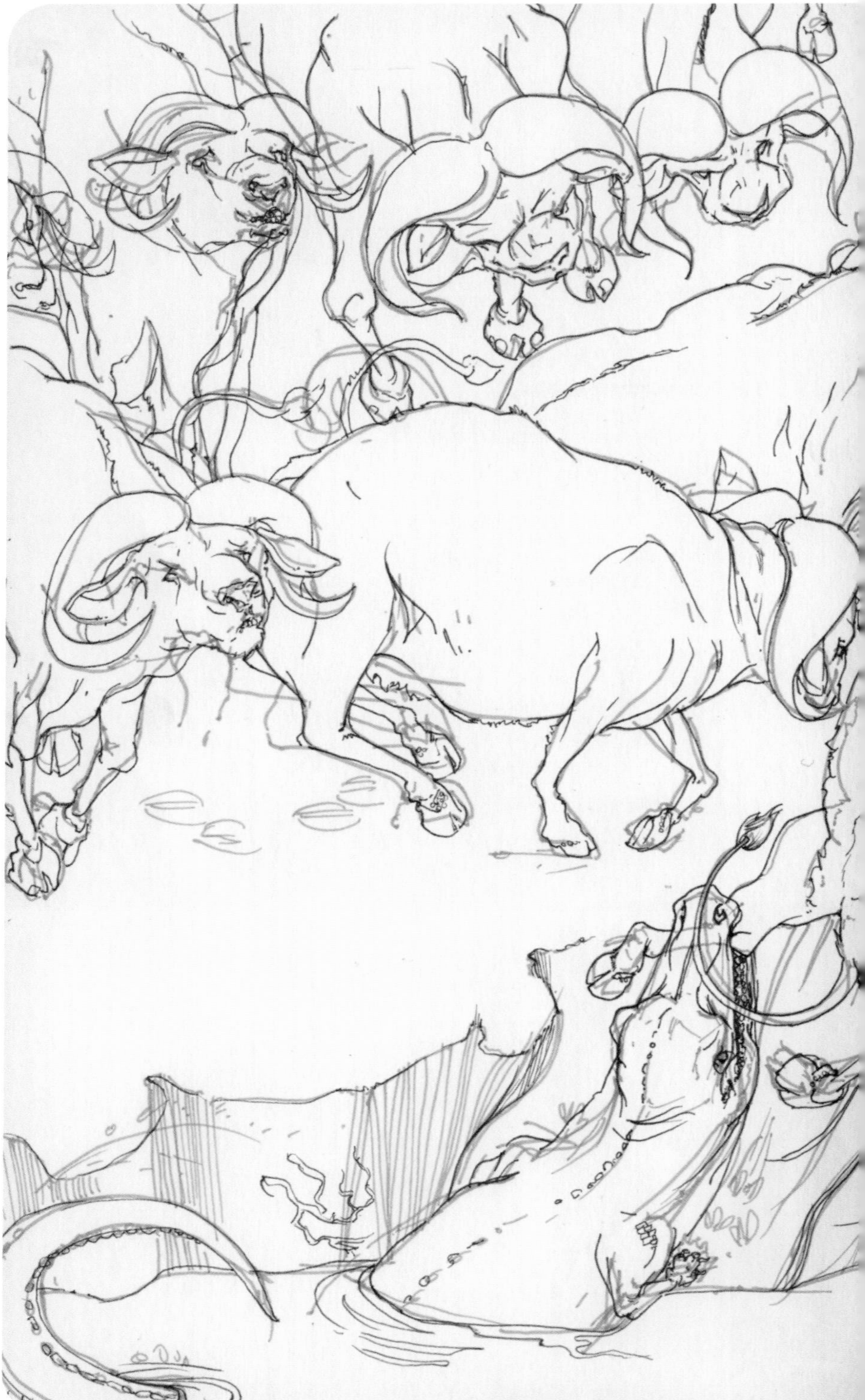

HOBBES VS · TOES
PAWS

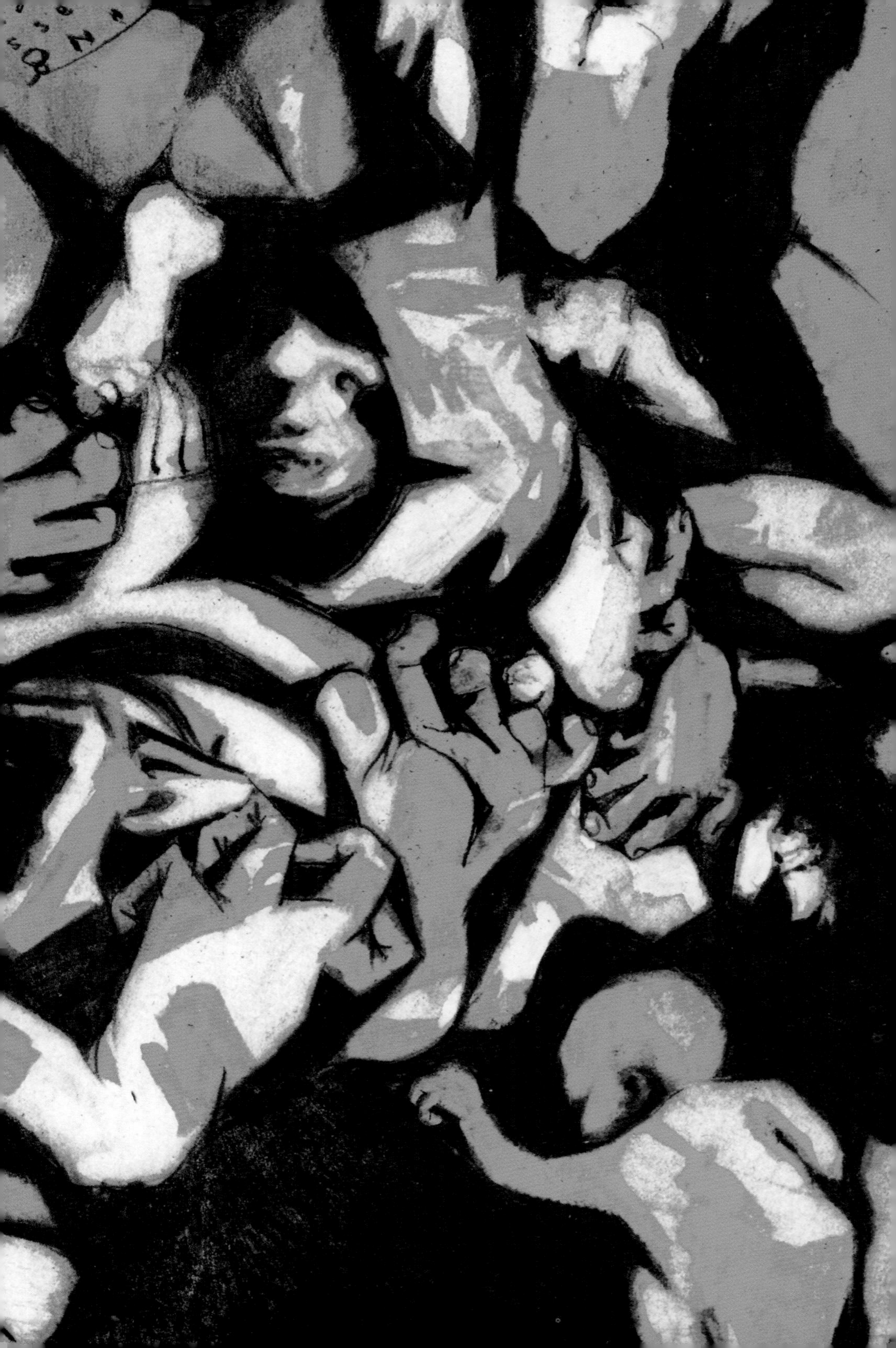

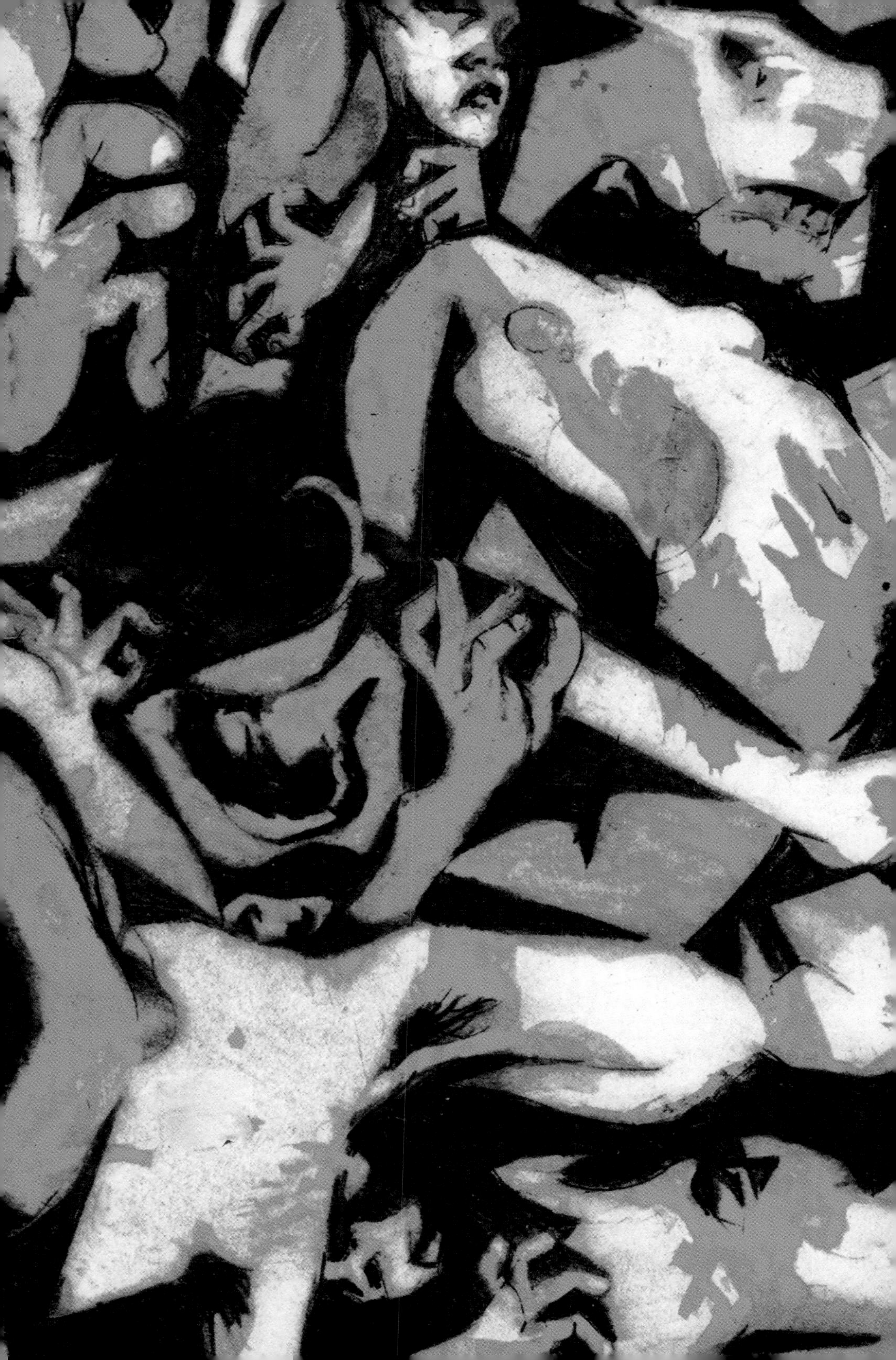

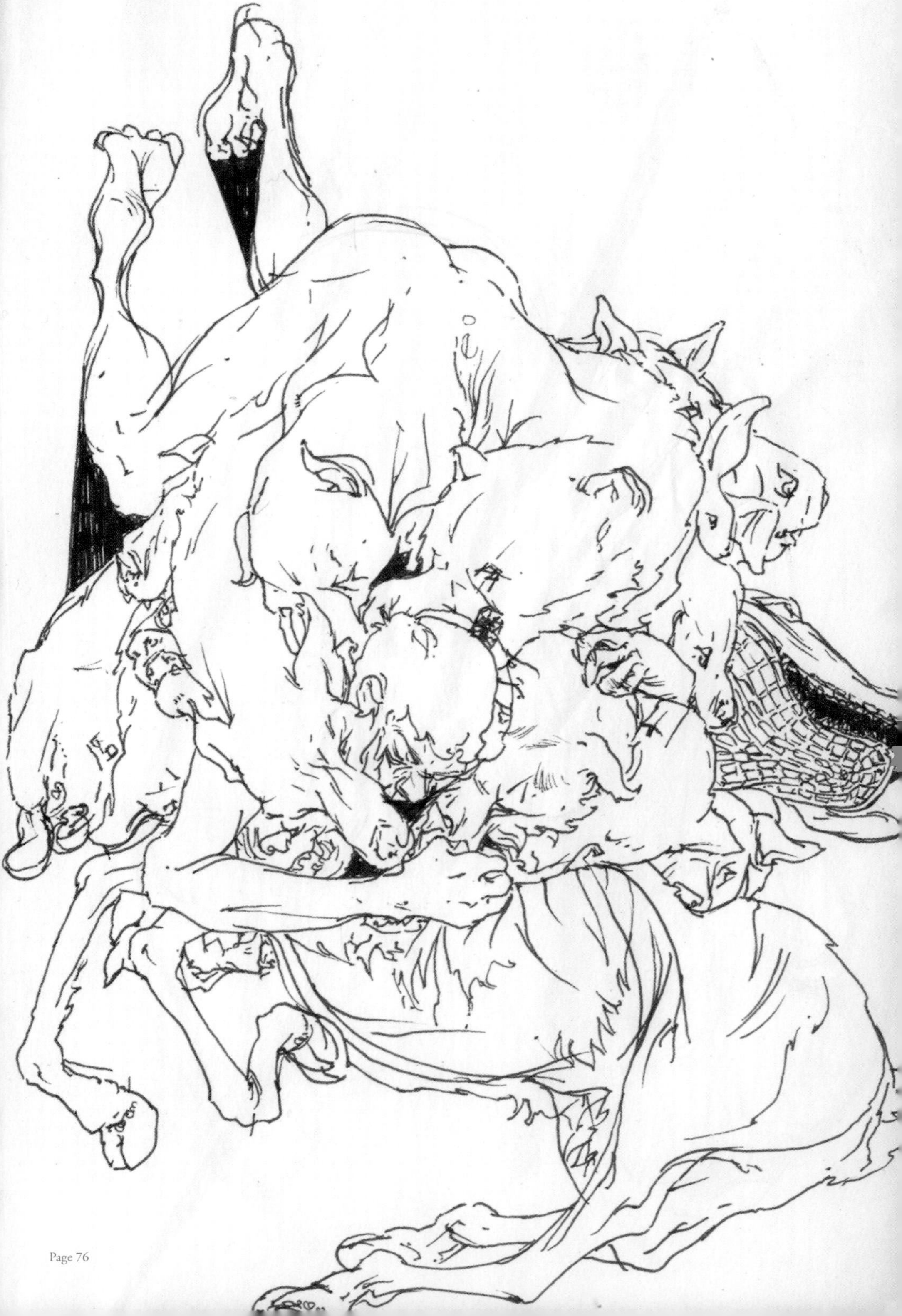

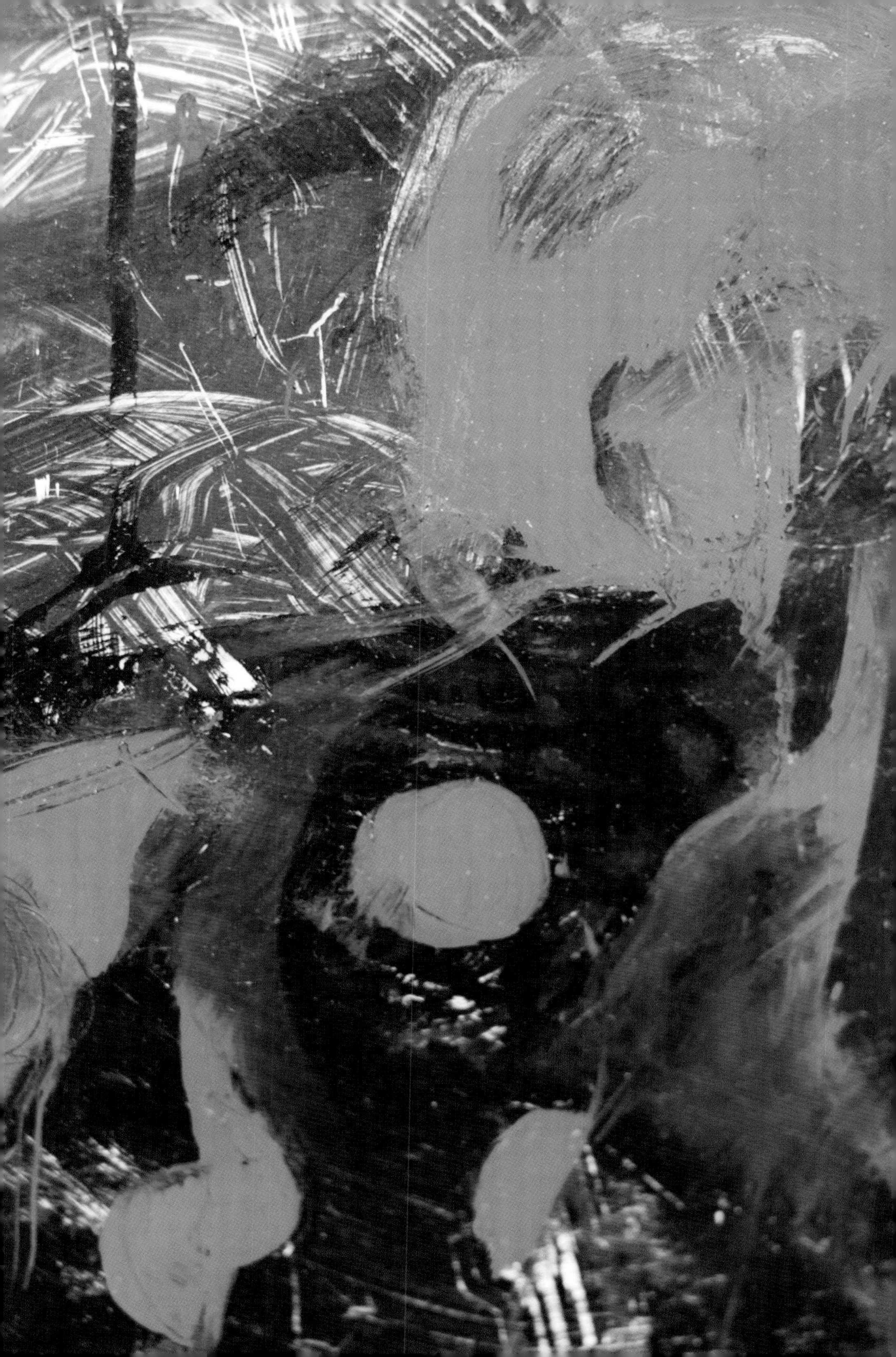

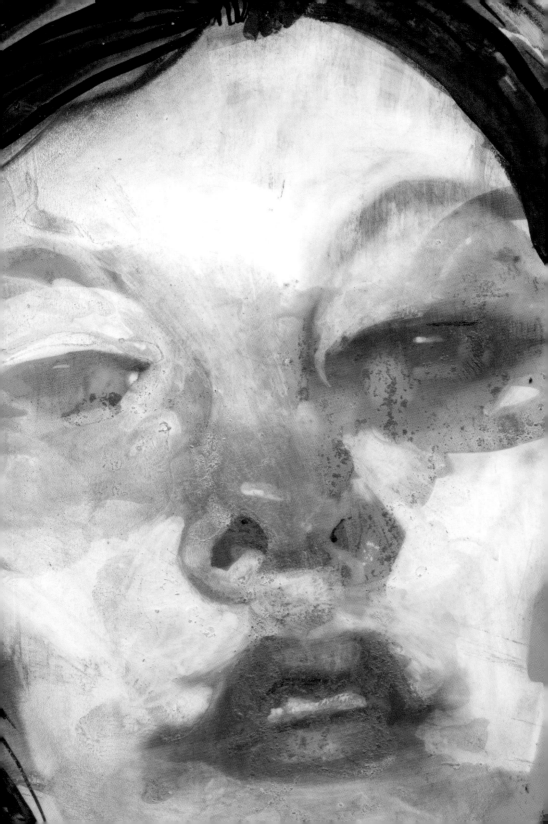

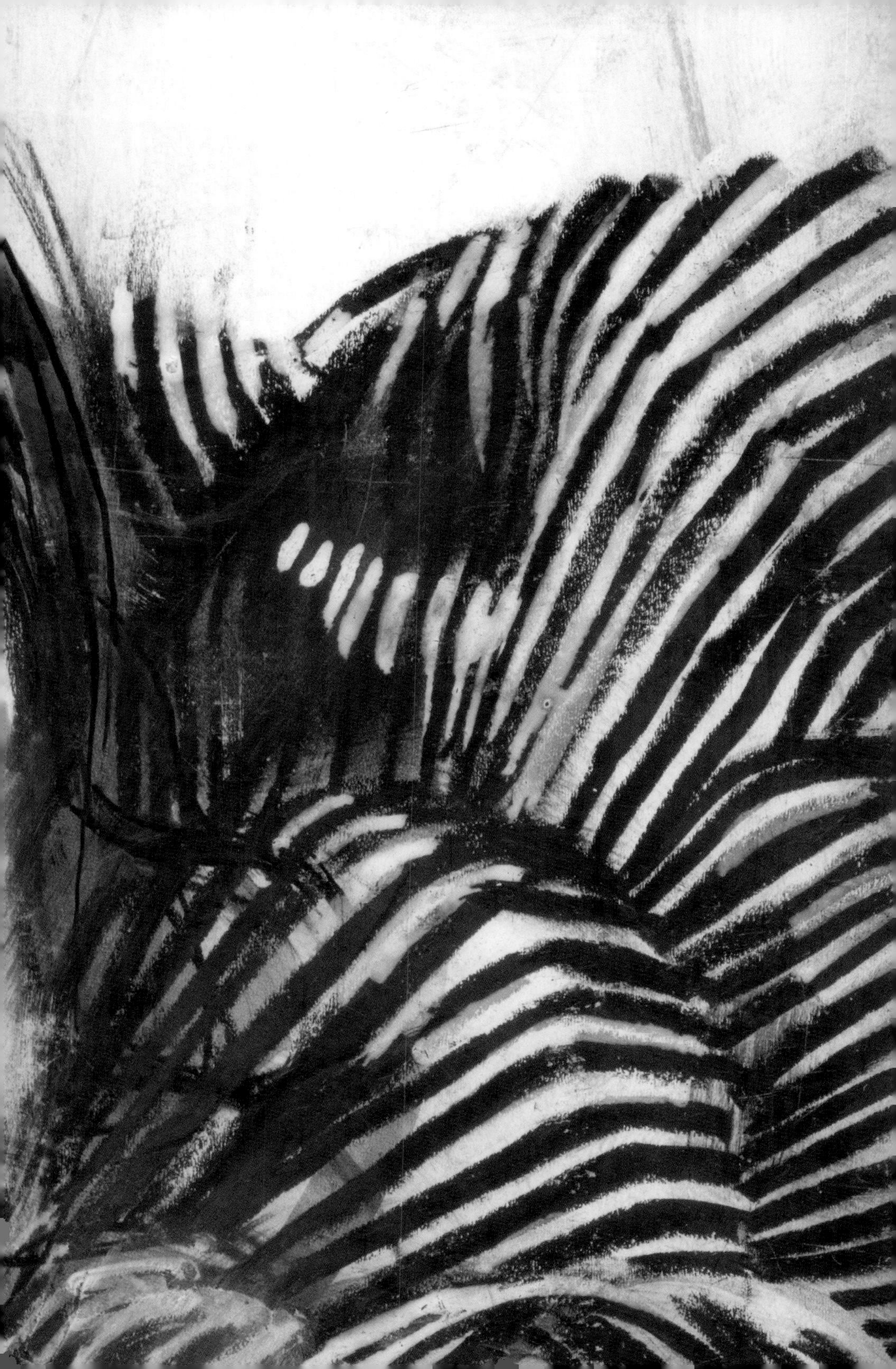

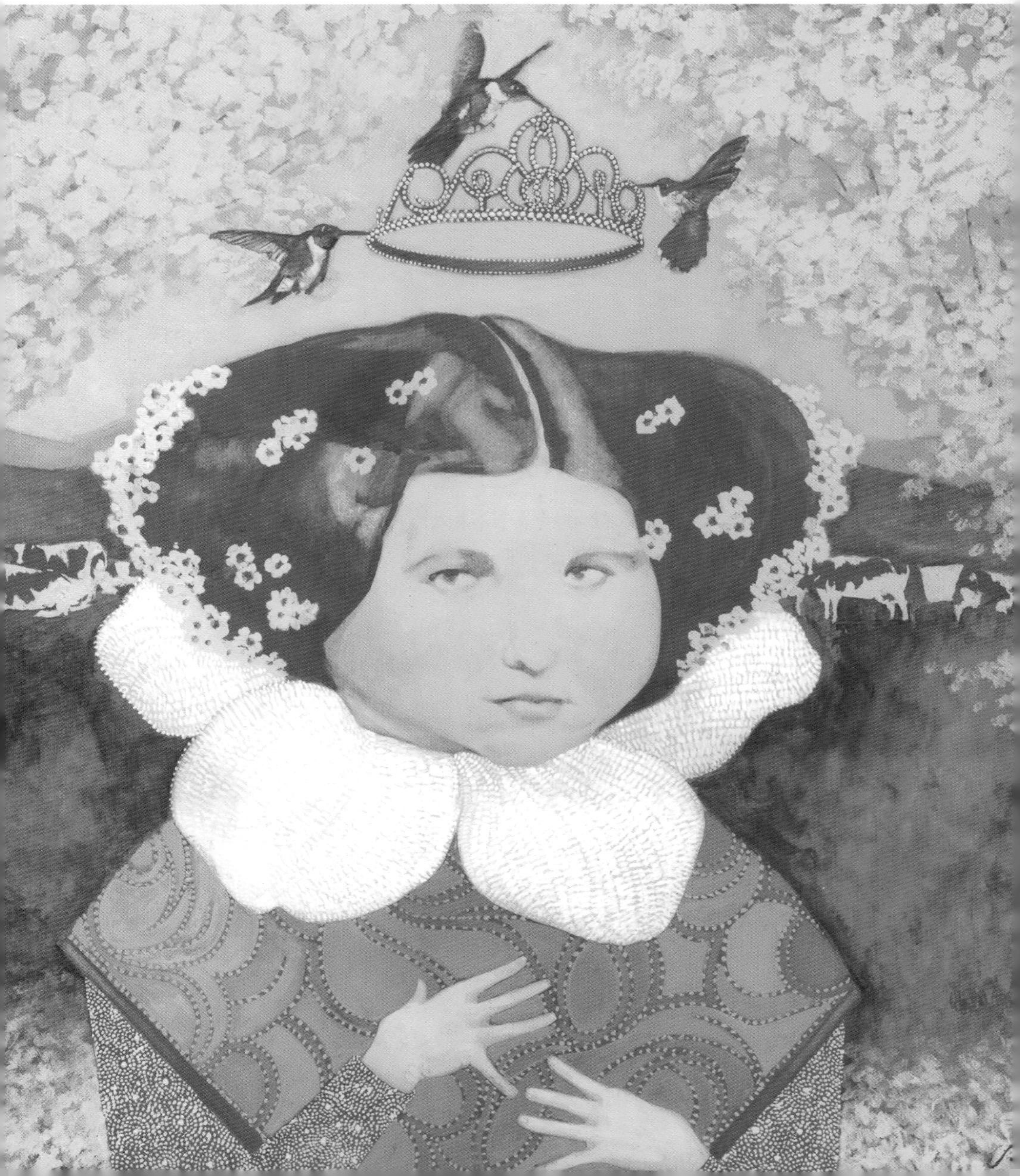

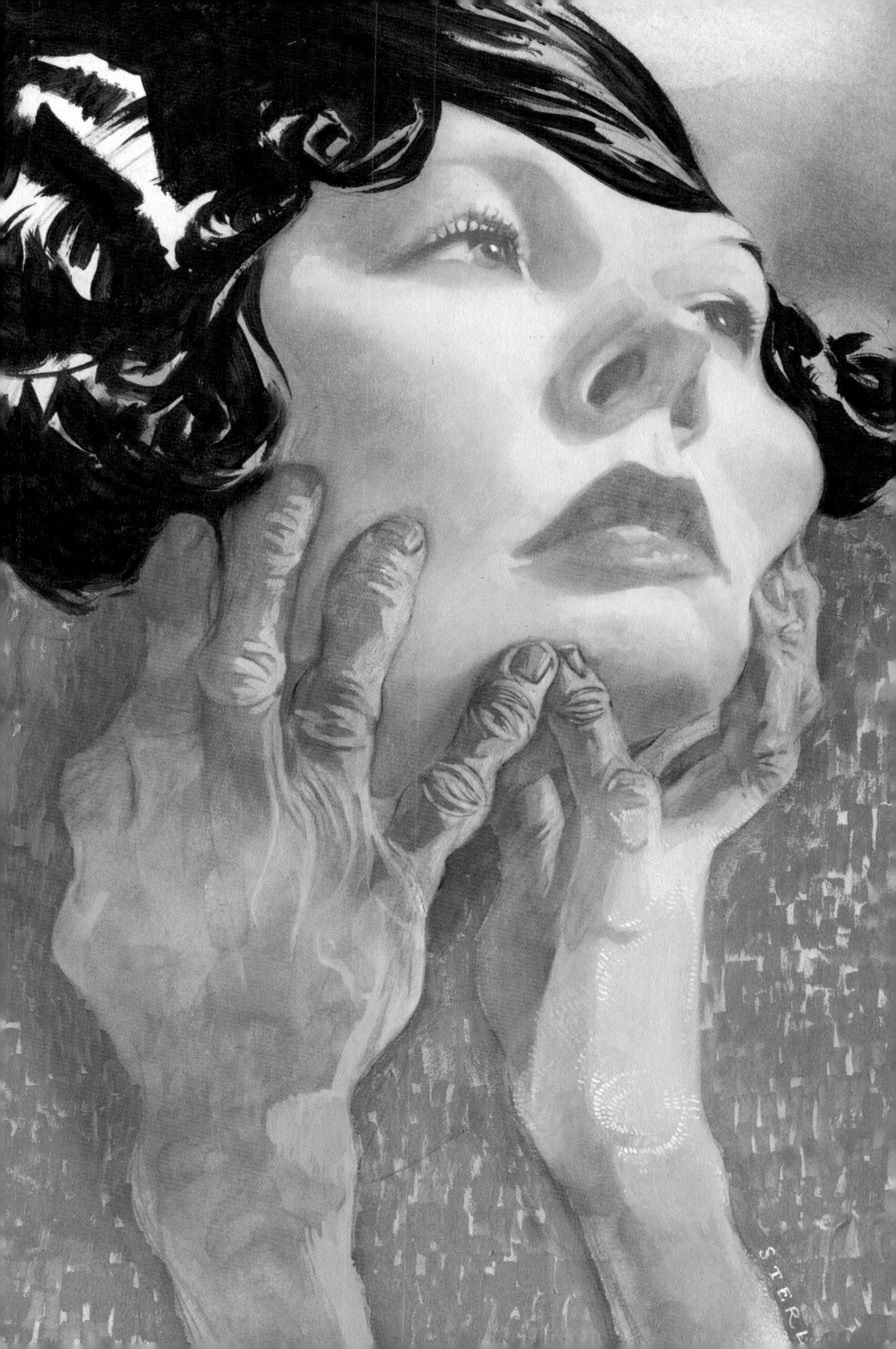

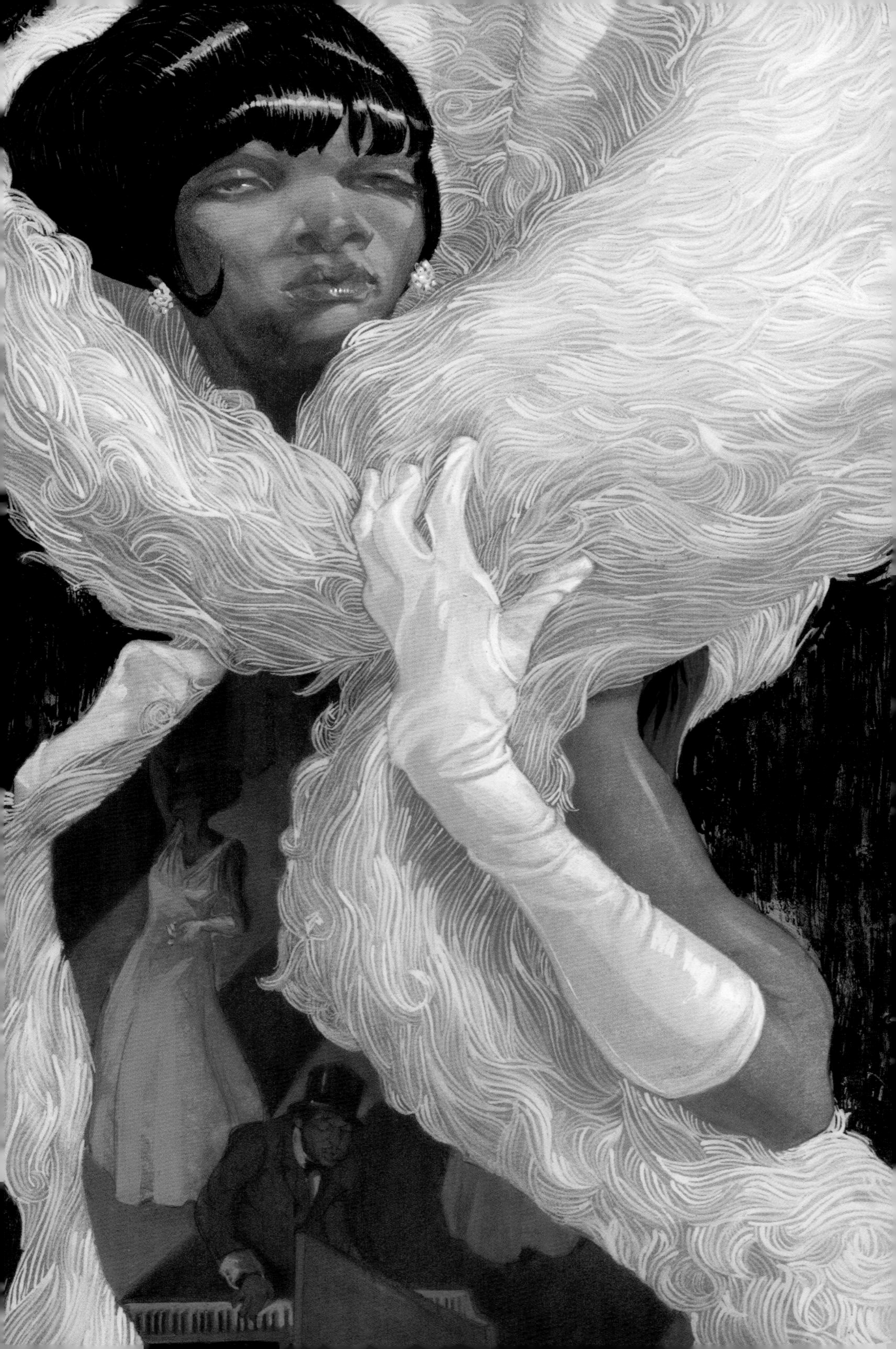

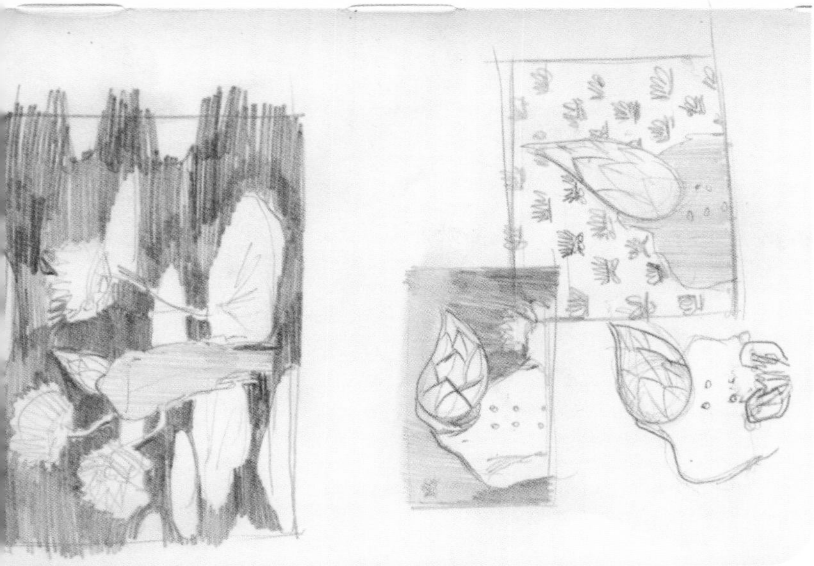

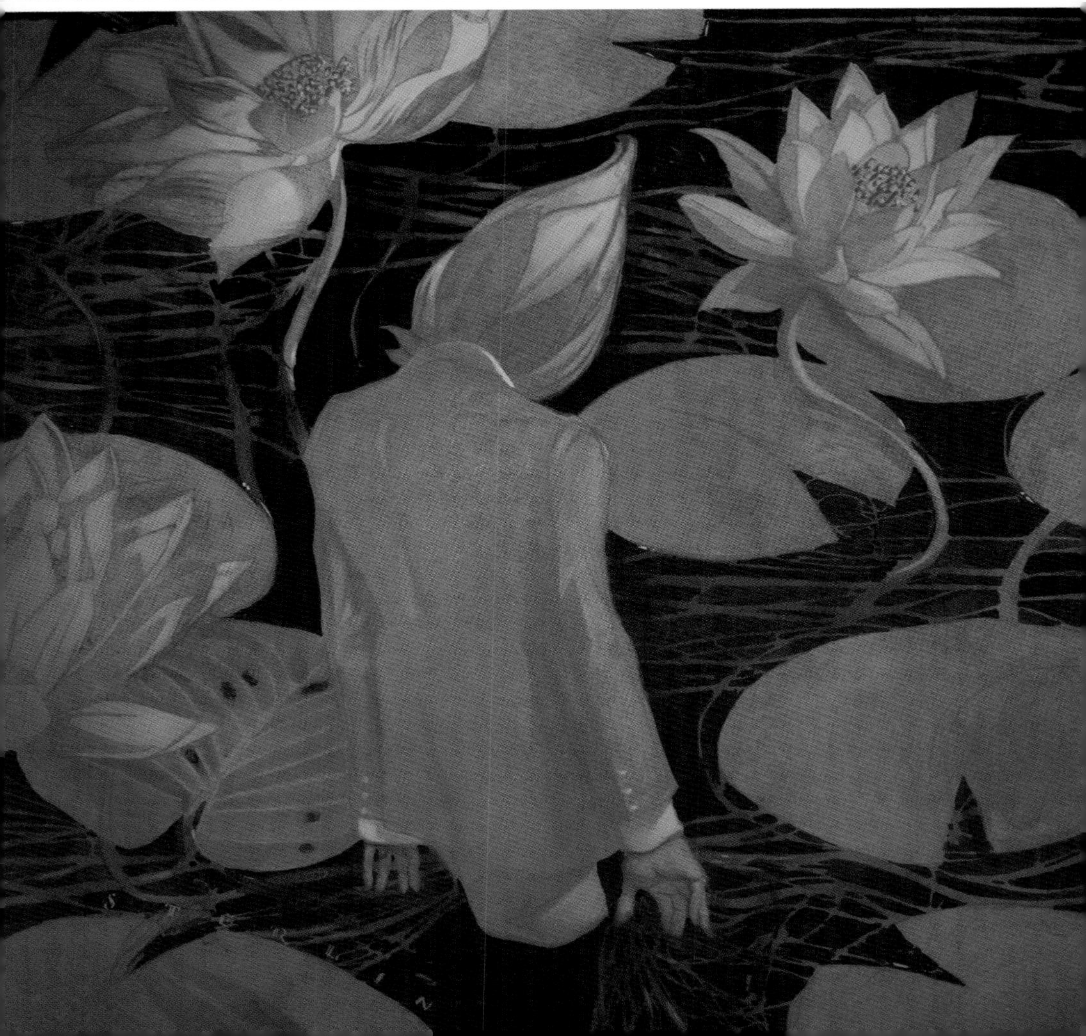

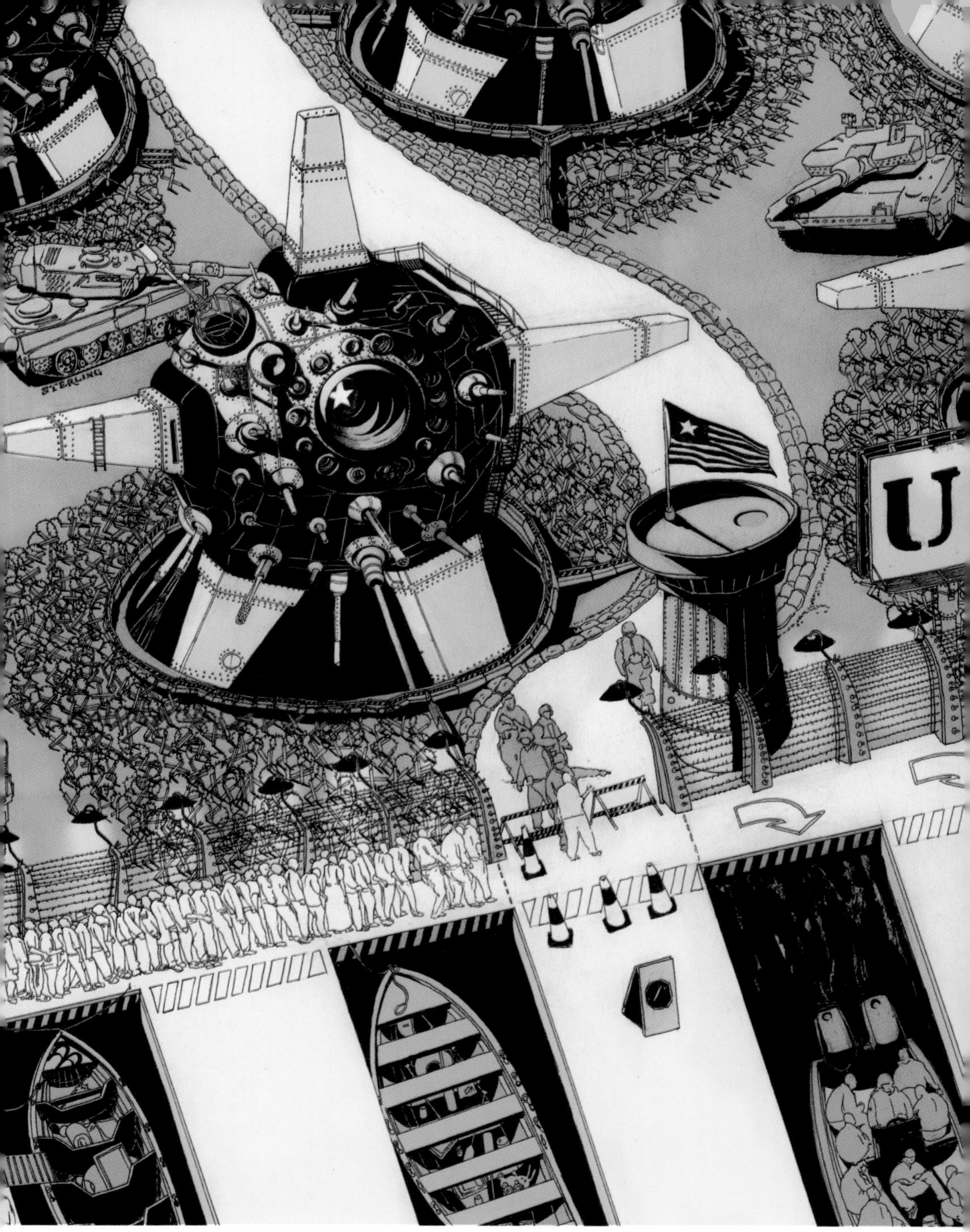
STERLING
U

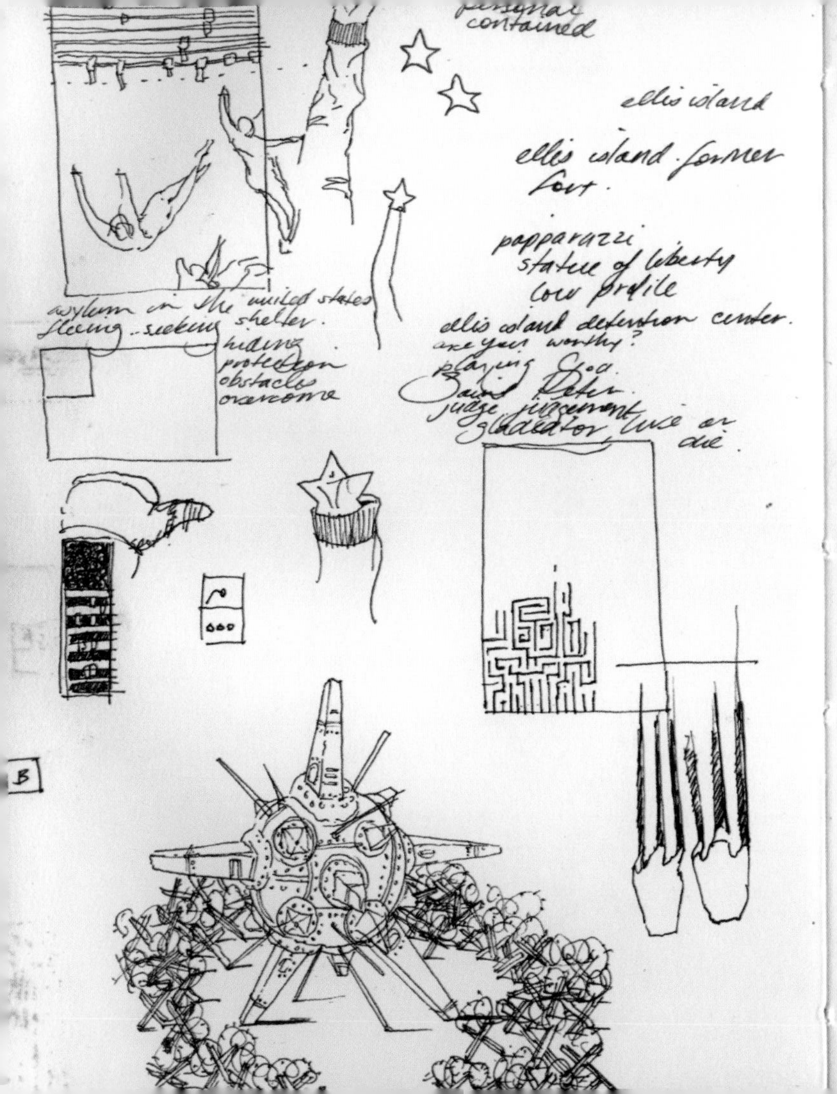

personal
contained
ellis island
ellis island former
fort.
papparazzi
statue of liberty
low profile
asylum in the united states
fleeing - seeking shelter.
hiding
protection
obstacles
overcome
ellis island detention center.
are you worthy?
playing God
Saint Peter
judge judgement
gladiator, live or die
B

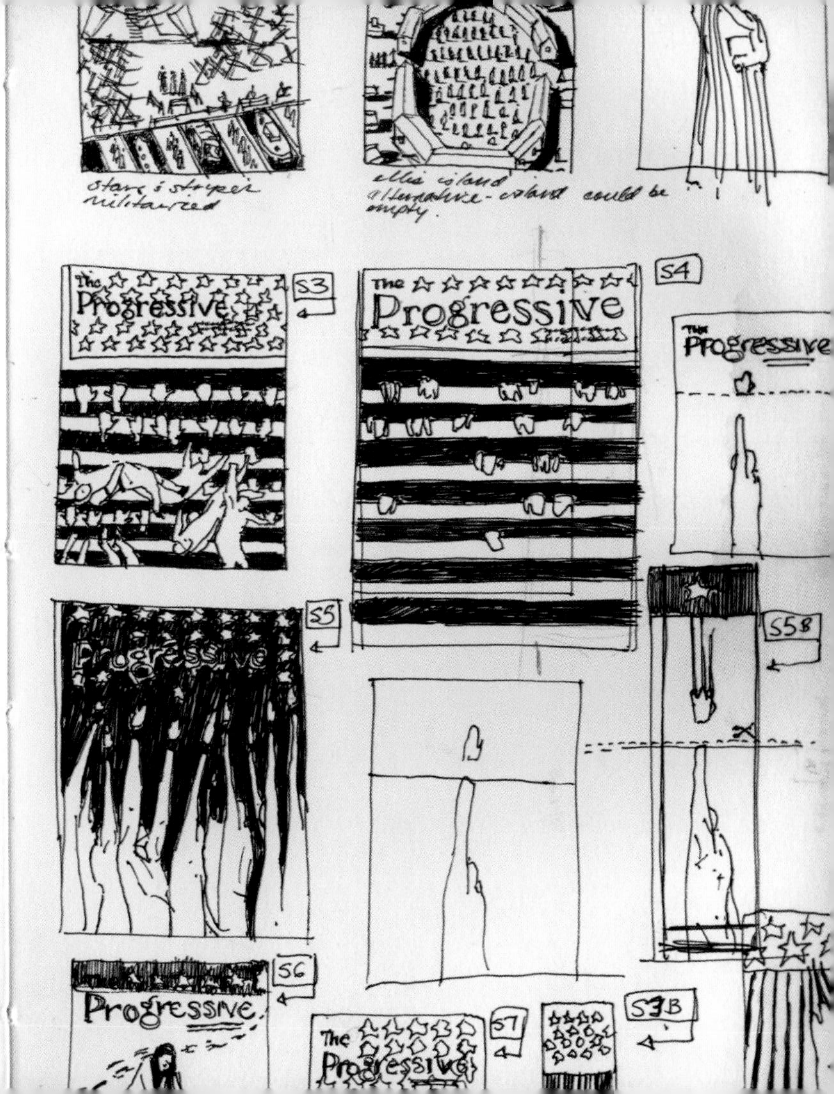

stars i stripes
militarized
ellis island
alternative - island could be
empty.
S3
The Progressive
S4
The Progressive
The Progressive
S5
Progressive
S5B
S6
Progressive
S7
The Progressive
S3B

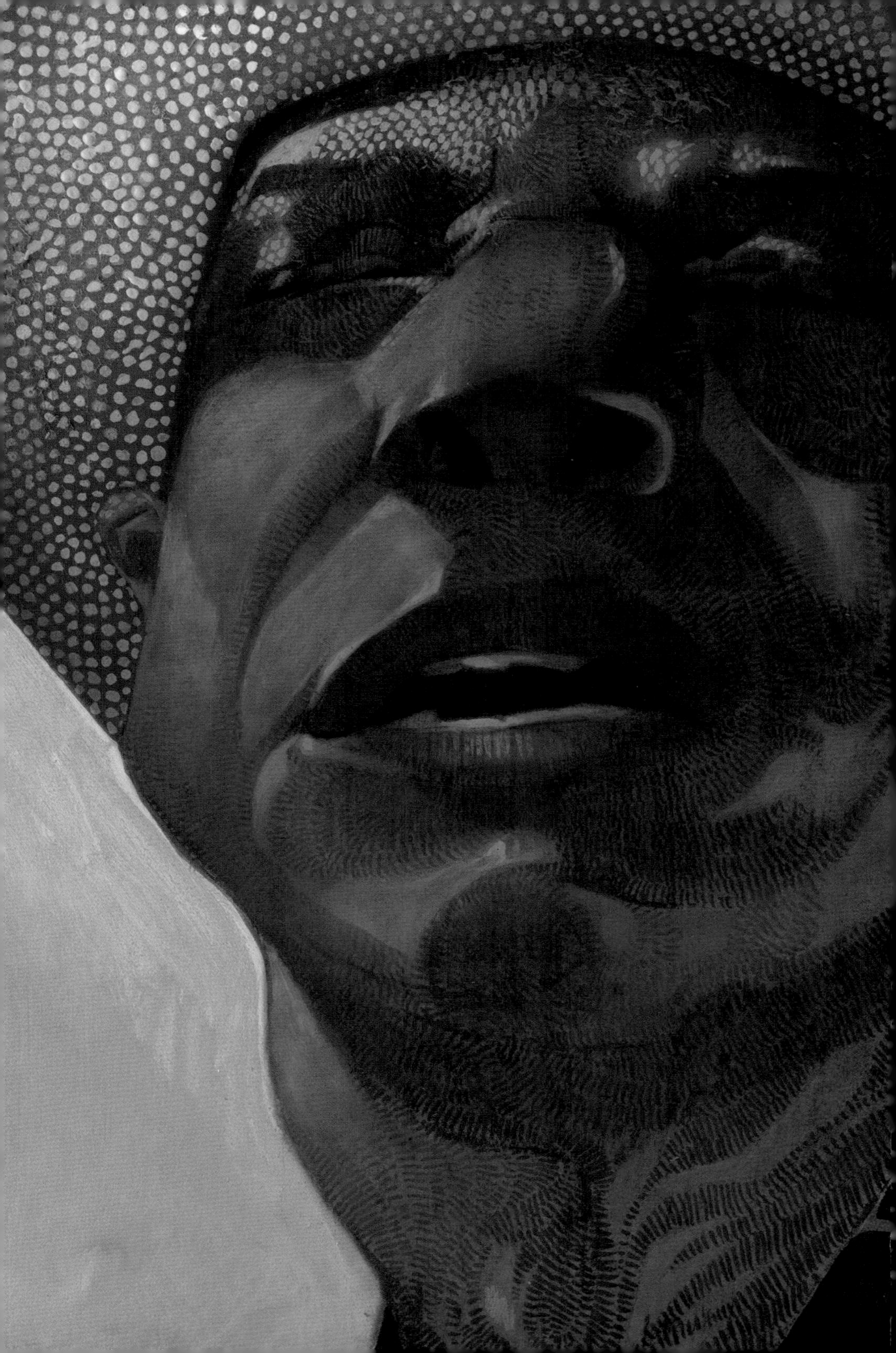

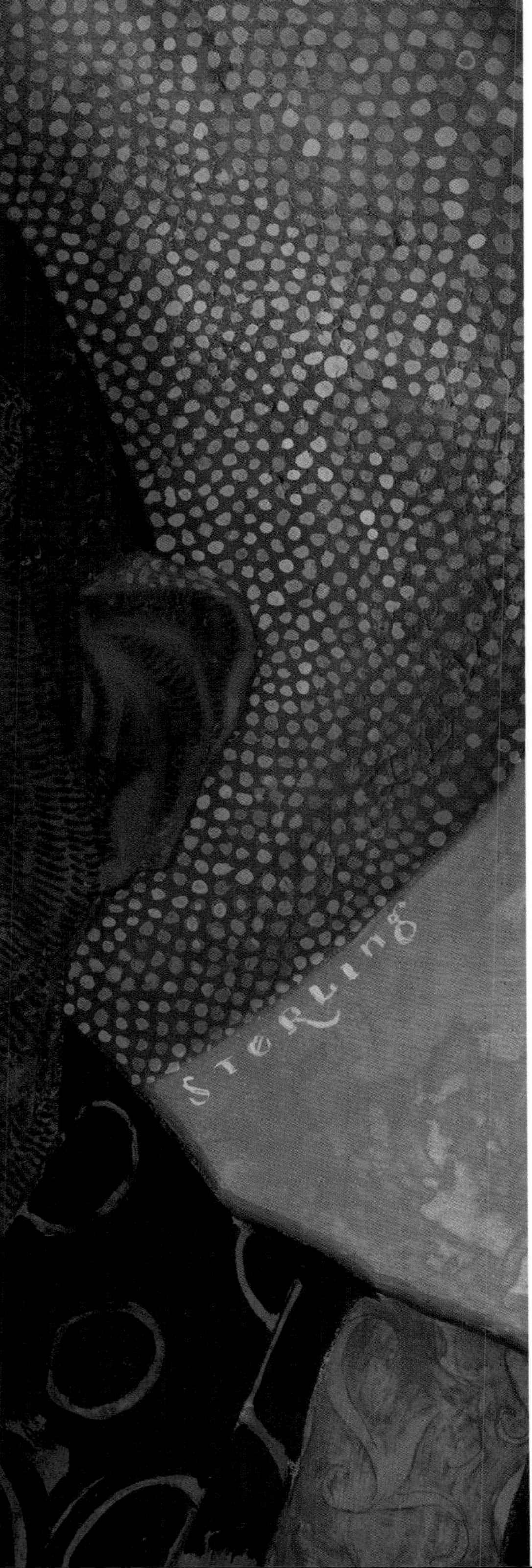
Sterling

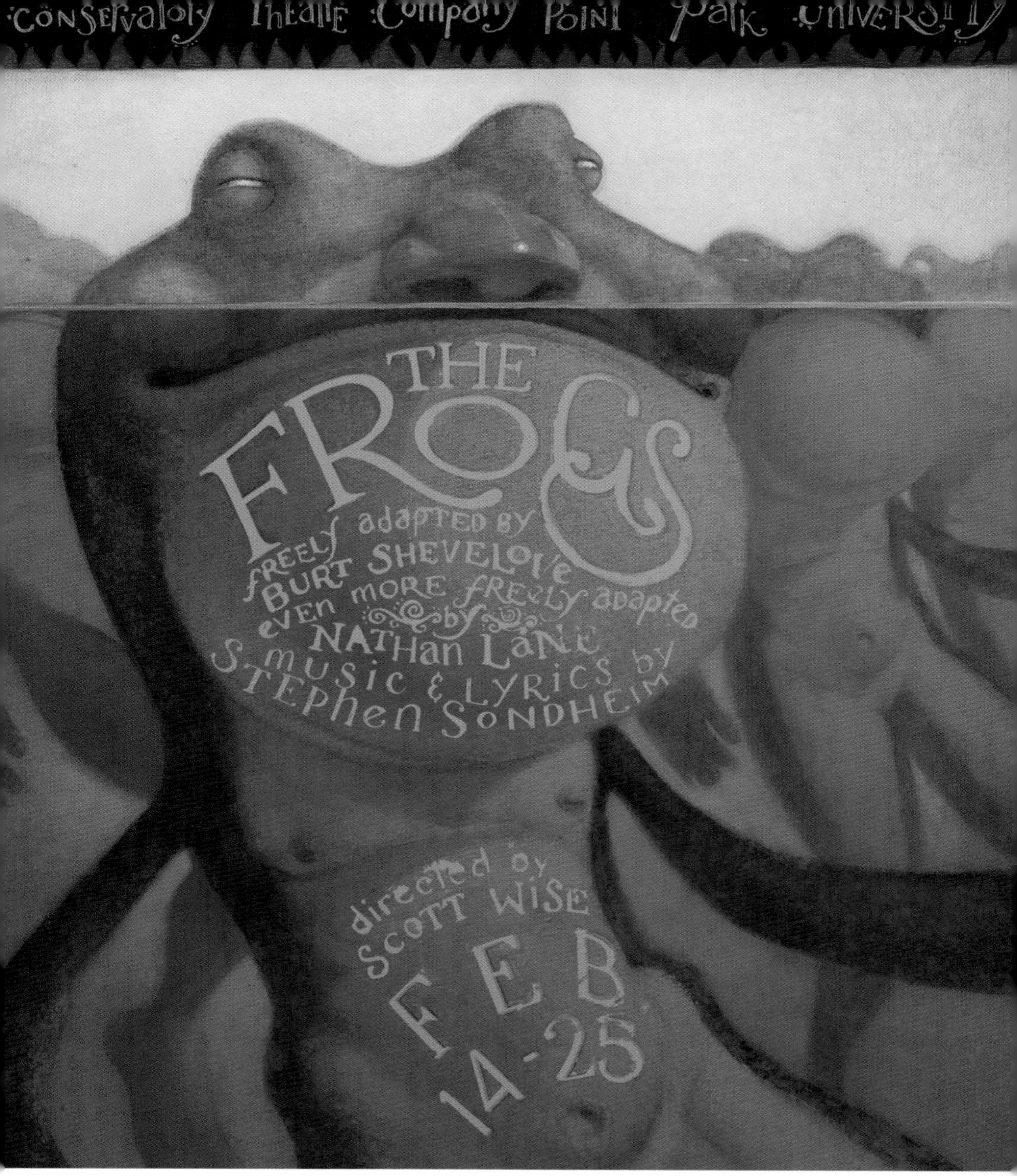
Conservatory Theatre Company Point Park University
THE FROGS
freely adapted by
BURT SHEVELOVE
even more freely adapted
by
NATHAN LANE
music & lyrics by
STEPHEN SONDHEIM
directed by
SCOTT WISE
FEB
14-25

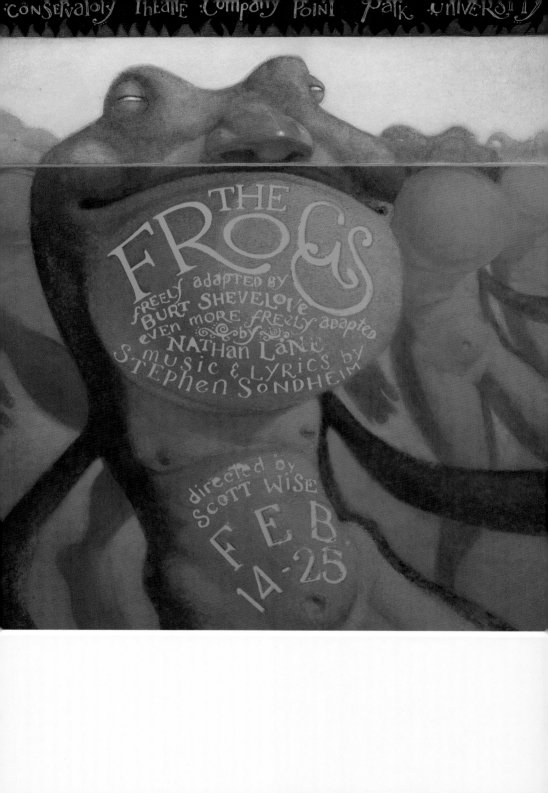

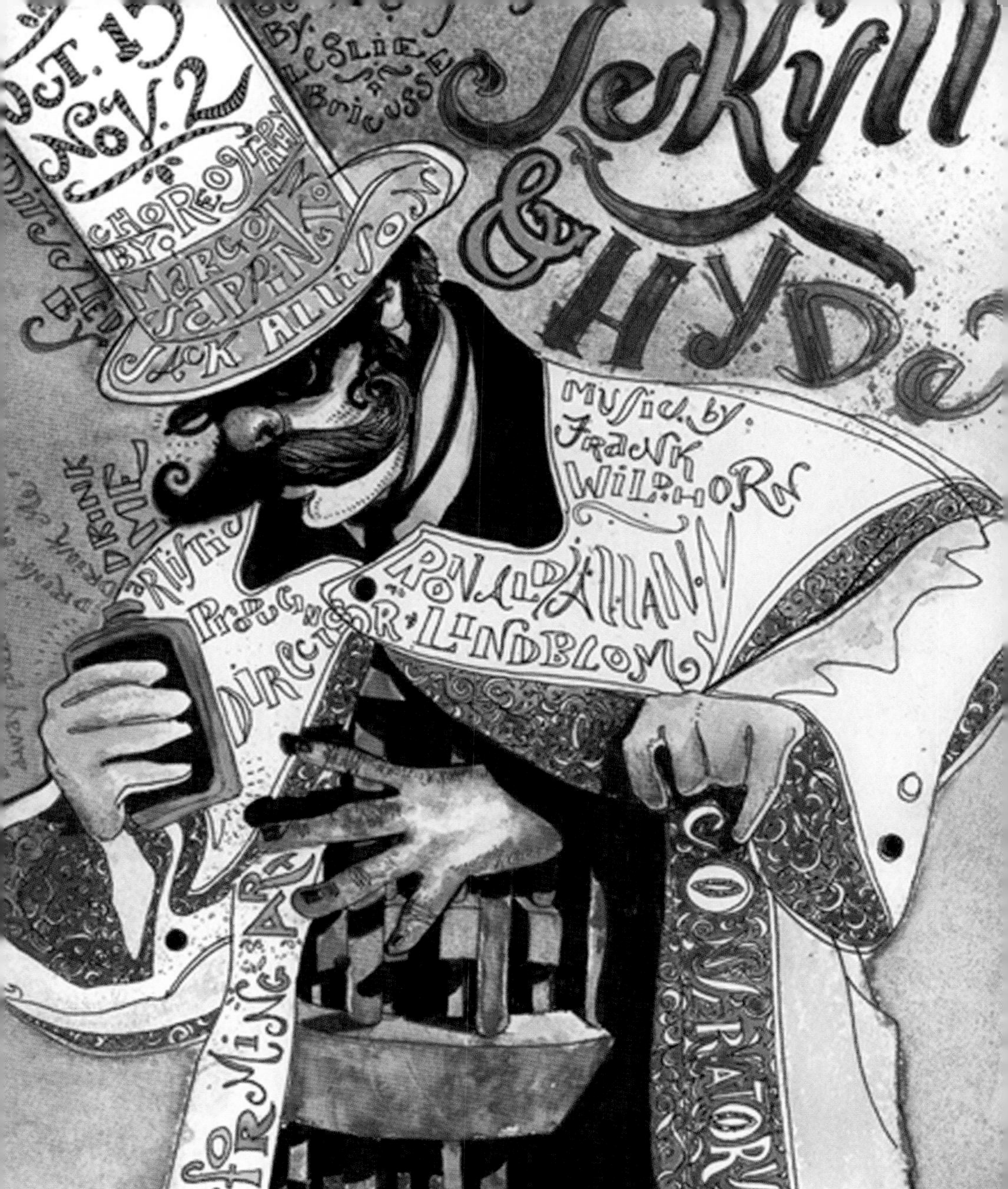
Oct. 15
Nov. 2
By Leslie Bricusse
Jekyll
& Hyde
Jack Allison
Music by Frank Wildhorn
Ronald Allan Lindblom

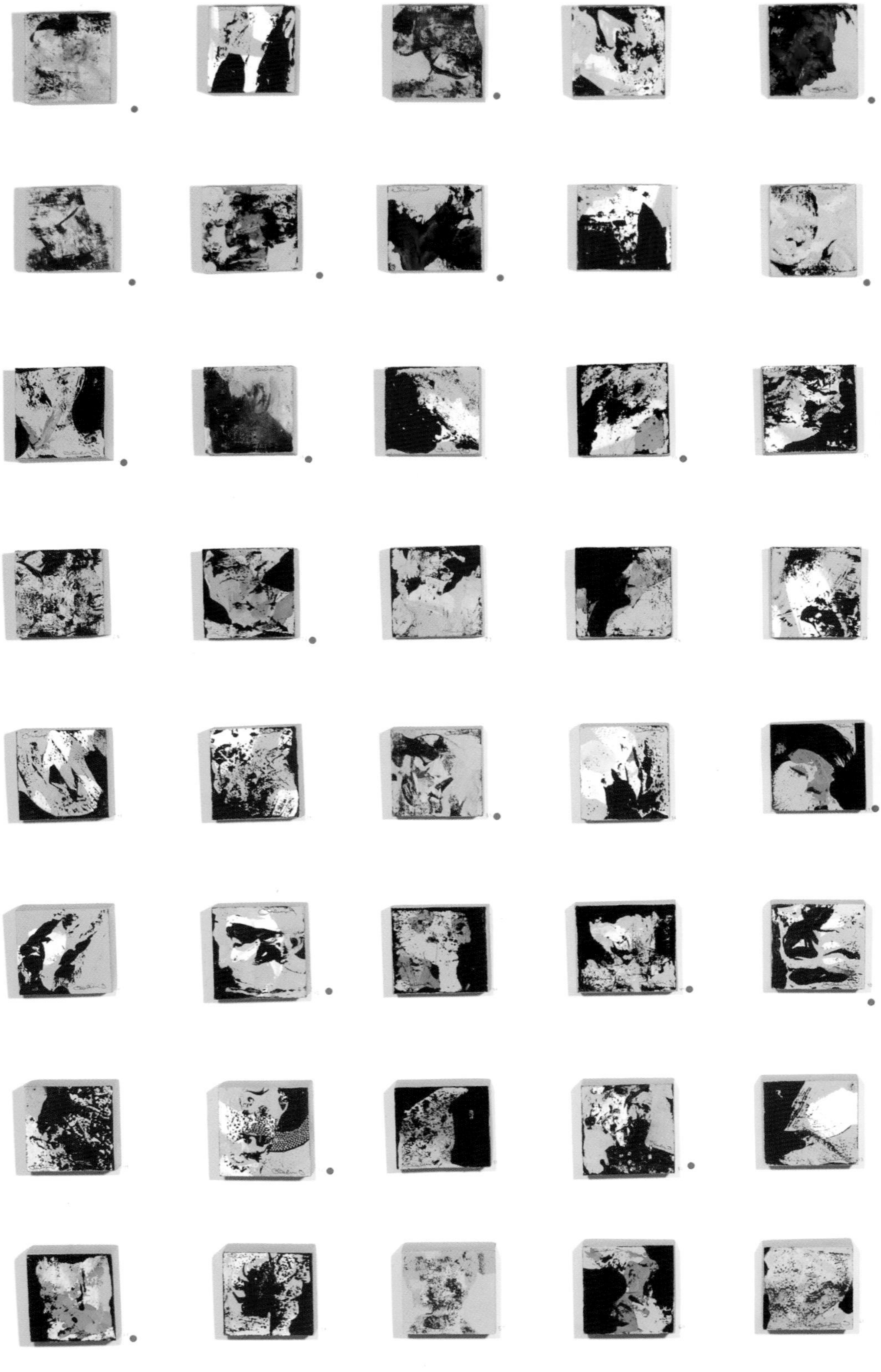

PAINTING

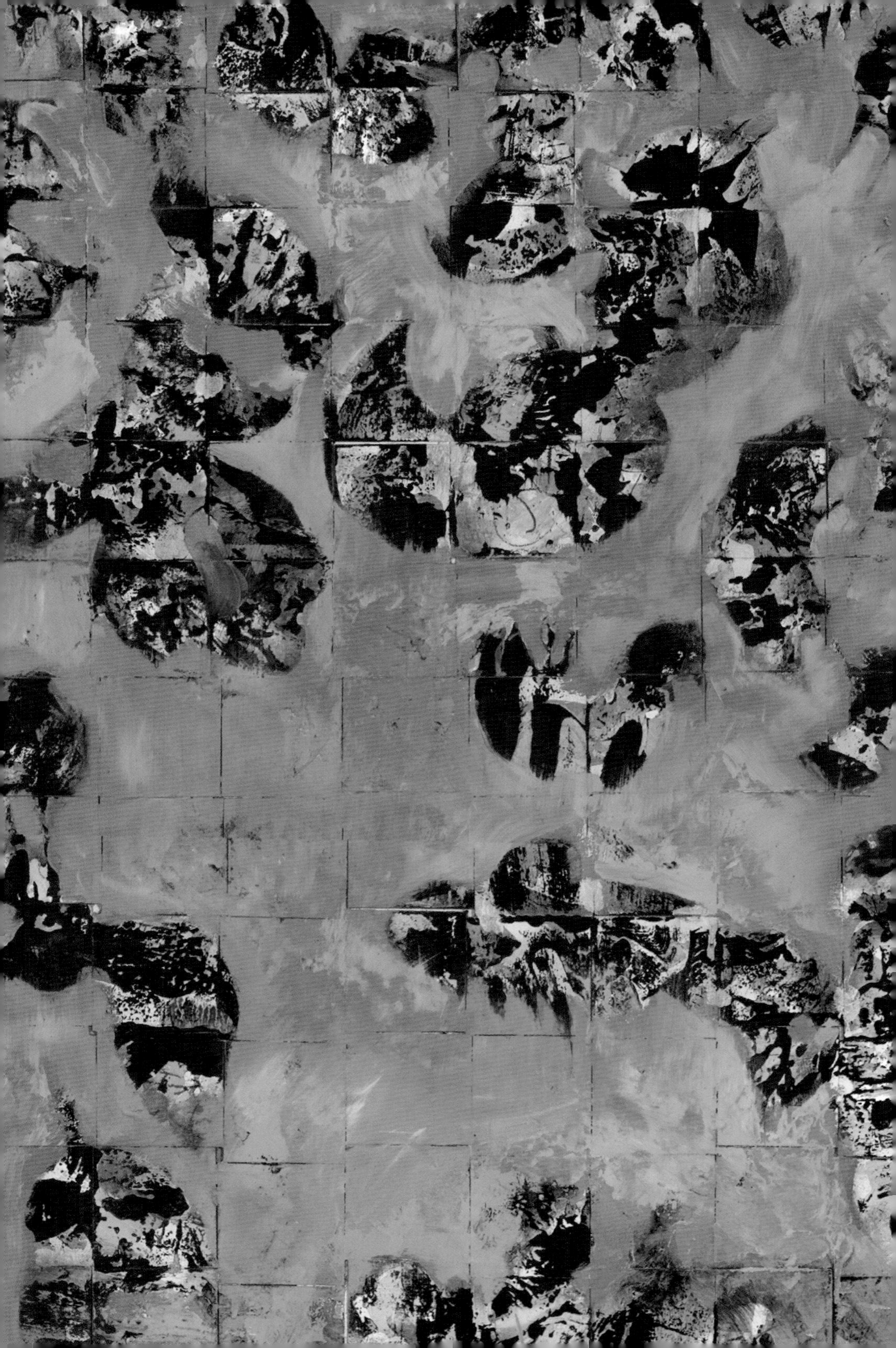

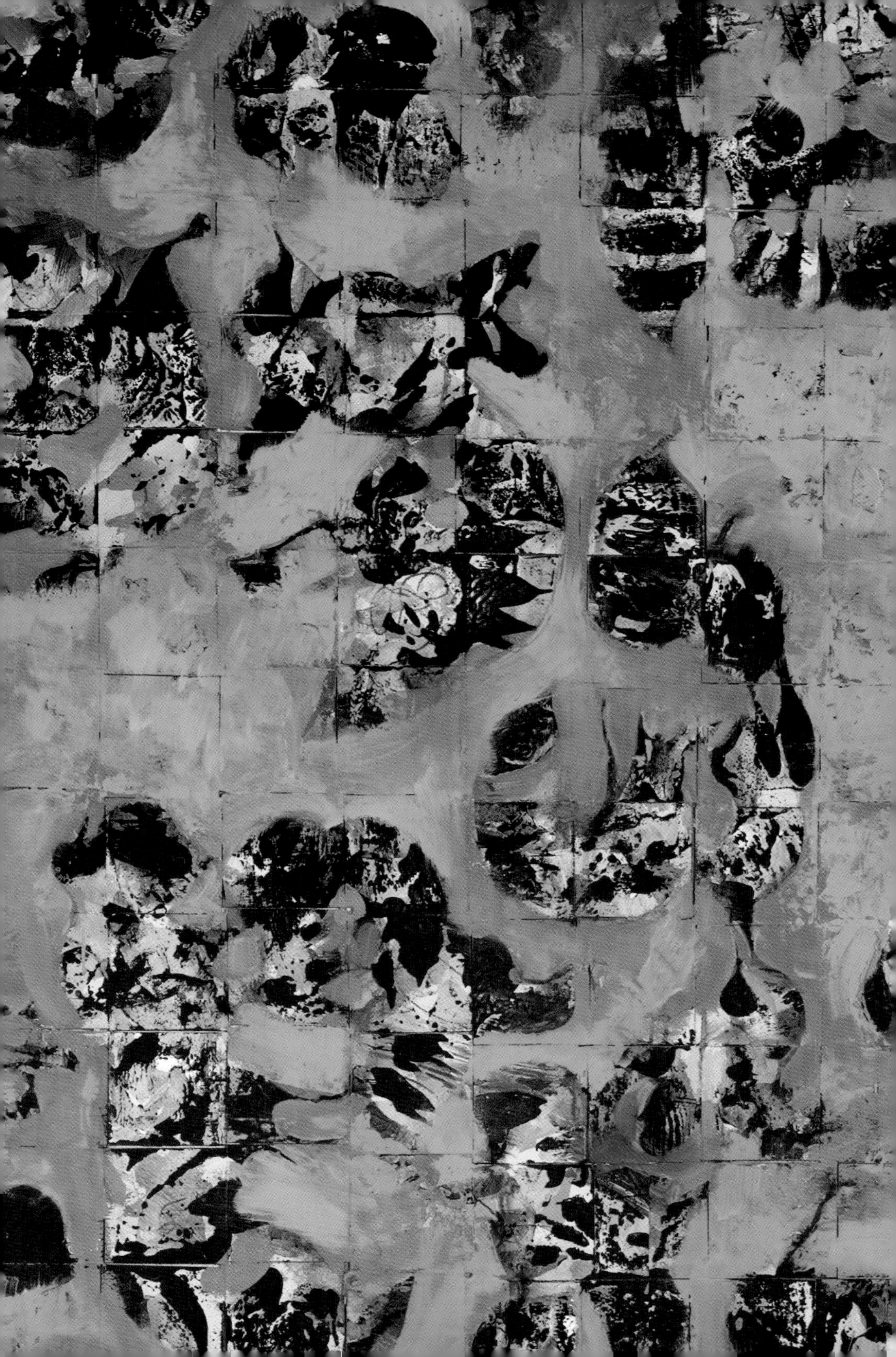

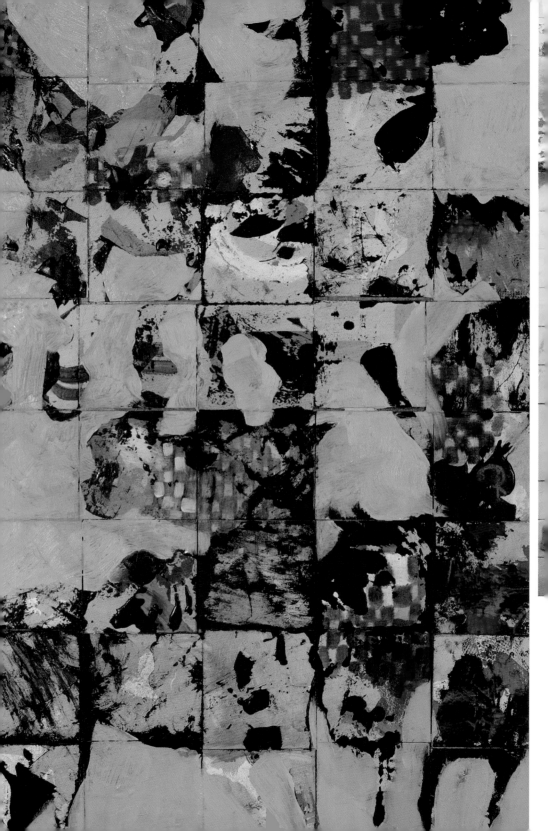

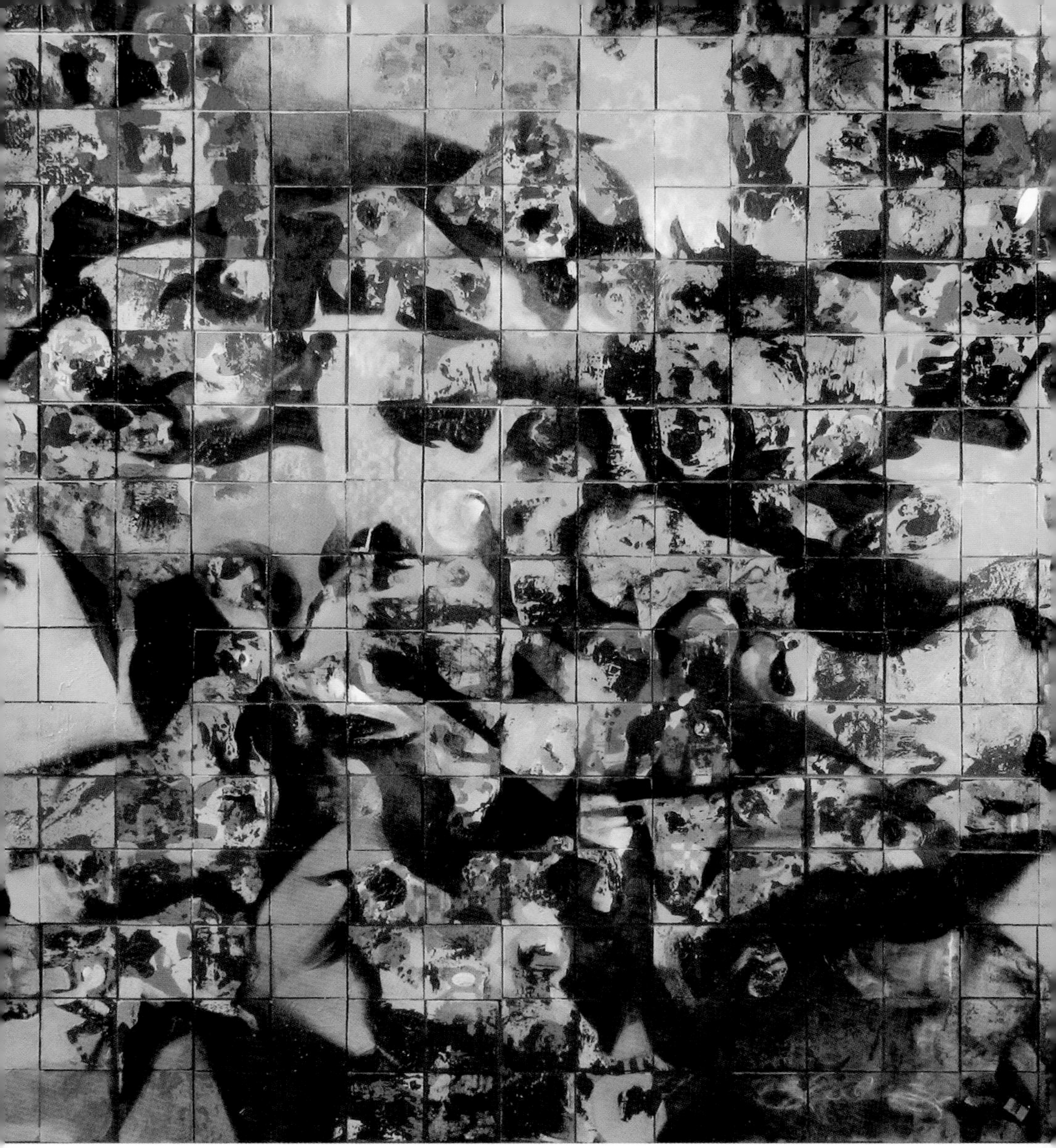

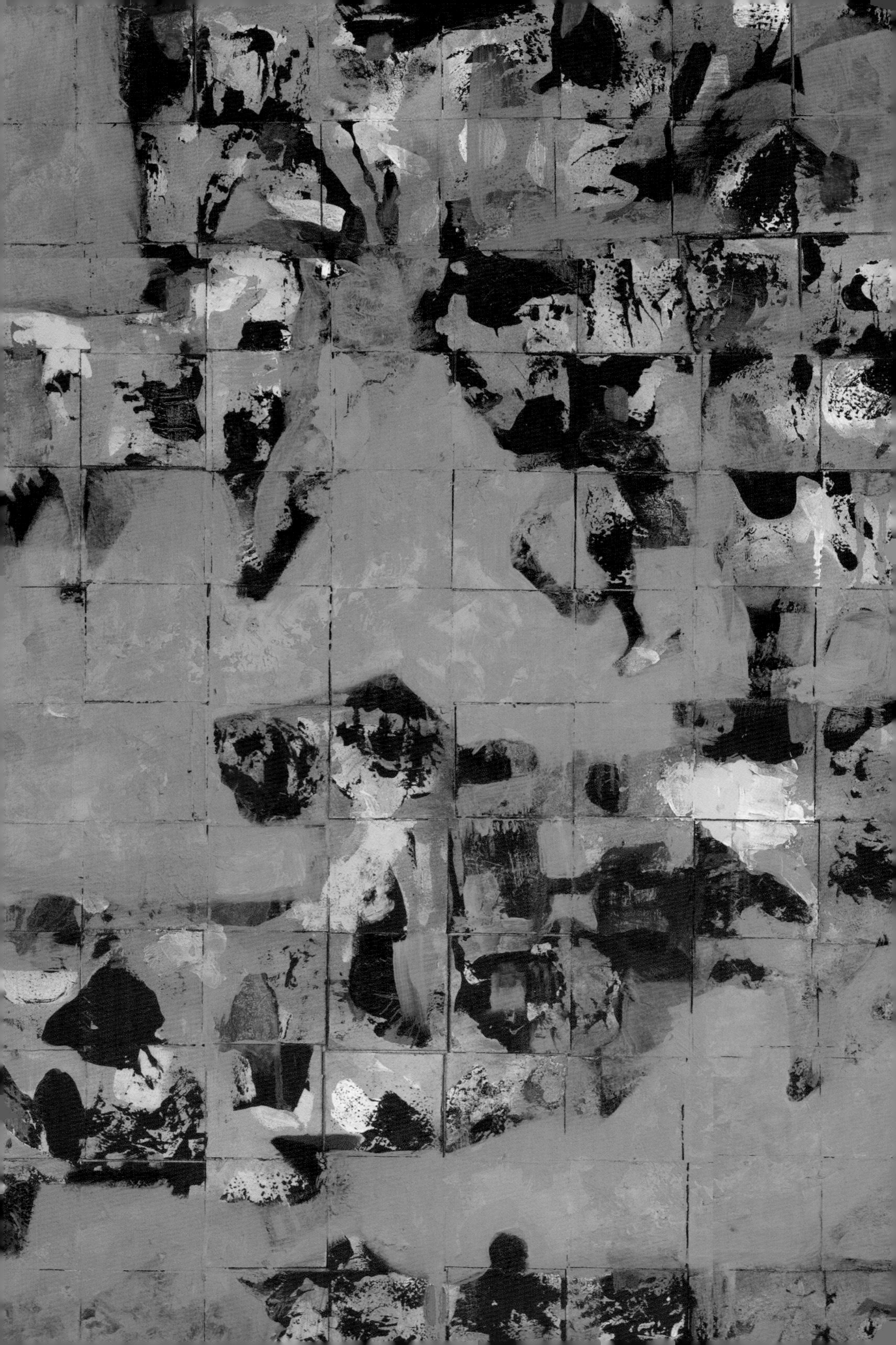

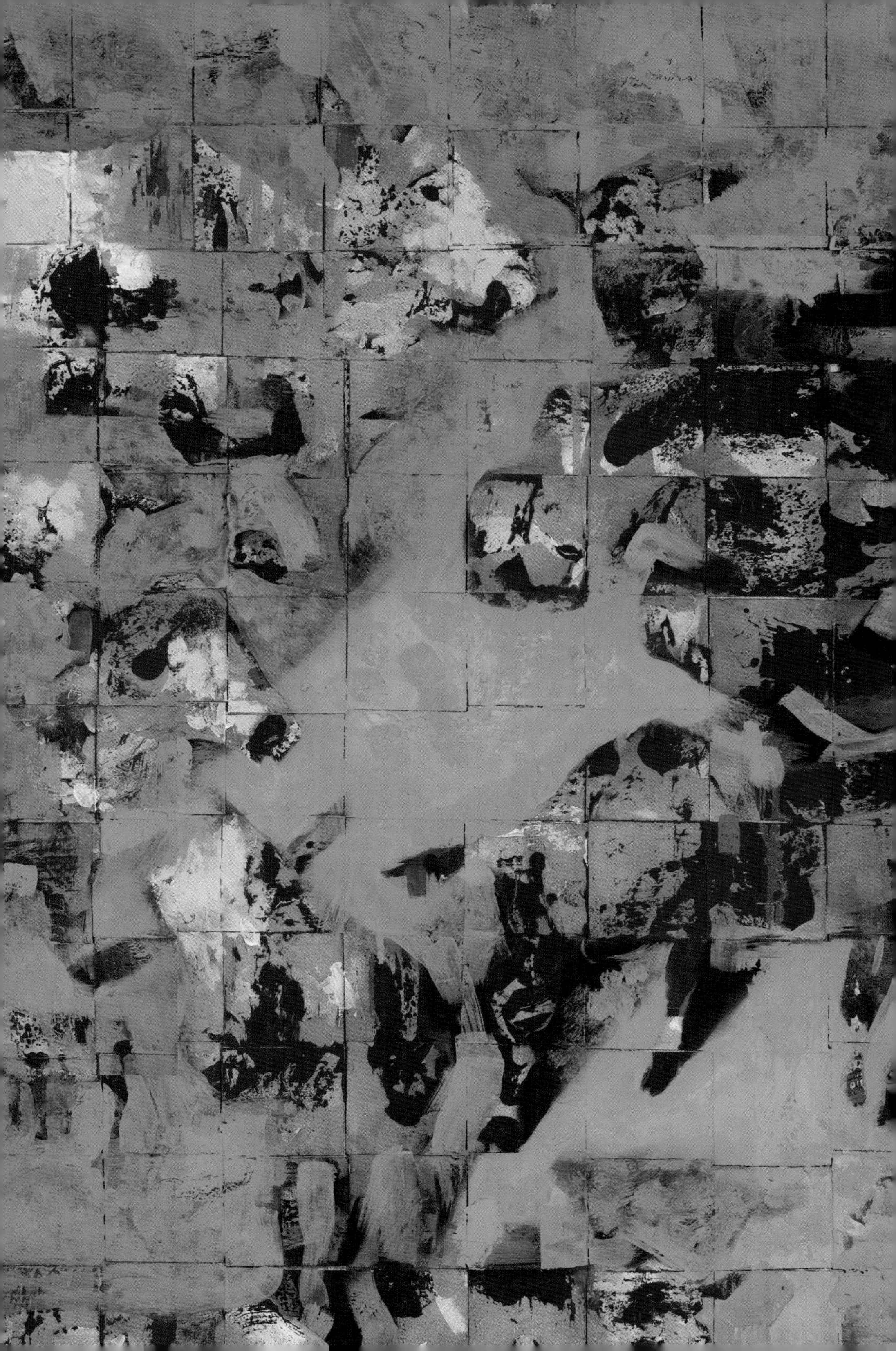

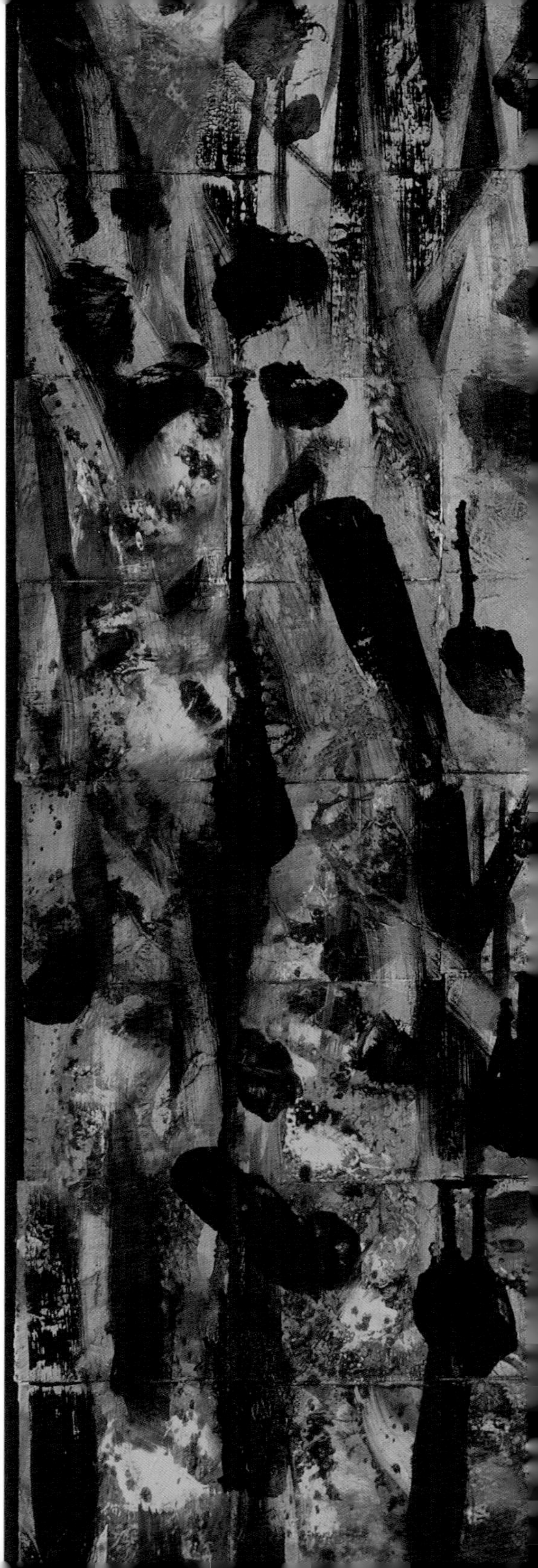

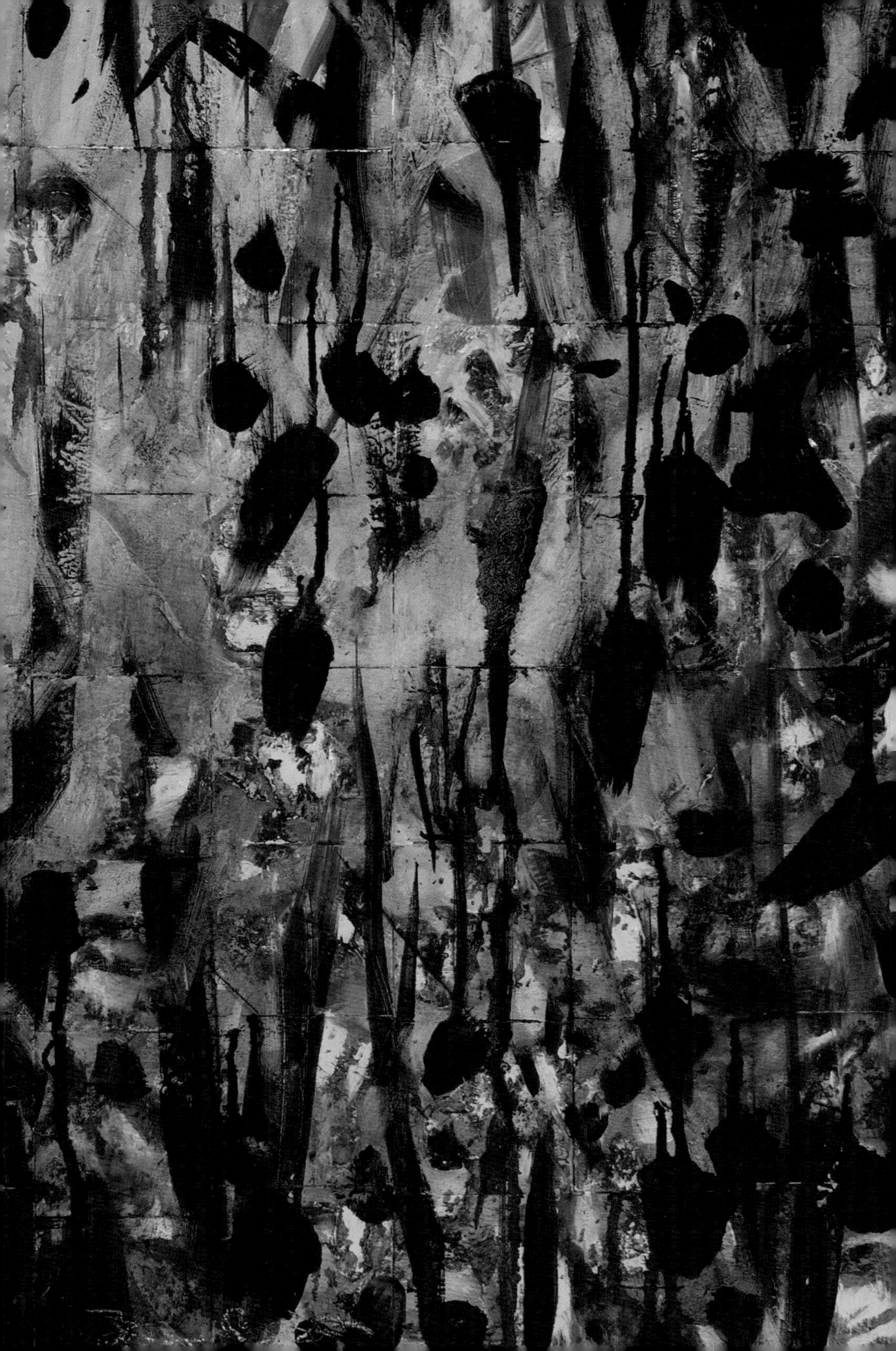

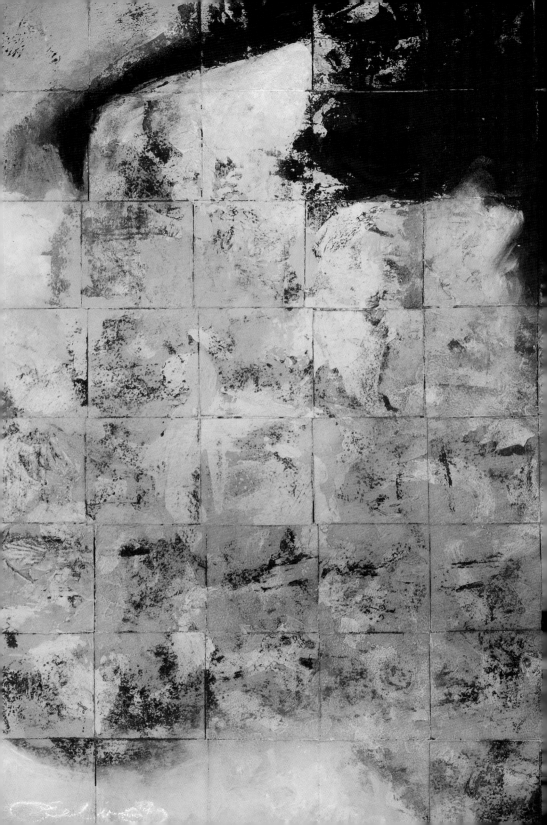

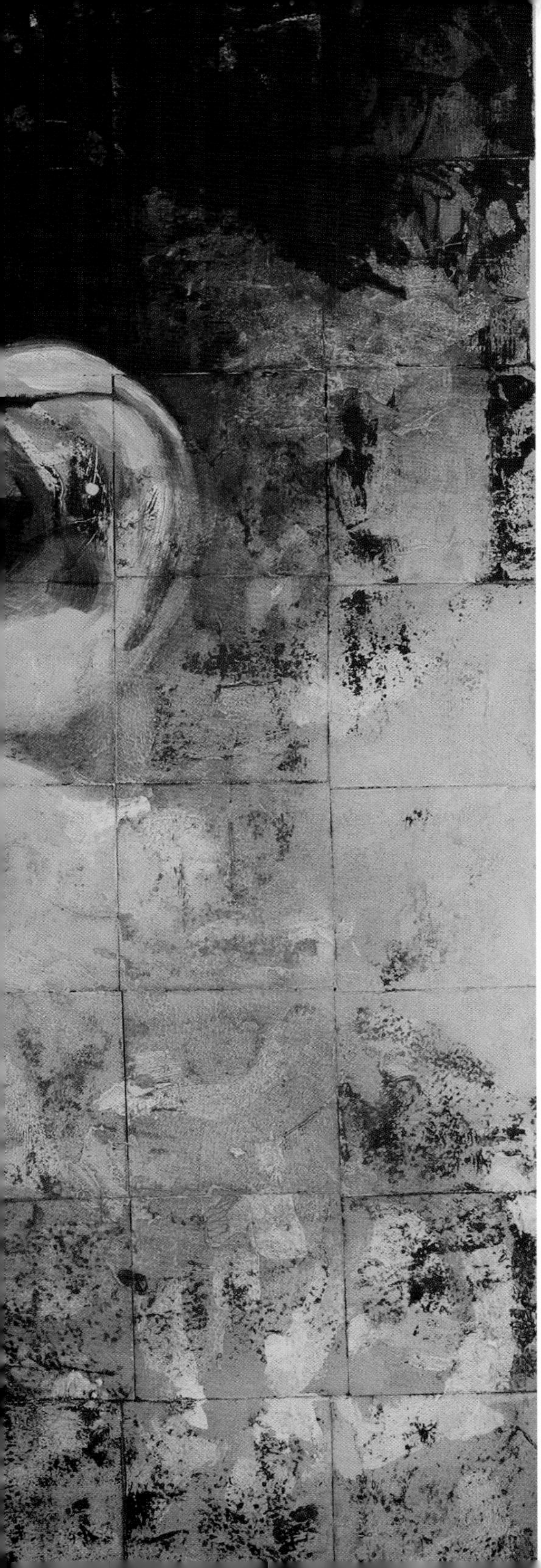

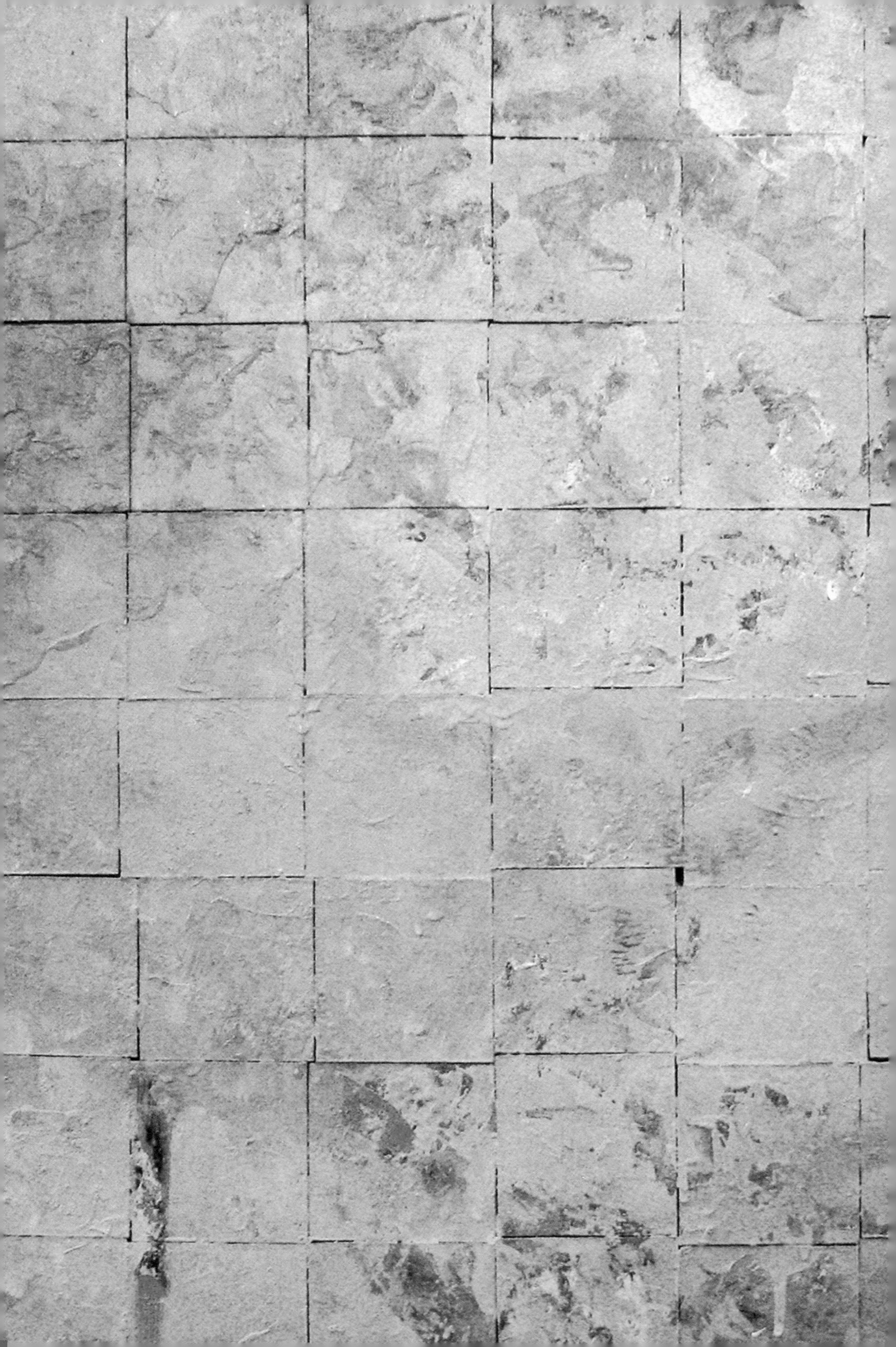

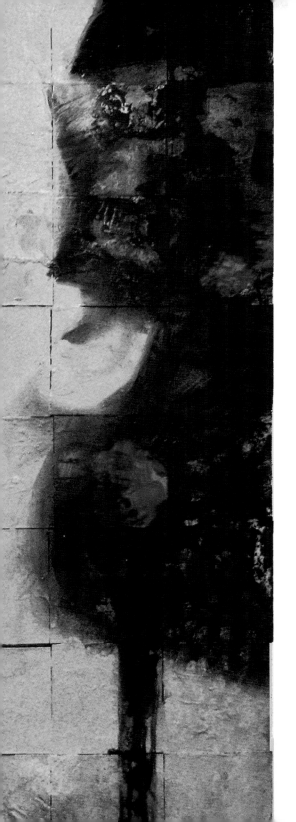

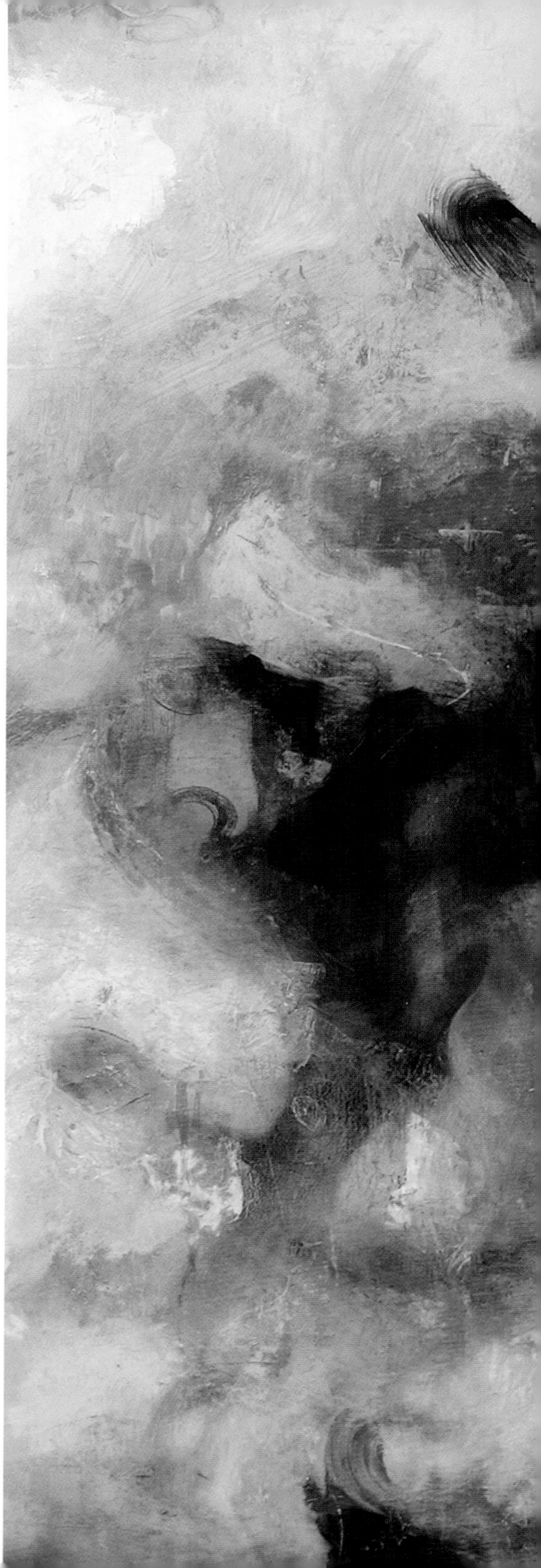

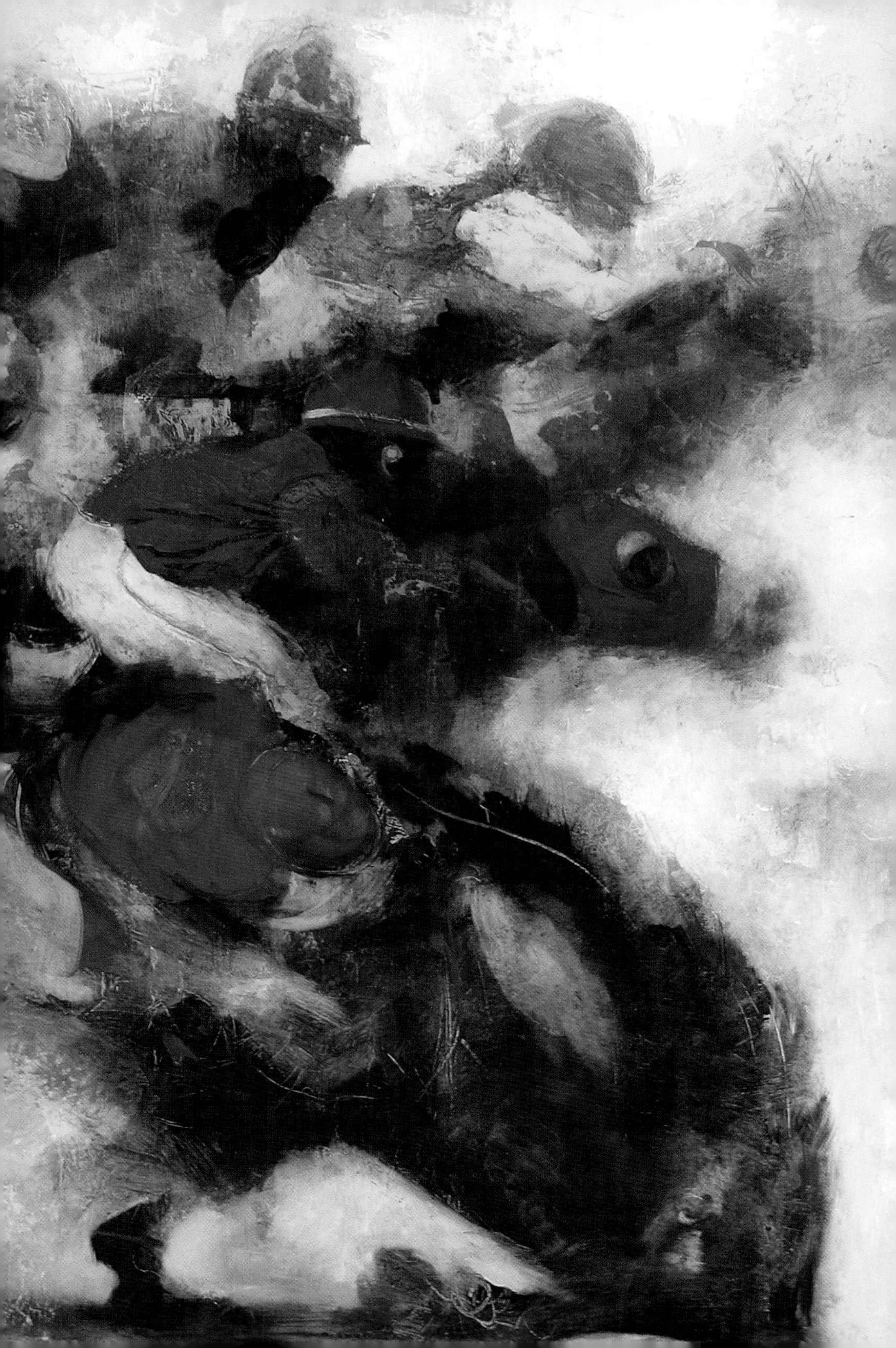

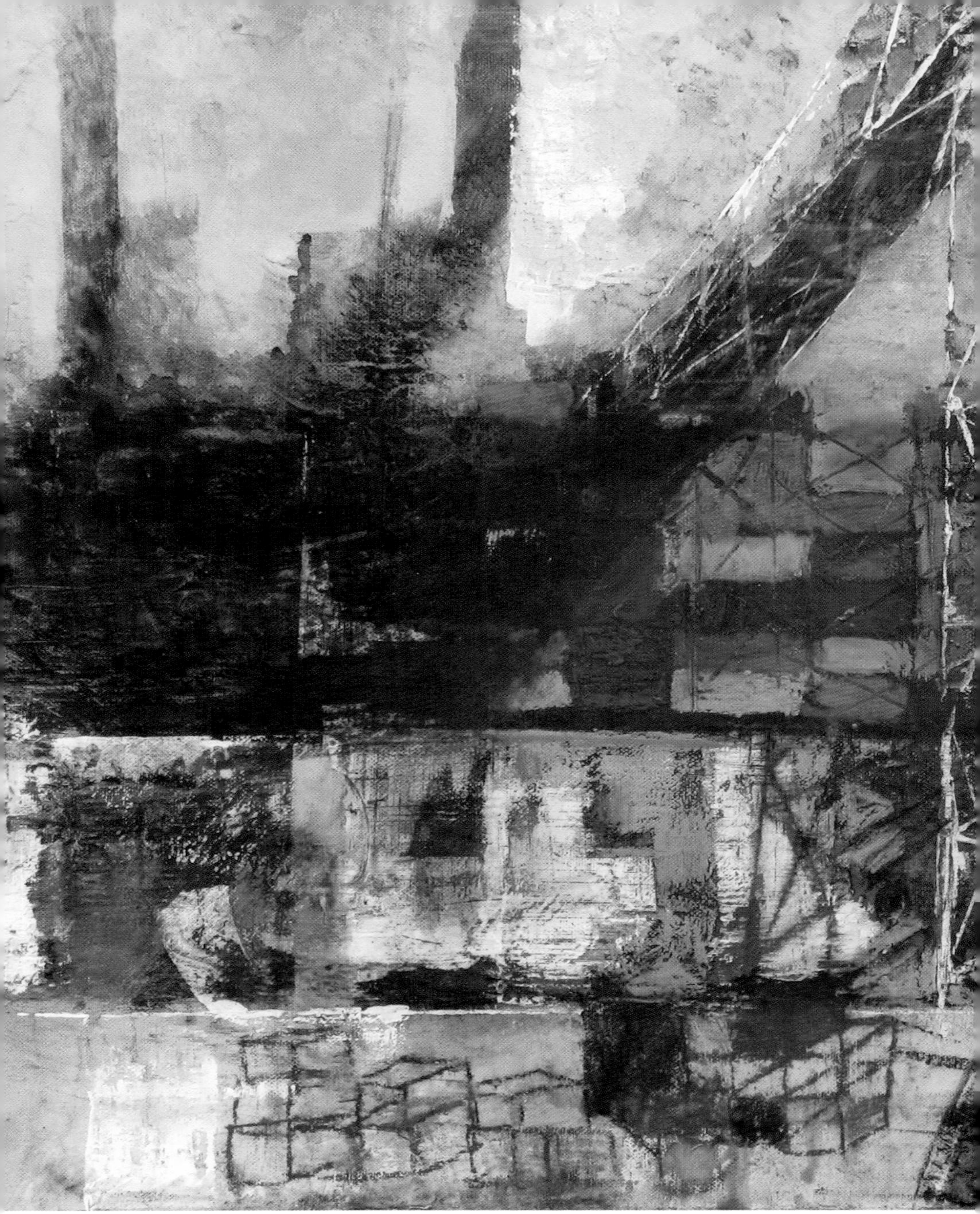

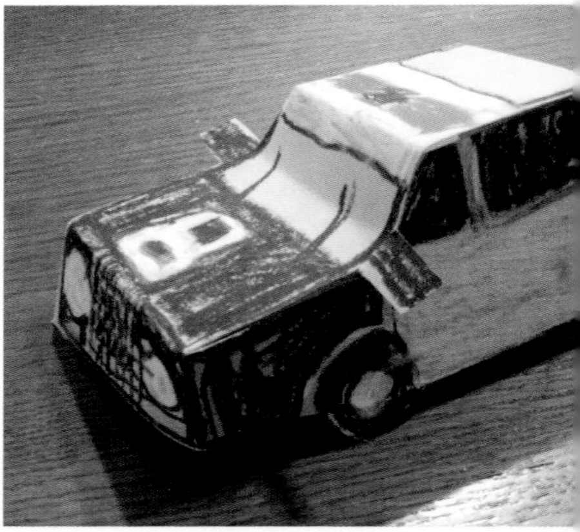

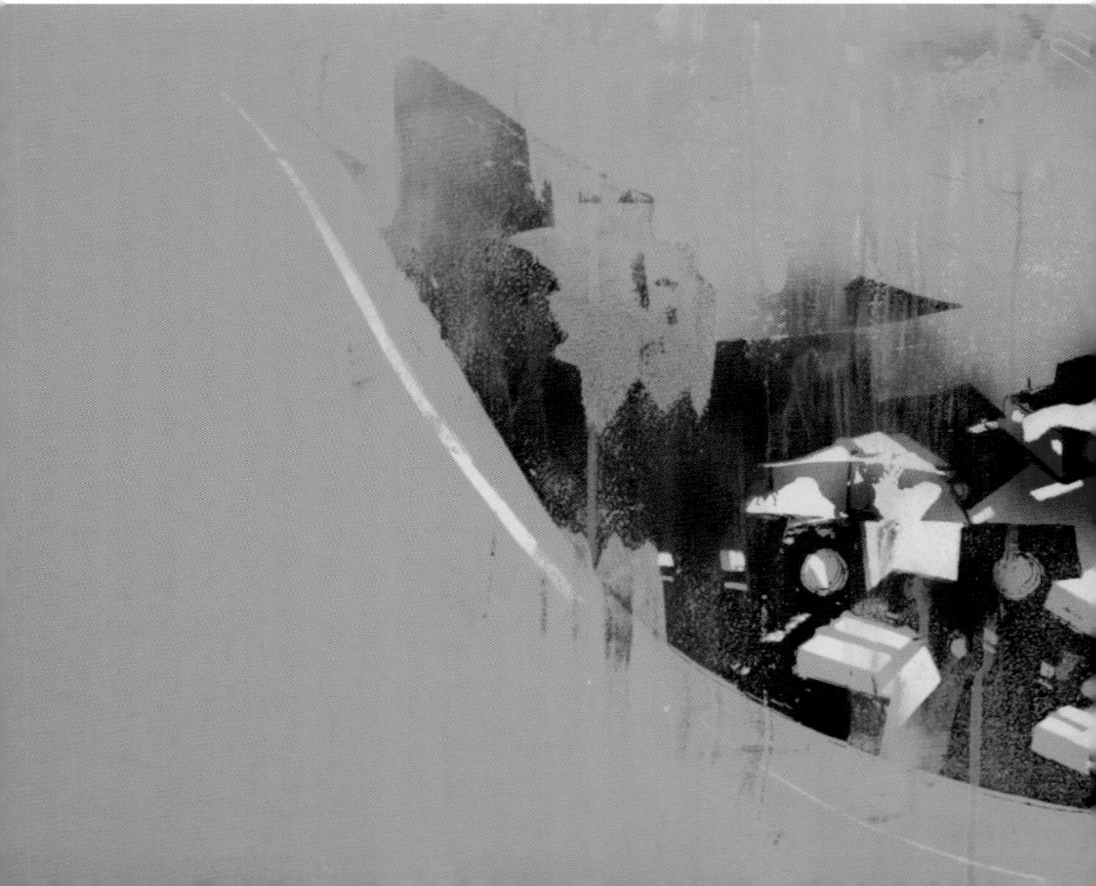

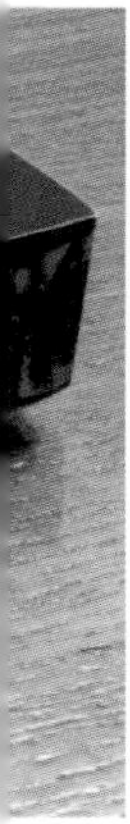

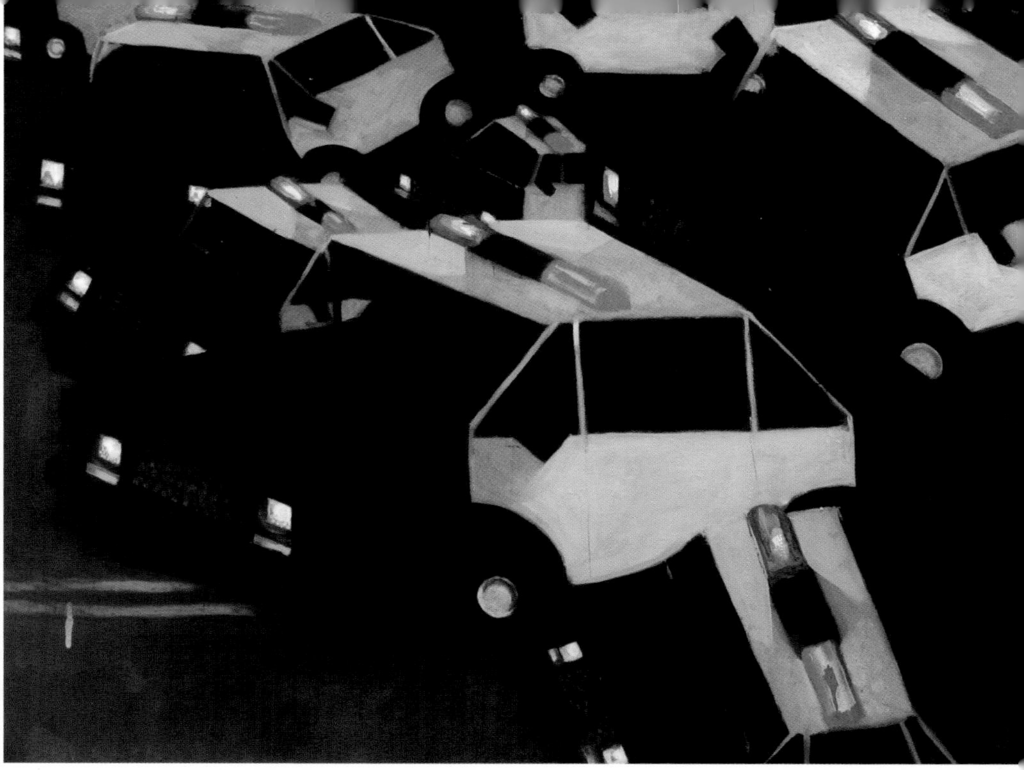

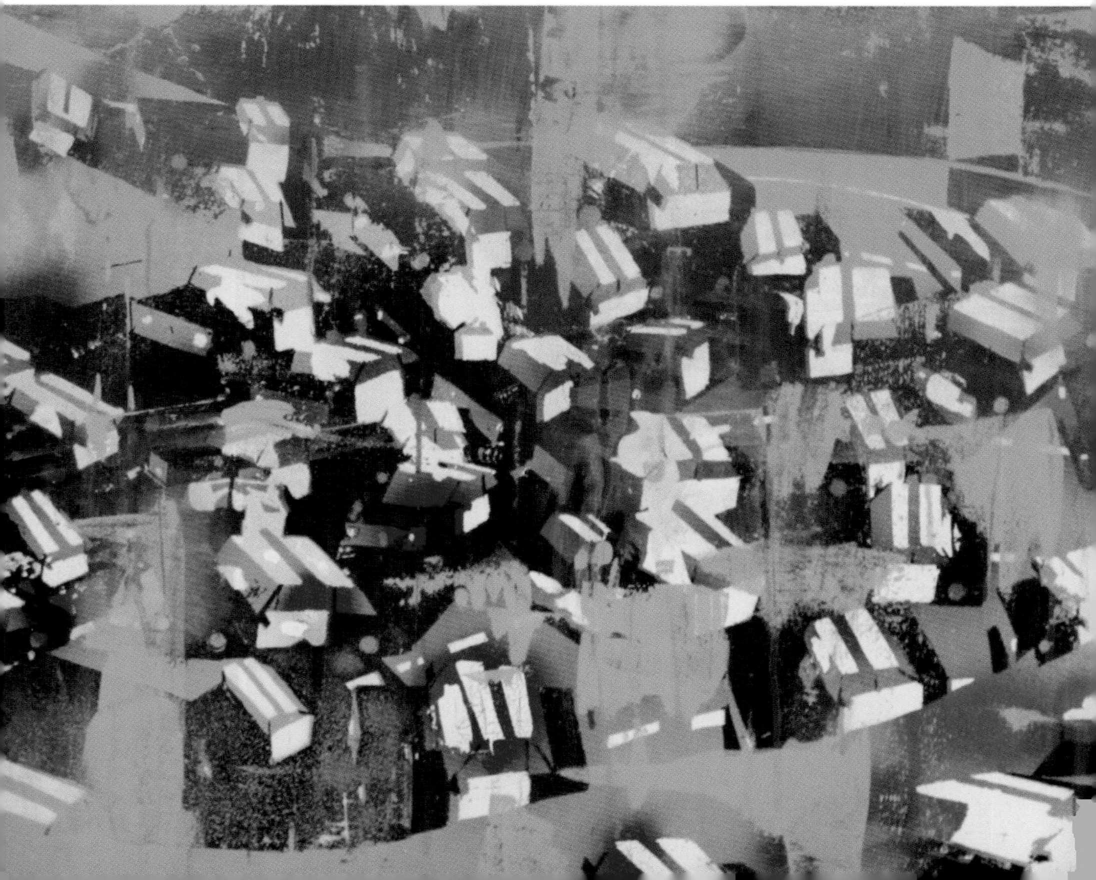

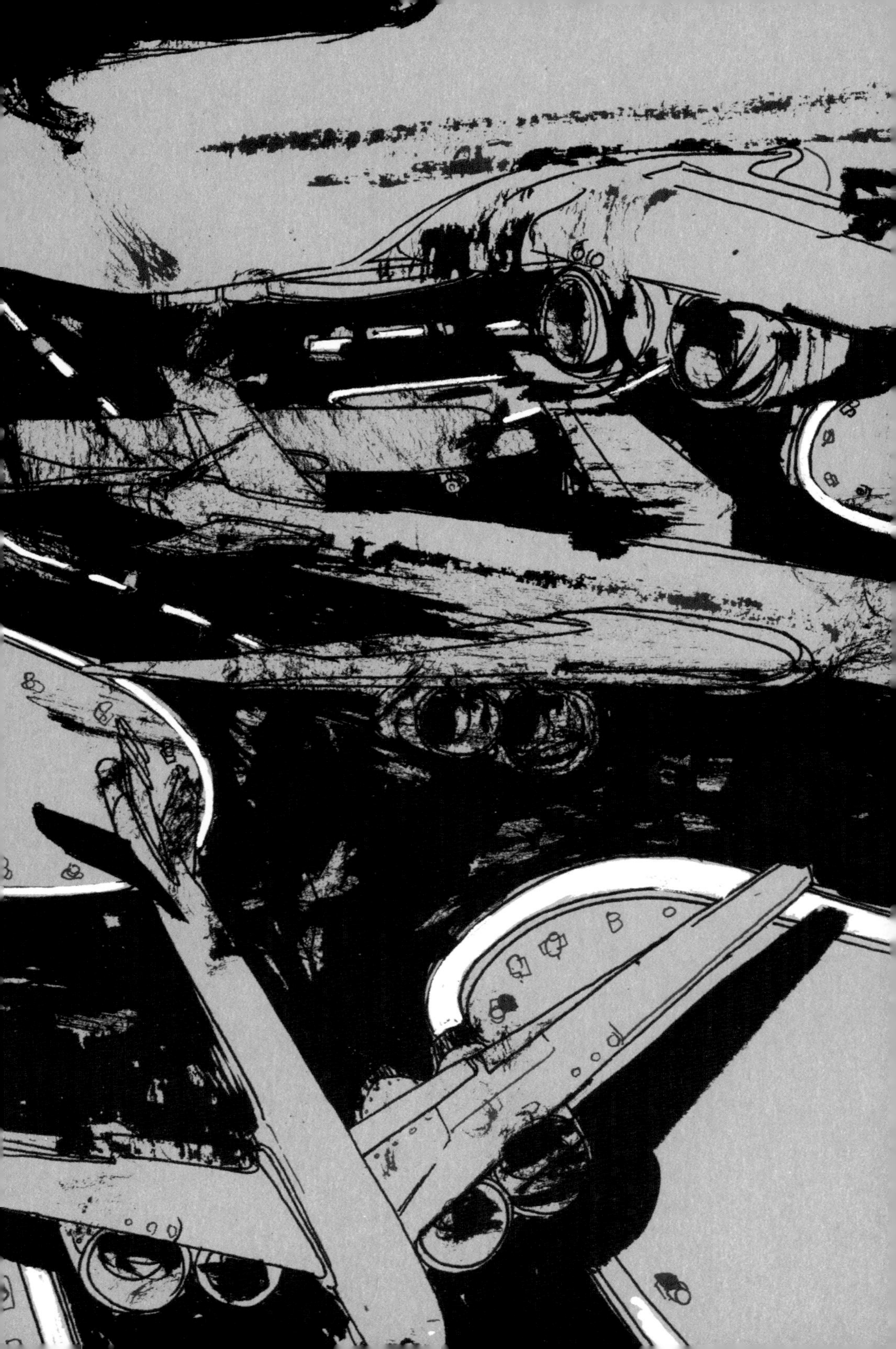

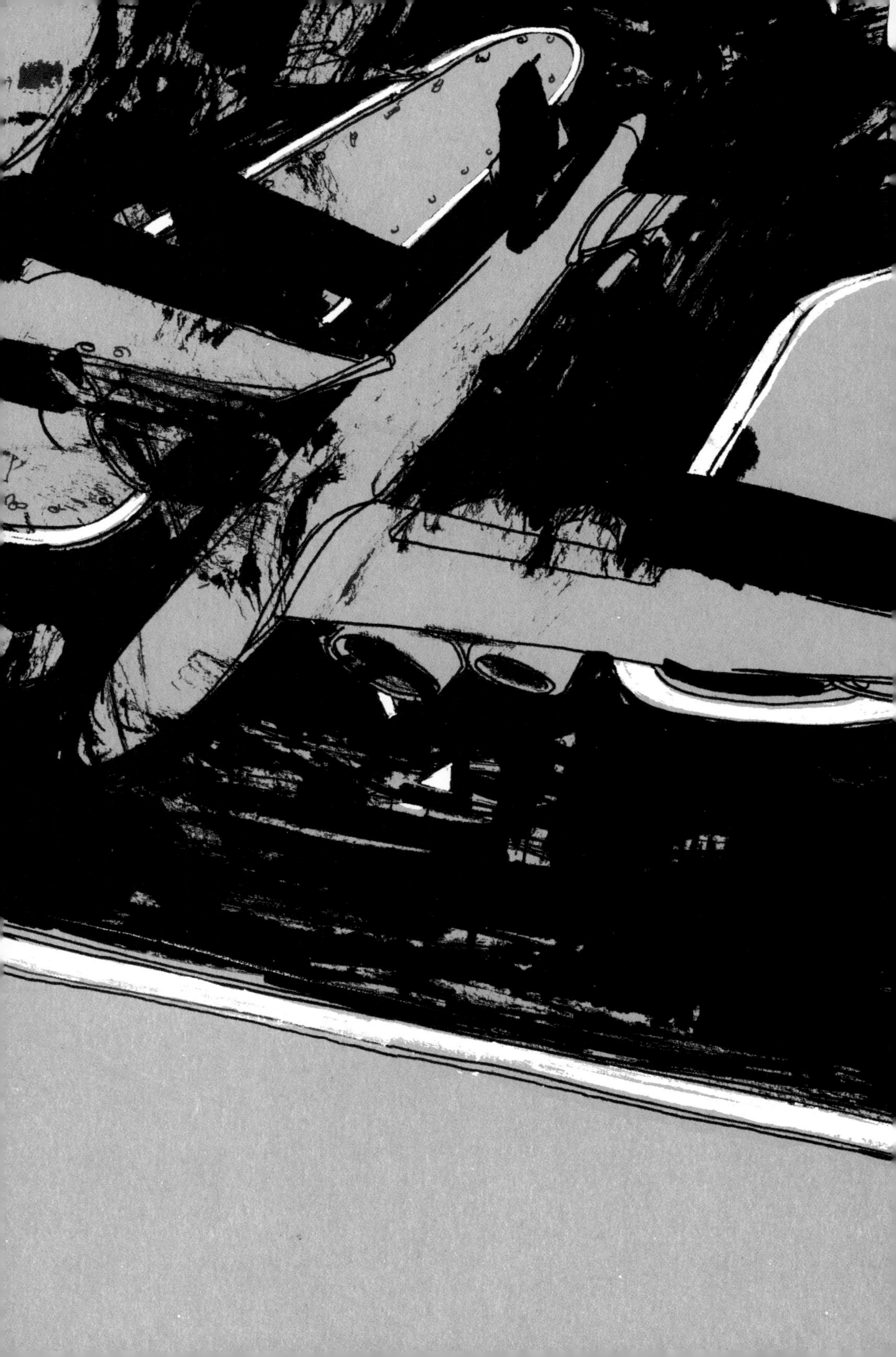

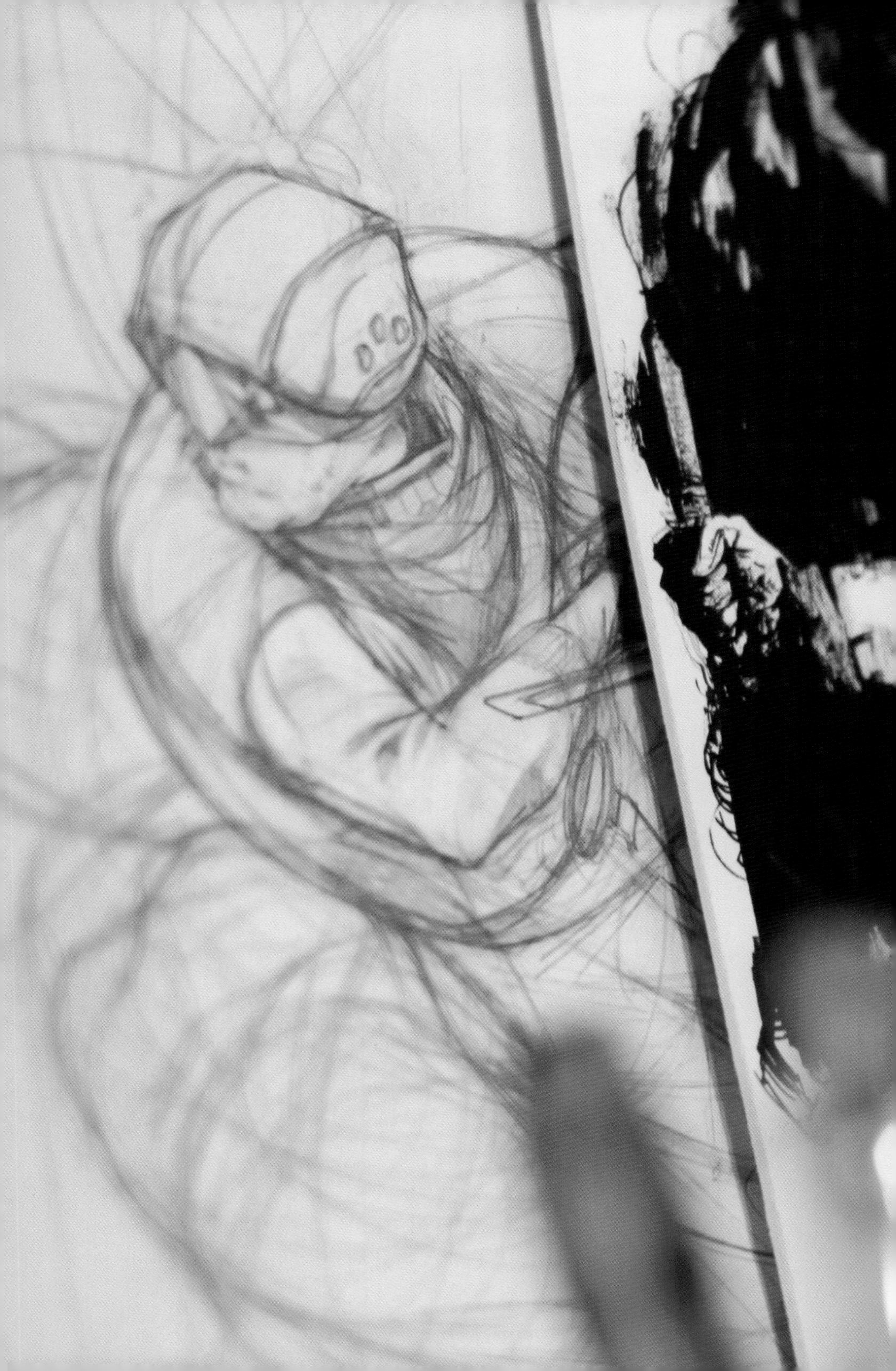

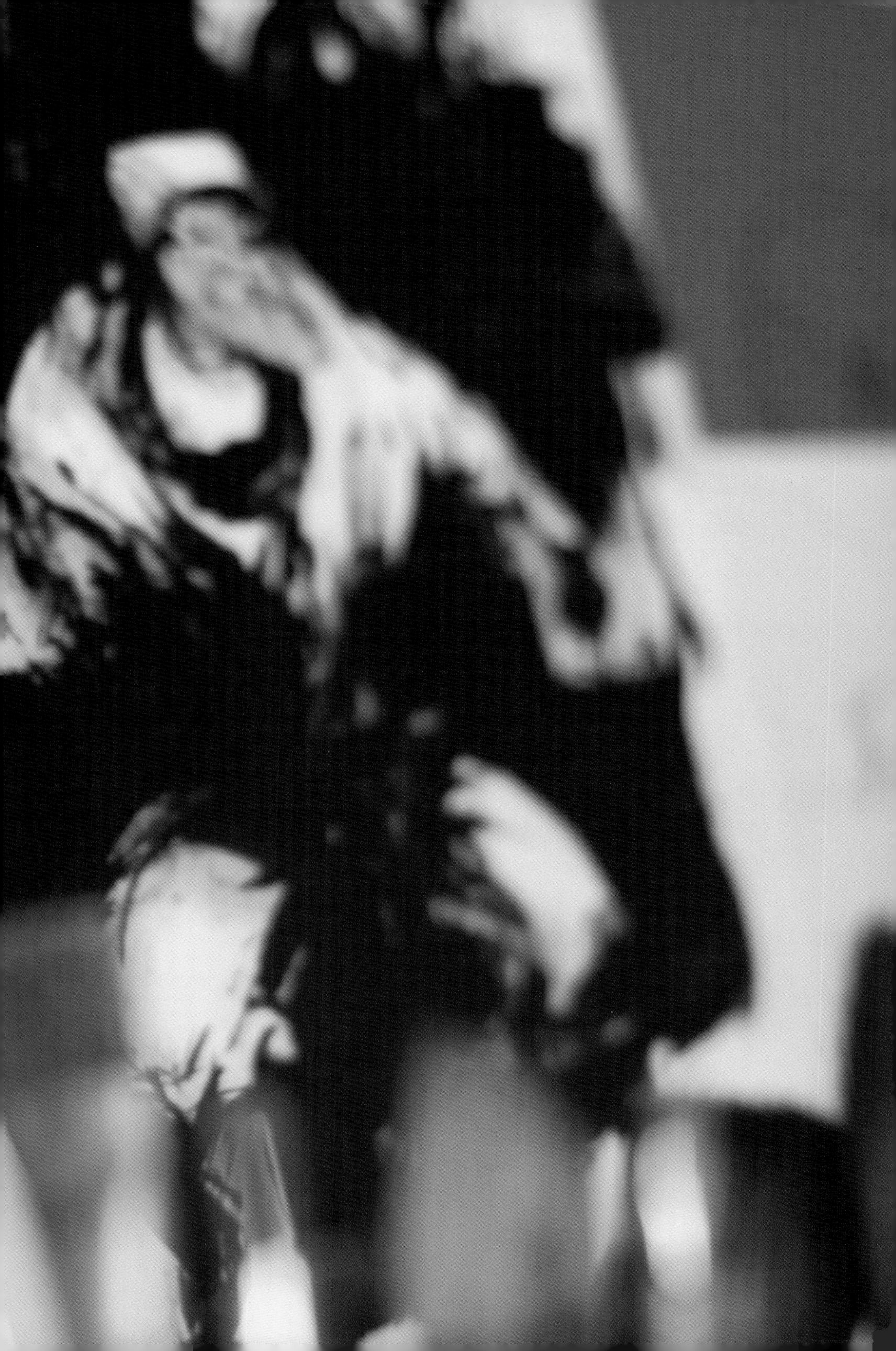

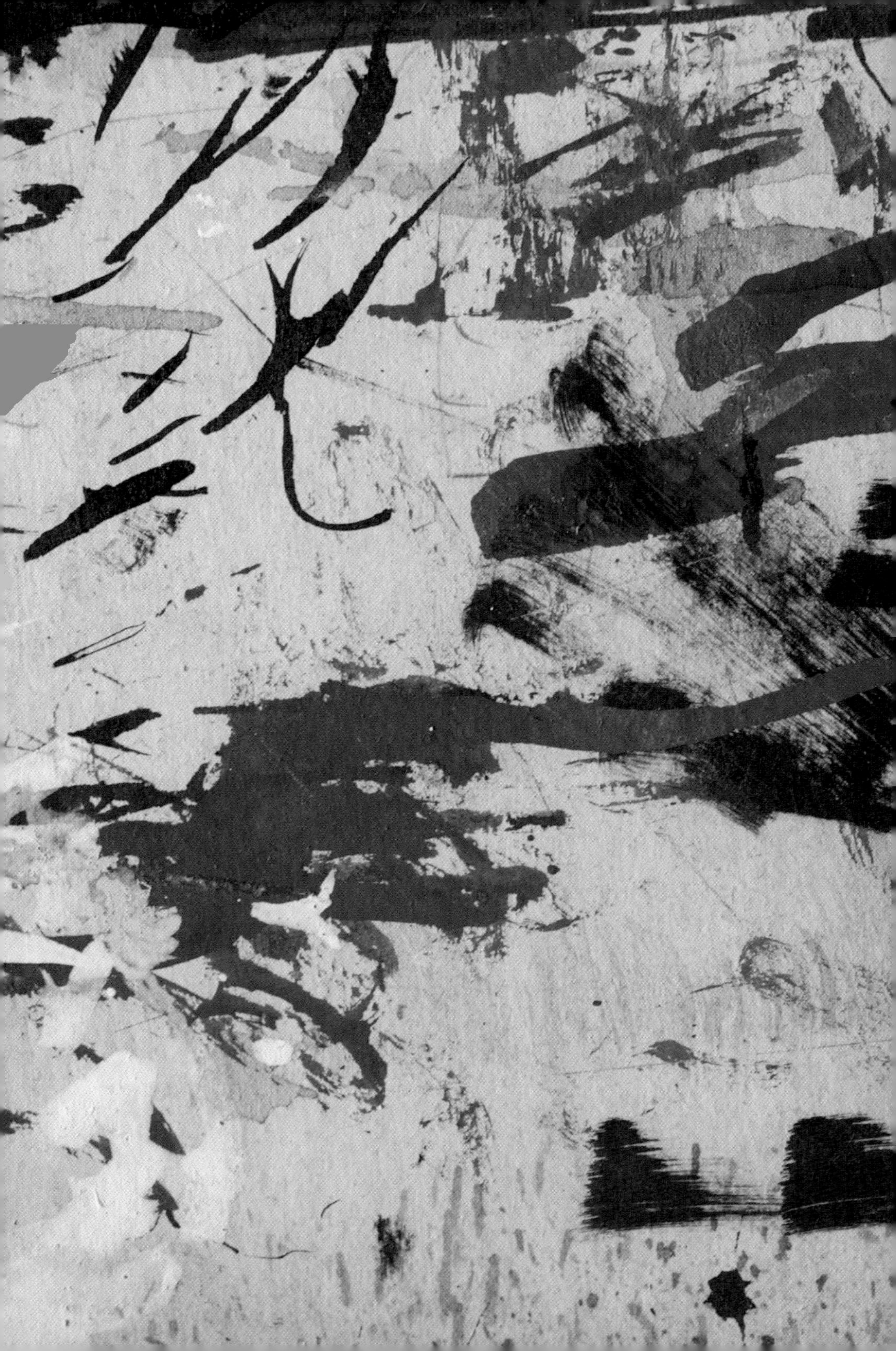

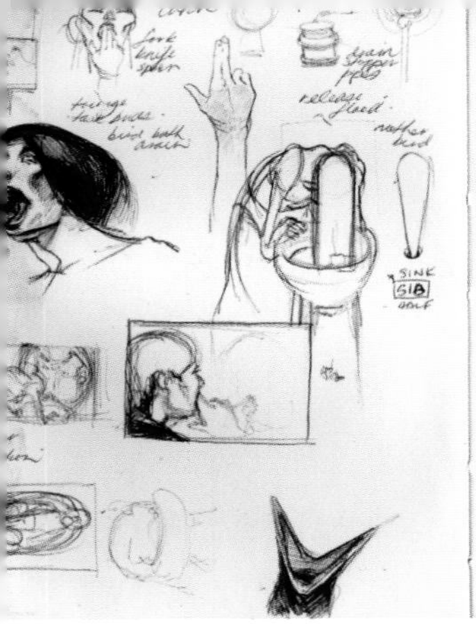
SINK
S1B
HALF

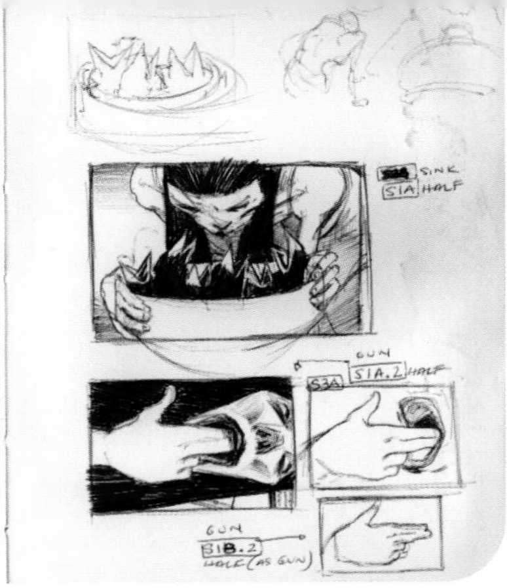
SINK
S1A HALF
GUN
S3A
S1A.2 HALF
GUN
B1B.2
HALF (AS GUN)

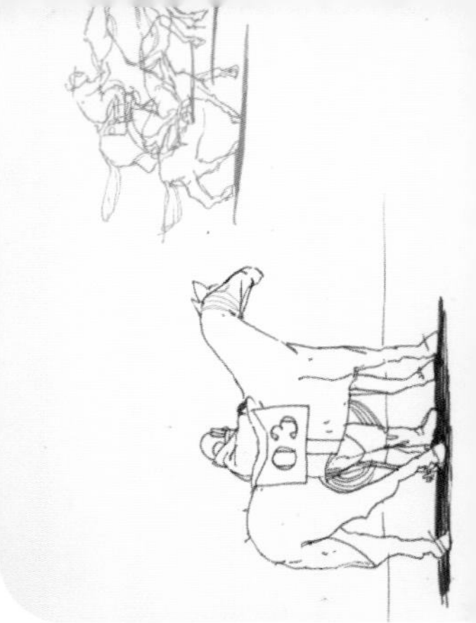

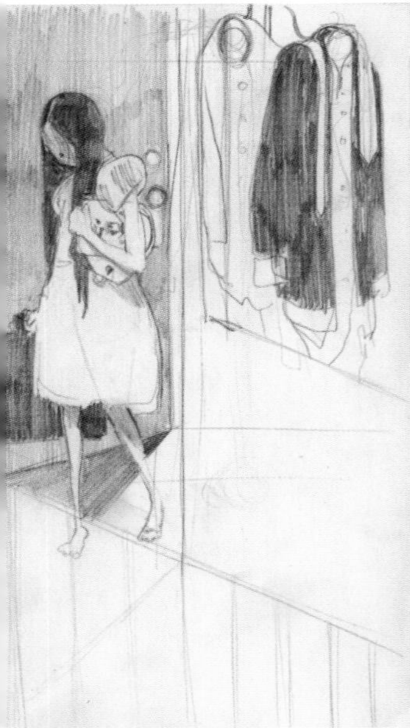

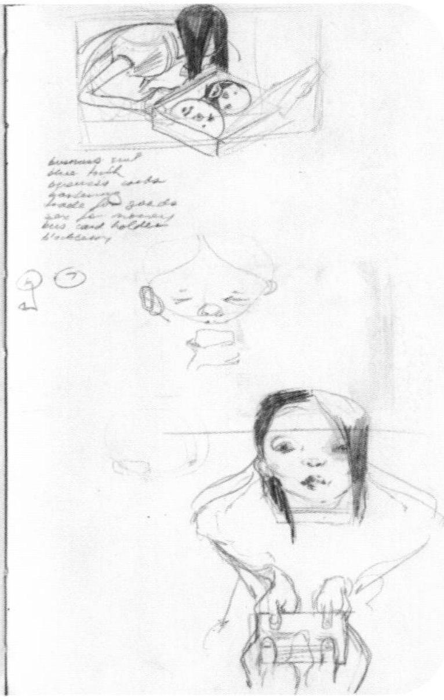

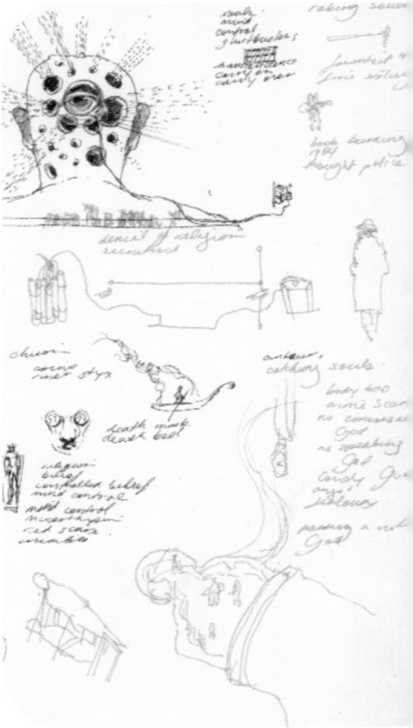

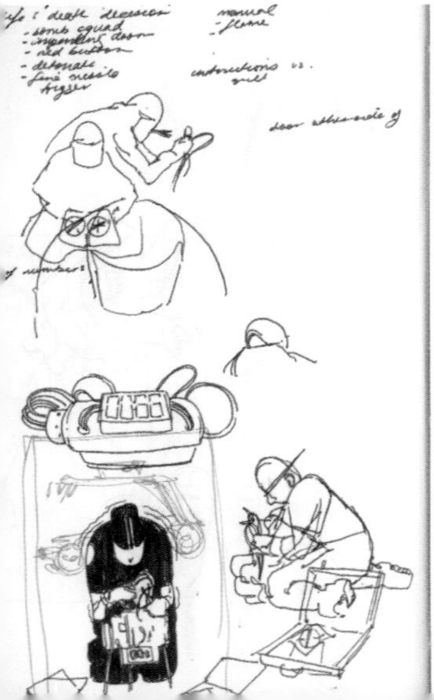

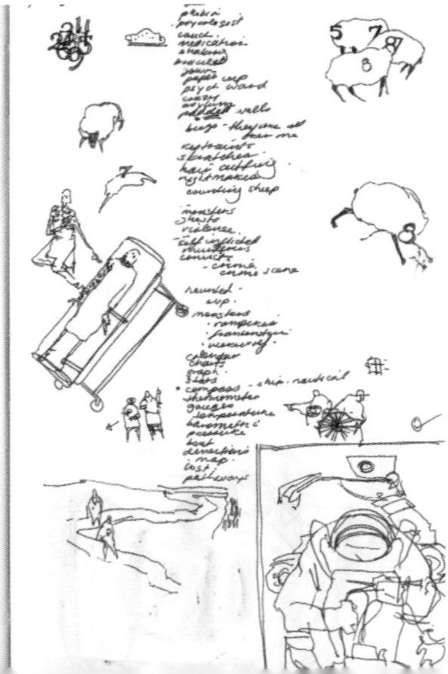

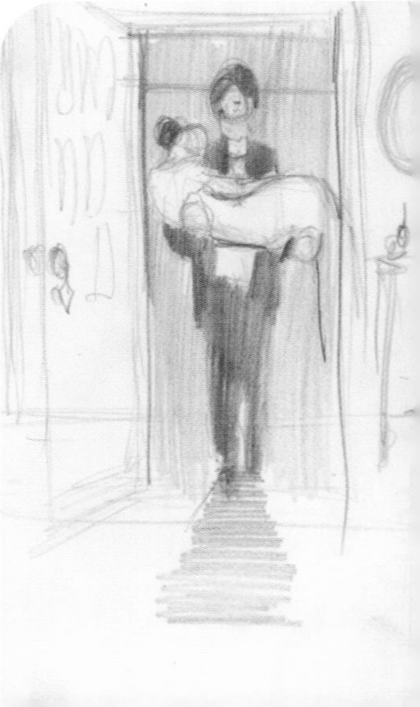

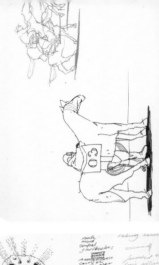

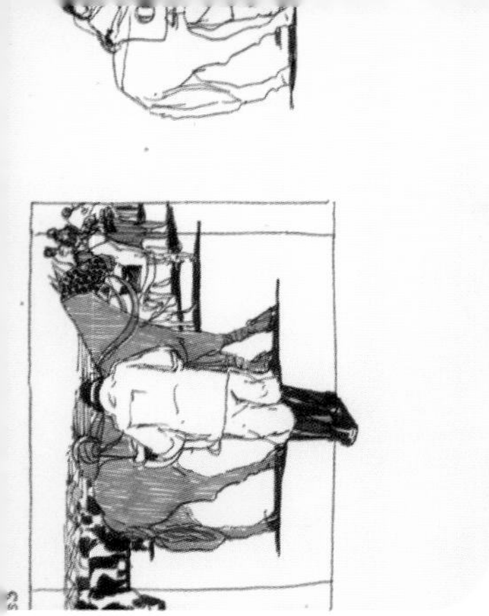

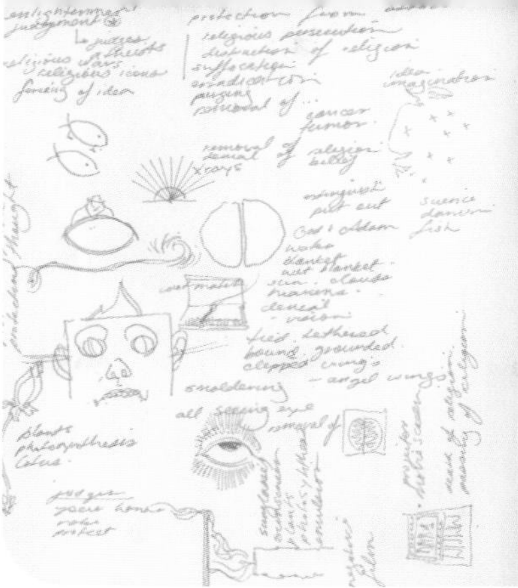
protection from
religious persecution
destruction of religion
eradication
purging
removal of
cancer
tumor
removal of religion
xrays
all seeing eye
plants
photosynthesis
lotus

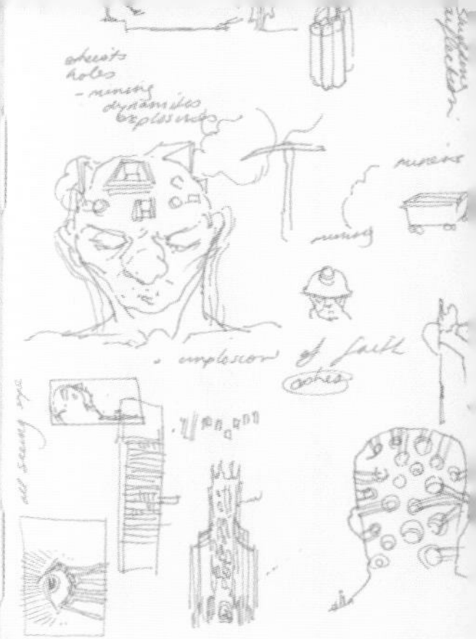
atheists
holes
mining
dynamites
explosions
mining
implosion of faith
ashes

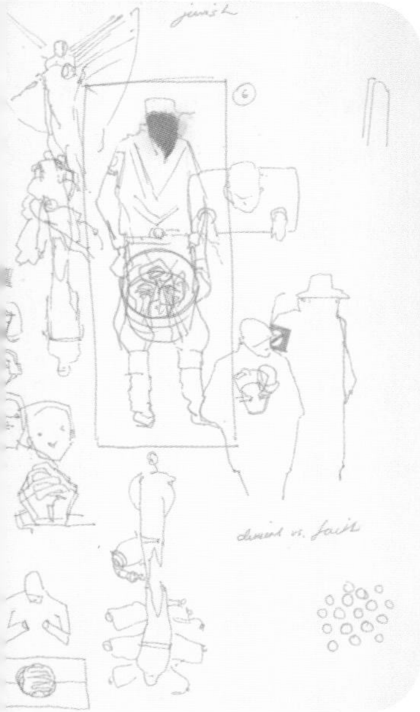
jewish
denial vs. faith

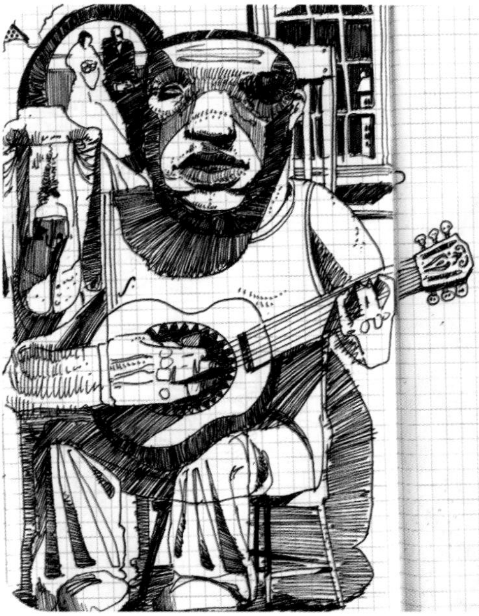

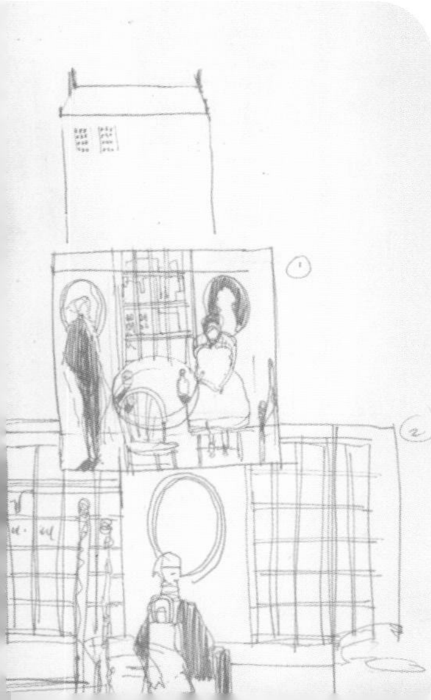

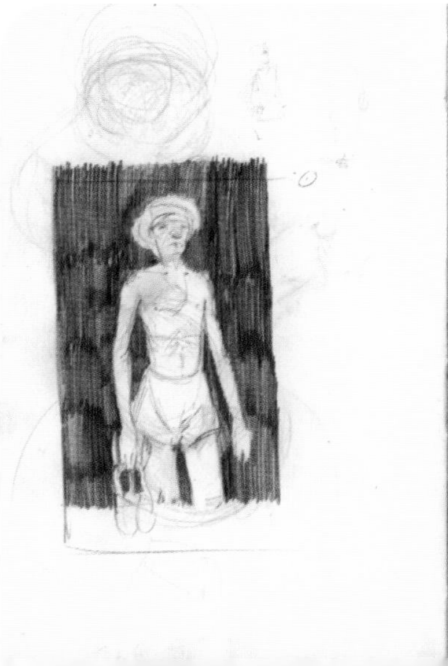

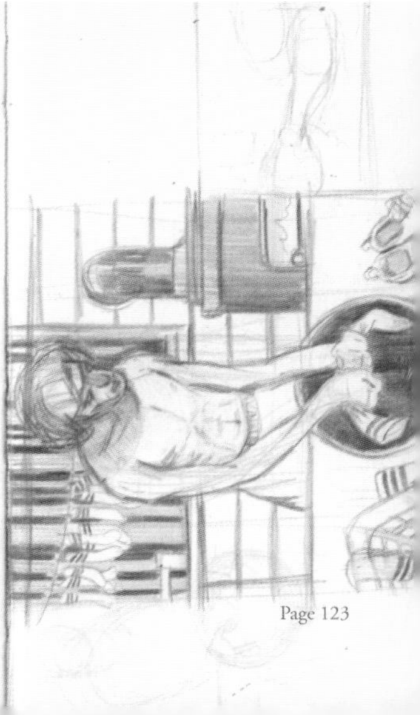

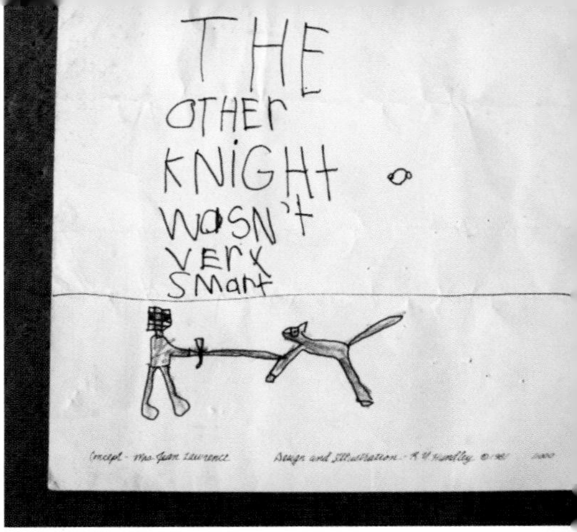
THE
OTHER
KNIGHT
WASN'T
VERY
SMART

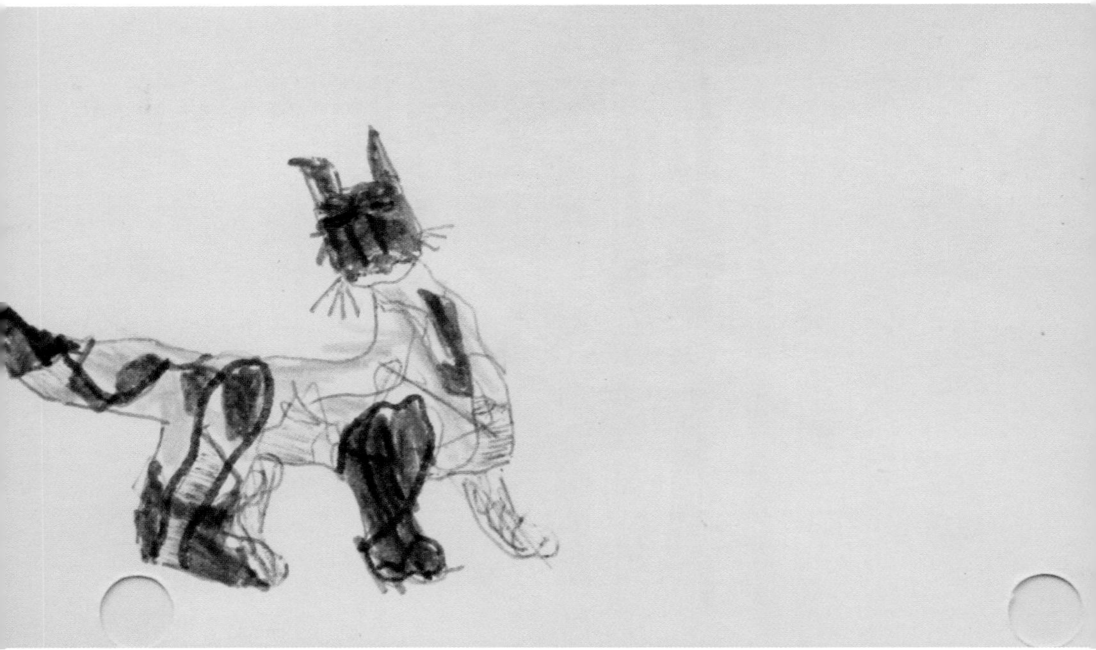

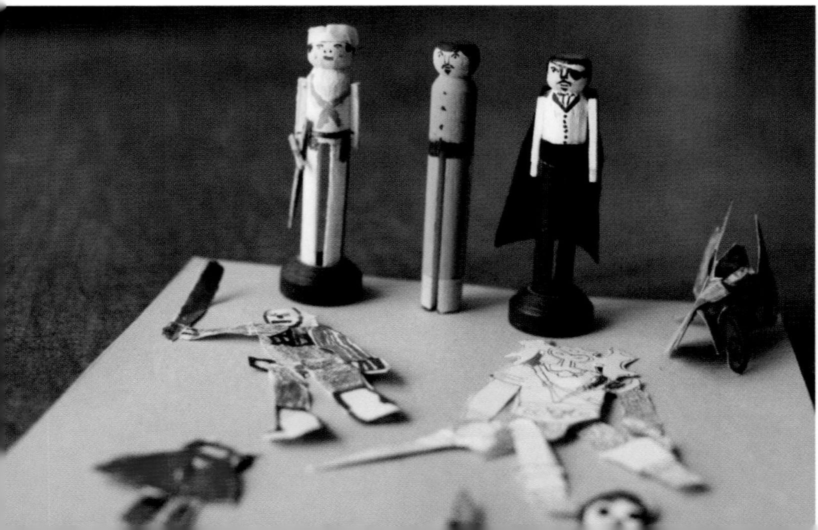

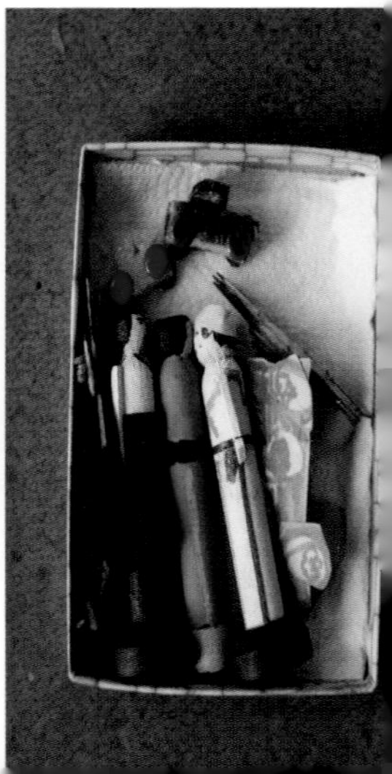

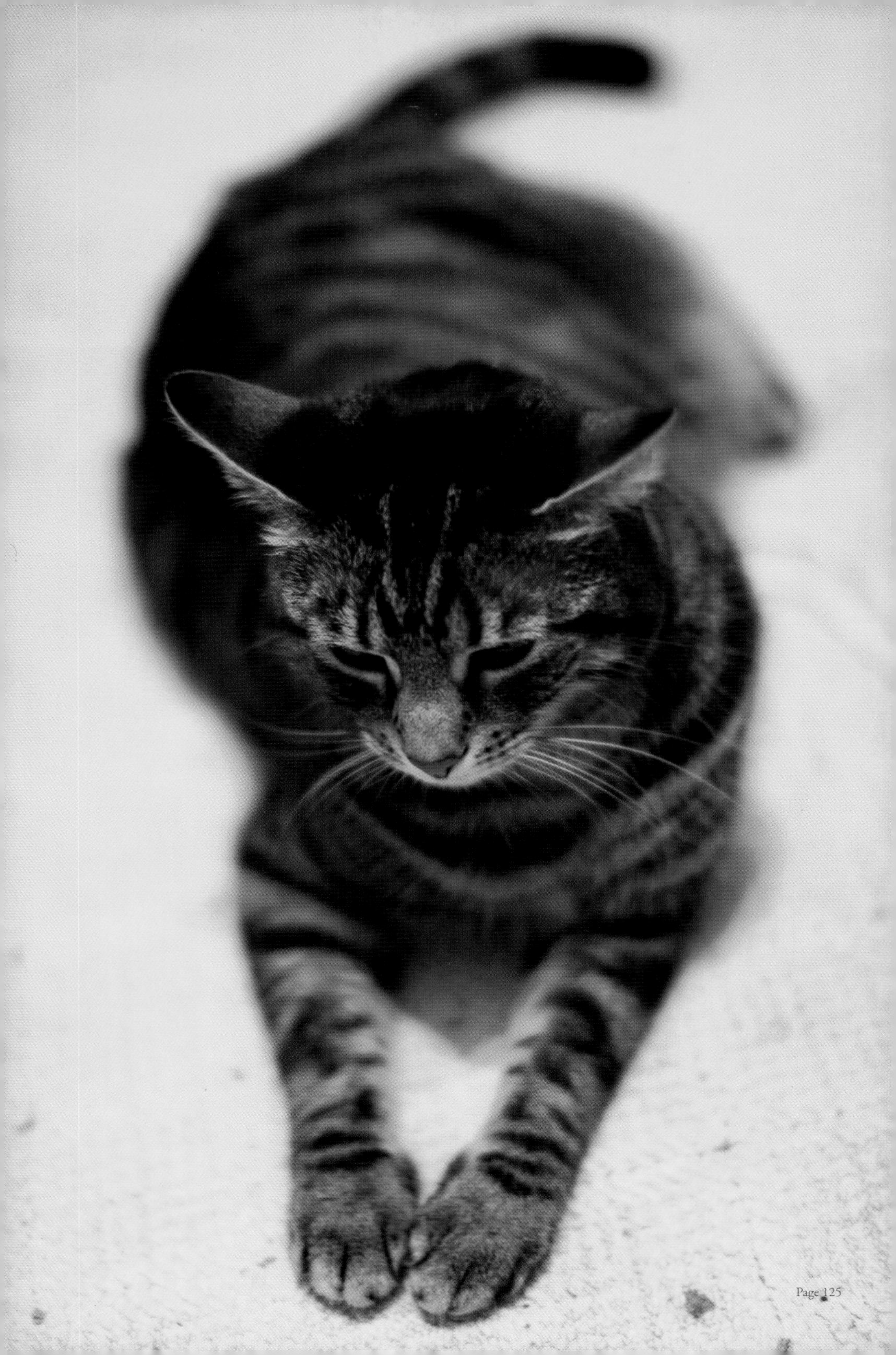

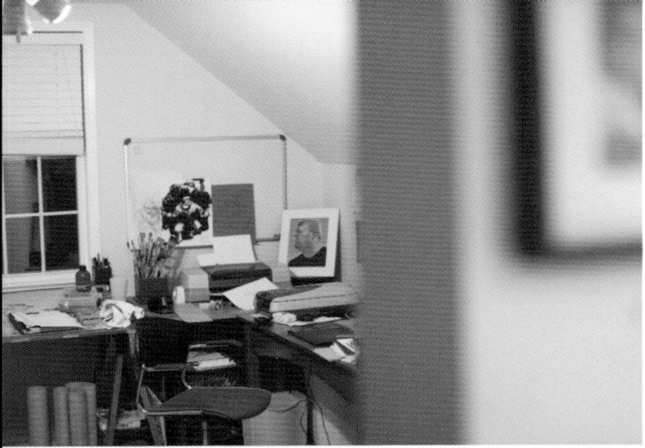

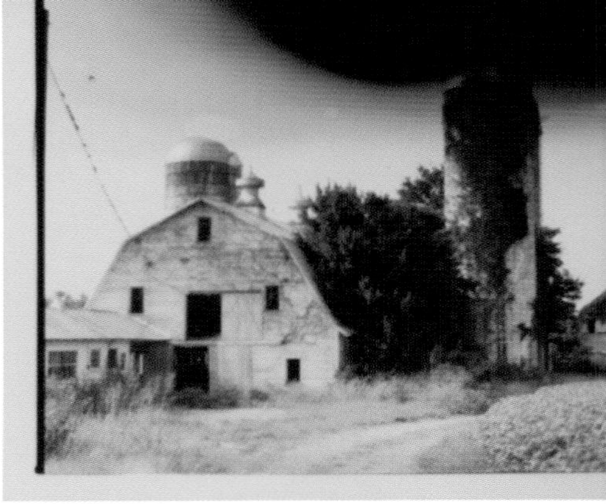

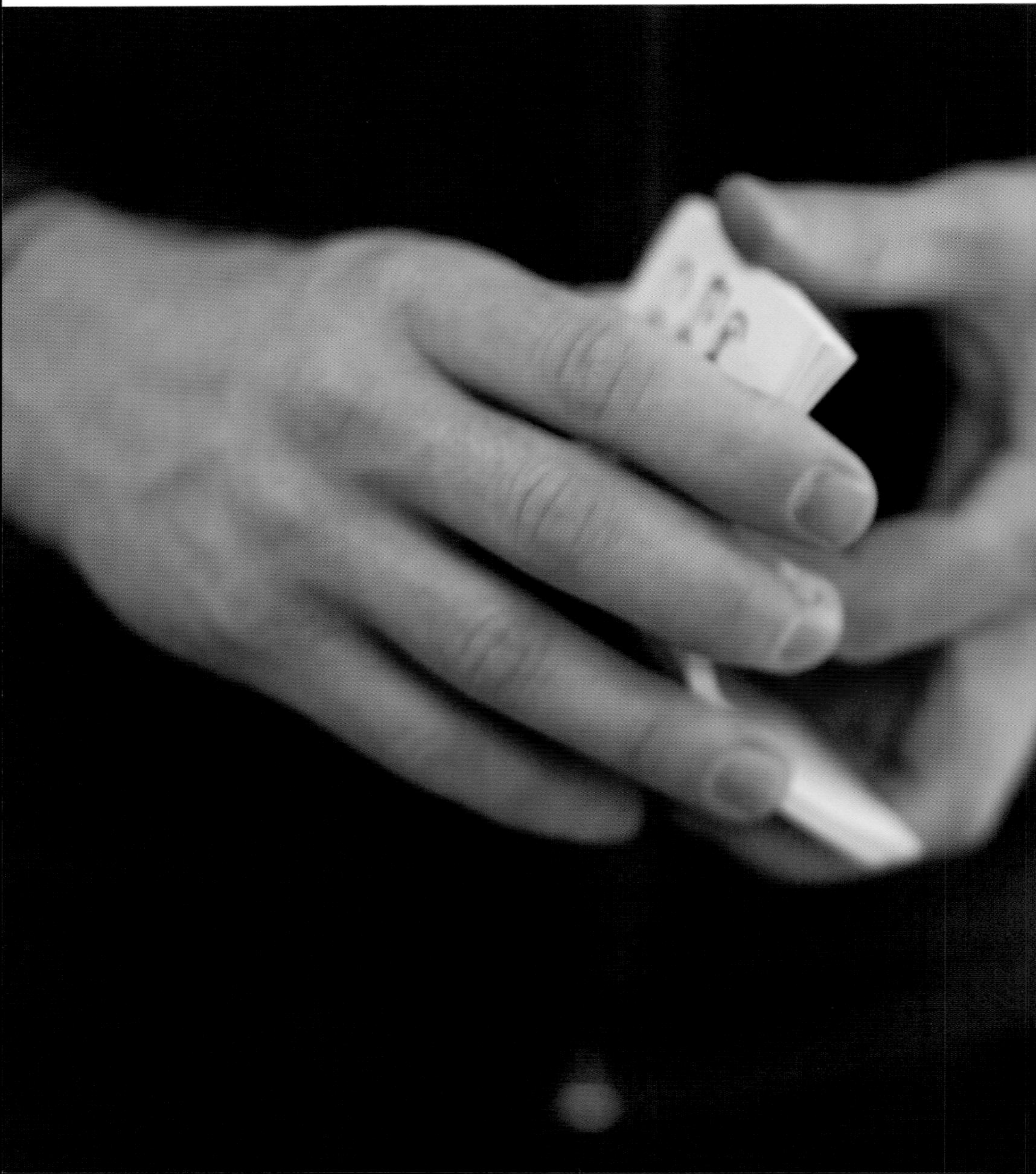

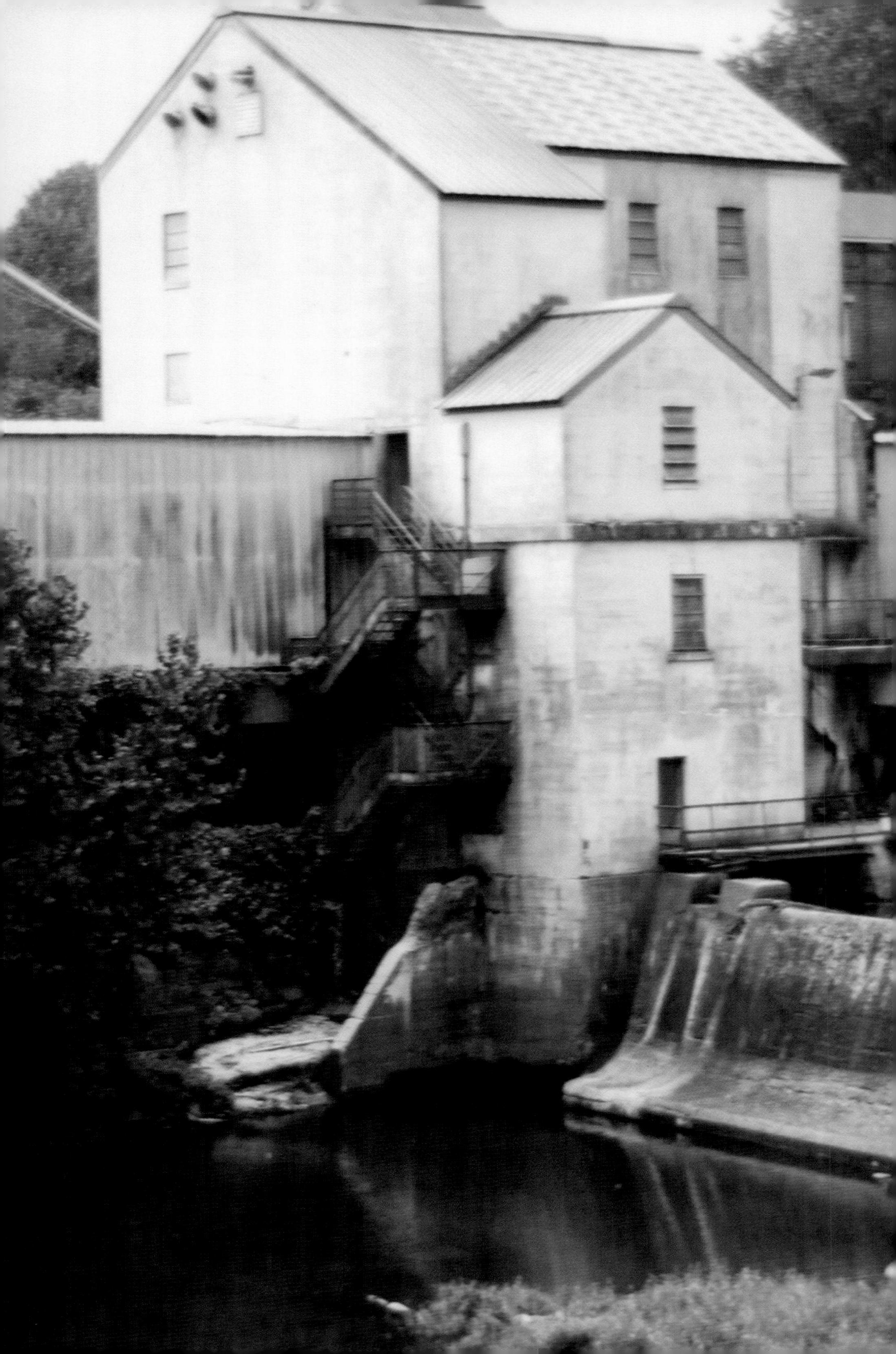

Index

PLACEMENT: PAGE 32
TITLE: Mickey Mouse Club
as led by David Carr Glover, Jr.
MEDIUM: Acrylic and gouache on panel
CLIENT: Virginia Living Magazine
DATE: 2007

PLACEMENT: PAGE 33
TITLE: Dinosaurland
MEDIUM: Acrylic, gouache, oil,
collage and ink on board
CLIENT: Virginia Living Magazine
DATE: 2006

PLACEMENT: PAGE 34
TITLE: Shipwreck
MEDIUM: Acrylic, gouache,
collage and ink on board
CLIENT: Virginia Living Magazine
DATE: 2007

PLACEMENT: PAGE 35
TITLE: Gibson's Gal
MEDIUM: Acrylic, gouache and ink on board
CLIENT: Virginia Living Magazine
DATE: 2007

PLACEMENT: PAGE 36-37
TITLE: My Lady Richmond
MEDIUM: Acrylic, gouache and ink on board
CLIENT: Arnika
DATE: 2001

PLACEMENT: PAGE 38
TITLE: Jane Eyre
MEDIUM: Acrylic, gouache, oil and ink on board
CLIENT: Point Park University
DATE: 2006

PLACEMENT: PAGE 39
TITLE: The Pearl Fishers
MEDIUM: Acrylic, gouache and ink on board
CLIENT: Lyric Opera of Kansas City
DATE: 2007

PLACEMENT: PAGE 40-41
TITLE: Mayo Island Homer
MEDIUM: Ink and digital
CLIENT: Virginia Living Magazine
DATE: 2010

PLACEMENT: PAGE 42
TITLE: Hair
MEDIUM: Acrylic, gouache and ink on board
CLIENT: Point Park University
DATE: 2005

PLACEMENT: PAGE 43 (top)
TITLE: The Skin of Our Teeth
MEDIUM: Acrylic, gouache and ink on board
CLIENT: Point Park University
DATE: 2006

PLACEMENT: PAGE 43 (bottom)
TITLE: King of Hearts
MEDIUM: Acrylic, gouache and ink on board
CLIENT: Point Park University
DATE: 2005

PLACEMENT: PAGE 44
TITLE: Marat/Sade
MEDIUM: Acrylic, gouache, oil, tar, collage
and ink on board
CLIENT: Point Park University
DATE: 2006

PLACEMENT: PAGE 45
TITLE: Sheep Dung Tea
MEDIUM: Acrylic, gouache and ink on board
CLIENT: Virginia Living Magazine
DATE: 2009

PLACEMENT: PAGE 46
TITLE: Magic Flute
MEDIUM: Acrylic, gouache and ink on board
CLIENT: Lyric Opera of Kansas City
DATE: 2007

PLACEMENT: PAGE 47
TITLE: Vertical Hold
MEDIUM: Acrylic, gouache, oil and ink on board
CLIENT: The Illustration Academy
DATE: 2009

PLACEMENT: PAGE 48
TITLE: Jerry Garcia
MEDIUM: Acrylic, gouache, oil,
collage and ink on board
CLIENT: AARP Magazine
DATE: 1999

PLACEMENT: PAGE 49 (top)
TITLE: Santana 1
MEDIUM: Acrylic, gouache, oil, collage
and ink on board
CLIENT: Entertainment Weekly Magazine
DATE: 1999

PLACEMENT: PAGE 49 (bottom)
TITLE: Santana 2
MEDIUM: Acrylic, gouache and ink on board
CLIENT: Rolling Stone Magazine
DATE: 2008

PLACEMENT: PAGES 50-51
TITLE: Omar Garcia
MEDIUM: Acrylic, gouache and ink on board
CLIENT: Rolling Stone Magazine
DATE: 2007

PLACEMENT: PAGE 51
TITLE: Kurt Cobain
MEDIUM: Acrylic, gouache, oil and ink on board
CLIENT: Rolling Stone Magazine
DATE: 1998

PLACEMENT: PAGE 52
TITLE: Stevie Wonder
MEDIUM: Acrylic, gouache, oil and ink on board
CLIENT: Rolling Stone Magazine
DATE: 2004

PLACEMENT: PAGE 53
TITLE: Prince
MEDIUM: Acrylic, gouache, collage, oil
and ink on board
CLIENT: Rolling Stone Magazine
DATE: 1999

PLACEMENT: PAGE 54-55
TITLE: Jam Master Jay
MEDIUM: Acrylic, gouache and ink on board
CLIENT: Scratch Magazine
DATE: 2005

PLACEMENT: PAGE 56
TITLE: Hemingway and Faulkner
(Cats and Dogs)
MEDIUM: Acrylic, gouache, oil and ink on board
CLIENT: Hemispheres Magazine
DATE: 2005

PLACEMENT: PAGE 57
TITLE: Audio Detective
MEDIUM: Acrylic and ink on board
CLIENT: Virginia Living Magazine
DATE: 2004

PLACEMENT: PAGE 58
TITLE: Lone Ranger
MEDIUM: Acrylic, gouache, oil and ink on board
CLIENT: American Cowboy Magazine
DATE: 2009

PLACEMENT: PAGE 59
TITLE: William Henry Harrison (vertical)
MEDIUM: Acrylic, gouache and ink on board
CLIENT: Virginia Living Magazine
DATE: 2006

PLACEMENT: PAGE 60-61
TITLE: William Henry Harrison (horizontal)
MEDIUM: Acrylic, gouache and ink on board
CLIENT: Virginia Living Magazine
DATE: 2006

PLACEMENT: PAGE 62-63
TITLE: Labyrinth
MEDIUM: Mixed
CLIENT: Deloitte Review
DATE: 2010

PLACEMENT: PAGE 64
TITLE: Virginia Giant (detail)
MEDIUM: Acrylic and ink on board
CLIENT: Virginia Living Magazine
DATE: 2008

PLACEMENT: PAGE 65
TITLE: Virginia Giant sketches
MEDIUM: Pencil on paper
CLIENT: Virginia Living Magazine
DATE: 2008

PLACEMENT: PAGE 66-67
TITLE: Pea Green Boat
MEDIUM: Acrylic, gouache, ink and digital
CLIENT: Saturday Evening Post
DATE: 2010

PLACEMENT: PAGE 68-69
TITLE: Tori Amos
MEDIUM: Acrylic, gouache, tape and ink
on board
CLIENT: RAINN
DATE: 2007

PLACEMENT: PAGE 70
TITLE: George Rogers Clark
MEDIUM: Acrylic, gouache and ink on board
CLIENT: Virginia Living Magazine
DATE: 2009

PLACEMENT: PAGE 71
TITLE: Shakespeare in the Park
MEDIUM: Acrylic, gouache, oil, collage
and ink on board
CLIENT: Los Angeles Times
DATE: 2003

PLACEMENT: PAGE 72-73
TITLE: Kruger National Park
MEDIUM: Ink on paper
CLIENT: Personal
DATE: 2008

PLACEMENT: PAGE 74-75
TITLE: Monolith (detail)
MEDIUM: Acrylic, ink and pencil on board
CLIENT: commissioned for
Stanley Kubrick Anthology
DATE: 2009

PLACEMENT: PAGE 76
TITLE: Food Chain (study)
MEDIUM: Ink on paper
CLIENT: Personal
DATE: 2008

PLACEMENT: PAGE 77
TITLE: Rouge et Noir (detail)
MEDIUM: Oil and charcoal on panel
CLIENT: Virginia Living Magazine
DATE: 2010

PLACEMENT: PAGE 78-79
TITLE: Fashion 1(detail)
MEDIUM: Ink and pencil on paper
CLIENT: Personal
DATE: 2009

PLACEMENT: PAGE 80
TITLE: Apple Blossom Queen
MEDIUM: Acrylic, ink and gouache on board
CLIENT: Virginia Living Magazine
DATE: 2006

PLACEMENT: PAGE 81
TITLE: Sweet Bird of Youth (detail)
MEDIUM: Acrylic, gouache and ink on board
CLIENT: Arena Stage
DATE: 2008

PLACEMENT: PAGE 82
TITLE: Duke Ellington's Sophisticated Ladies (detail)
MEDIUM: Acrylic, ink and digital
CLIENT: Arena Stage
DATE: 2009

PLACEMENT: PAGE 83 (top)
TITLE: We Are All Businessmen sketches
MEDIUM: Ink and graphite on paper
CLIENT: Atlantic Monthly Magazine
DATE: 2008

PLACEMENT: PAGE 83 (bottom)
TITLE: We Are All Businessmen
MEDIUM: Acrylic, watercolor and oil on board
CLIENT: Atlantic Monthly Magazine
DATE: 2008

PLACEMENT: PAGE 84
TITLE: Immigration
MEDIUM: Ink and digital
CLIENT: The Progressive Magazine
DATE: 2006

PLACEMENT: PAGE 85
TITLE: Immigration sketches
MEDIUM: Ink on paper
CLIENT: The Progressive Magazine
DATE: 2006

PLACEMENT: PAGE 86-87
TITLE: Buddy Guy
MEDIUM: Oil, acrylic and ink on board
CLIENT: Rolling Stone Magazine
DATE: 2008

PLACEMENT: PAGE 88
TITLE: Frogs (detail)
MEDIUM: Acrylic, ink, watercolor and oil on board
CLIENT: Point Park University
DATE: 2005

PLACEMENT: PAGE 89
TITLE: Jeckyll and Hyde (detail)
MEDIUM: Watercolor on board
CLIENT: Point Park University
DATE: 2005

PLACEMENT: PAGE 90
TITLE: anon series (detail)
MEDIUM: Mixed
CLIENT: Personal
DATE: 2009

PLACEMENT: PAGE 91
TITLE: anon 64.2
MEDIUM: Oil and acrylic on panel
SIZE: 1' x 1'
CLIENT: Personal
DATE: 2009

PLACEMENT: PAGE 92-93
TITLE: God Save the Queen 1.4 (detail)
MEDIUM: Oil and acrylic on panel
SIZE: 4' x 4'
CLIENT: Personal
DATE: 2009

PLACEMENT: PAGE 94
TITLE: Another Black Sunday 1.3 (detail)
MEDIUM: Oil and acrylic on panel
SIZE: 2' x 2'
CLIENT: Personal
DATE: 2009

PLACEMENT: PAGE 95
TITLE: Another Black Sunday 1.4
MEDIUM: Oil and acrylic on panel
SIZE: 4' x 4'
CLIENT: Personal
DATE: 2009

PLACEMENT: PAGE 96-97
TITLE: Herd 1.4 (detail)
MEDIUM: Oil and acrylic on panel
SIZE: 4' x 4'
CLIENT: Personal
DATE: 2009

PLACEMENT: PAGE 98-99
TITLE: God Save the Queen 1.3
MEDIUM: Oil and acrylic on panel
SIZE: 2' x 2'
CLIENT: Personal
DATE: 2009

PLACEMENT: PAGE 100-101
TITLE: anon 1.3
MEDIUM: Oil and acrylic on panel
SIZE: 2' x 2'
CLIENT: Personal
DATE: 2009

PLACEMENT: PAGE 102-103
TITLE: anon 64.3
MEDIUM: Oil and acrylic on panel
SIZE: 2' x 2'
CLIENT: Personal
DATE: 2009

PLACEMENT: PAGE 104-105
TITLE: Muybridge Descending (detail)
MEDIUM: Oil on canvas
SIZE: 4' x 6'
CLIENT: Personal
DATE: 2010

PLACEMENT: PAGE 106-107
TITLE: Ship Yard
MEDIUM: Oil, acrylic, pastel and wax on canvas
SIZE: 18" x 24"
CLIENT: Personal
DATE: 2010

PLACEMENT: PAGE 108
TITLE: Untitled
MEDIUM: Construction paper and crayon
CLIENT: Personal

PLACEMENT: PAGE 108-109 (bottom)
TITLE: I Run Like a Coward 2 (detail)
MEDIUM: Acrylic and enamel on panel
SIZE: 18" x 48"
CLIENT: Personal
DATE: 2010

PLACEMENT: PAGE 109 (top)
TITLE: I Run Like a Coward 1
MEDIUM: Oil on canvas
SIZE: 2' x 4'
CLIENT: Personal
DATE: 2010

PLACEMENT: PAGE 110-111
TITLE: Runway (study)
MEDIUM: Ink on panel
SIZE: 12" x 12"
CLIENT: Personal
DATE: 2010

PLACEMENT: PAGE 112-113
TITLE: Air Traffic Control (study)
MEDIUM: Acrylic, ink and latex on panel
SIZE: 18" X 48"
CLIENT: Personal
DATE: 2010

PLACEMENT: PAGE 114-115
TITLE: Big Brother Hero studies (detail)
MEDIUM: Various
SIZE: Various
CLIENT: Personal
DATE: 2010

PLACEMENT: PAGE 118
TITLE: Tethered
MEDIUM: Oil on canvas
SIZE: 3' x 4'
CLIENT: Personal
DATE: 2010

PLACEMENT: PAGE119
TITLE: Reclining Nude 1
MEDIUM: Oil on canvas
SIZE: 5' x 6'
CLIENT: Personal
DATE: 2010

PLACEMENT: PAGE 120-121
TITLE: Rural (triptych)
MEDIUM: Oil, acrylic, pastel and wax on panel
SIZE: 18" x 24", 18" x 24", 18" x 24"
CLIENT: Personal
DATE: 2010

PLACEMENT: PAGE 122-123
TITLE: Process sketches
DATE: Various

PLACEMENT: PAGE 124
TITLE: Kid Art
MEDIUM:Various
DATE: Various

PLACEMENT: PAGE 125
TITLE: Cooper

PLACEMENT: PAGE 126-128
TITLE: Things I've Seen
MEDIUM:Various
DATE: Various

PLACEMENT: PAGE 132
TITLE: Ex Libris Sterling Hundley
MEDIUM: Drypoint on BFK Rives paper
DATE: 2009

+++

PLACEMENT: LIMITED (100) SLIP COVER (FRONT AND BACK)
TITLE: Another Black Sunday 1.4 (DETAIL)
MEDIUM: Oil and acrylic on panel
SIZE: 4' X 4'
DATE: 2009

PLACEMENT: LIMITED (100) PRINT
TITLE: Blue Collar/White Collar
MEDIUM: Serigraphy
SIZE: 5" X 5"
DATE: 2011

EX LIBRIS
STERLING
HUNDLEY

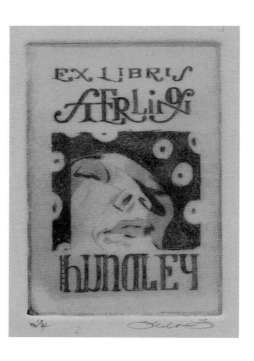

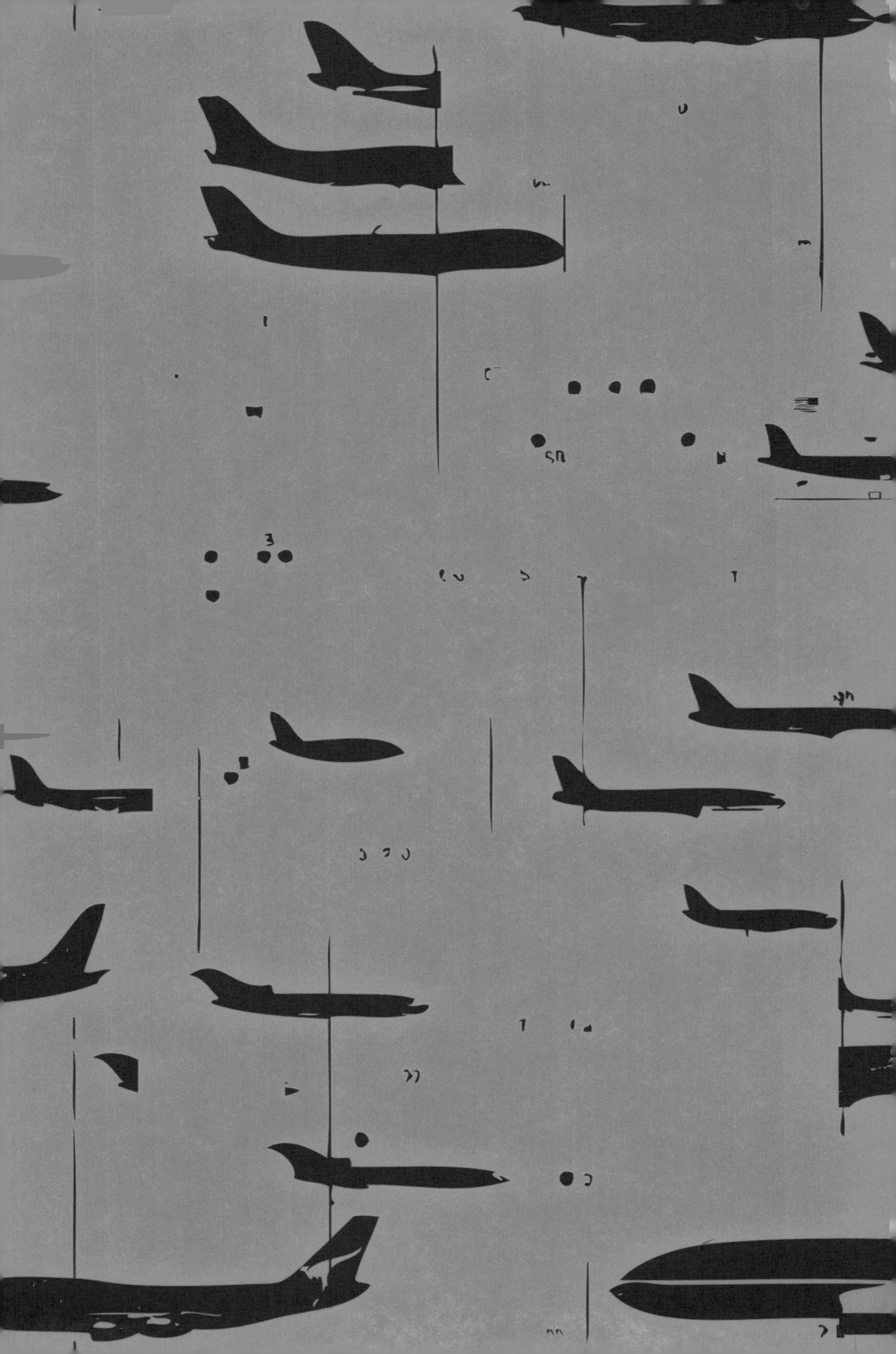